"Professor Shawn Wright has given us a good, reliable, readable, basic introduction to Calvinism, and some of the main questions that surround it. If you are a non-Calvinist seeking answers about Calvinism, you will find a clear and winsome presentation of the position, as well as a response to some key criticisms. If you are a Calvinist looking for a model of how to talk about these things with non-Calvinists, then you will find a helpful and humble model for explaining the Calvinist position and its points of disagreement with Arminianism, in a fair-minded, evenhanded way. If you are seeking something that will help you to understand, summarize, and explain these issues, you will find a welcome addition to your library. The biblical doctrines discussed in this book matter. They matter to our understanding of who God is, what he is like, and what he has graciously done. So read and be edified, and give all the glory to God."

—Ligon Duncan,
Chancellor/CEO, John E. Richards Professor of Systematic and Historical Theology,
Reformed Theological Seminary

"Shawn Wright's book on Calvinism is biblically rooted, theologically astute, historically informed, and pastorally shaped. Wright lucidly explains the tenets of Calvinism, answers common misconceptions about it, and refutes objections to Calvinist soteriology. Wright's book is the first book I would give to anyone with questions about Calvinism, for a pastoral, warmhearted love for the gospel, missions, and holiness pervades this work. I recommend this work enthusiastically."

—Thomas R. Schreiner,
James Buchanan Harrison Professor of New Testament Interpretation, Associate Dean,
The Southern Baptist Theological Seminary

"How we make the greatness of God central in our thought and in how we see ourselves and our world is at the very heart of biblically shaped faith. Over the ages, Calvinists have pondered these matters very deeply. In this book, Wright explains that for which Calvinism stands. It is a book that is informed and informative. It is lucid and forthright. And even when engaging ideas in conflict with Calvinistic beliefs it is fair and even gentle. It is a very commendable study."

—David F. Wells,
Distinguished Senior Research Professor,
Gordon-Conwell Theological Seminary

"The resurgence of Calvinism today has necessitated a book that painstakingly answers the many honest questions that are being asked about it. Thankfully, this book answers such questions with biblical and historical fidelity. Here is a book to put into the hands of such inquirers whose understanding of Calvinism may have been formed by those who caricature it. The fact that each chapter is a question helps readers go straight to the issue that is dogging them. Shawn Wright's book will also help young Calvinists to better understand and express the historic theological position they espouse—to the glory of God!"

—Conrad Mbewe,
Pastor, Kabwata Baptist Church,
Lusaka, Zambia

T0326946

"One of the most striking features of the writings of the apostle Paul is his willingness to raise the most strenuous questions against his doctrine, and then to answer those questions fully and powerfully. This follows the same pattern seen perfectly in our Lord Jesus Christ, who took on all comers and answered their deepest questions. The same spirit of courageous truth-telling fills Shawn Wright's excellent volume, *40 Questions About Calvinism*. The questions raised are comprehensive and well-organized, and each one is addressed with a wonderful balance of thoroughness and clarity. This volume will prove a helpful tool to all people seeking to understand Calvinism, and more importantly, biblical doctrine concerning God's sovereign actions in saving sinners."

—Andy Davis,
Senior Pastor, First Baptist Church,
Durham, North Carolina

"This is a clear and thoughtful book that fairly represents and quotes from alternative viewpoints, contains much informative historical material, and wisely counsels against common misunderstandings and misuses of Calvinist teaching. This book ultimately presents a highly persuasive argument that what is commonly called 'Calvinism' is, quite simply, a system of belief that is taught in the Bible from beginning to end."

—Wayne Grudem,
Distinguished Research Professor of Theology and Biblical Studies,
Phoenix Seminary

"For all those who want to understand what the Bible says about how we are saved, as well as the arguments surrounding that discussion, Shawn Wright has provided a valuable service. *40 Questions About Calvinism* provides both a clear and persuasive case for the sovereignty of God in salvation, and a helpful resource for specific questions raised by that fundamental truth. With clarity, brevity, accuracy, and always with an eye to pastoral relevancy, Dr. Wright addresses the major topics and objections to Calvinism. But the most pleasant surprise of the book, other than its positive and irenic tone, is the final section, aimed at encouraging Calvinists to be fruitful in gospel ministry because of, not in spite of, the doctrines of grace. This is a great book to hand to a church member with questions, or a young theology student in need of orientation. And it's a wonderful reminder to those of us long familiar with these doctrines that they are not only true, but beautiful, because they tend most to magnifying God's glory. I highly recommend it."

—Michael Lawrence,
Lead Pastor, Hinson Baptist Church,
Portland, Oregon

"This book is an excellent introduction to Calvinism by a seasoned scholar, Shawn Wright. Those looking for a solid overview of Calvinistic soteriology that is scholarly, yet clear and accessible, will find it here. Despite the obvious disagreements I—as an Arminian—have with Wright's Calvinistic theology, I highly recommend this erudite and well-written volume for those who want to gain a fuller understanding of the Calvinistic system of thought."

—Matthew Pinson,
President,
Welch College

40 QUESTIONS ABOUT
Calvinism

Shawn D. Wright

Benjamin L. Merkle, Series Editor

40 Questions About Calvinism
© 2019 Shawn D. Wright

Published by Kregel Academic, an imprint of Kregel Publications, 2450 Oak Industrial Dr. NE, Grand Rapids, MI 49505-6020.

This book is a title in the 40 Questions Series edited by Benjamin L. Merkle.

The Greek font GraecaU is available from www.linguistsoftware.com/lgku.htm, +1-425-775-1130.

ISBN 978-0-8254-4231-5

Printed in the United States of America

19 20 21 22 23 / 5 4 3 2 1

To Jonathan and Madison,
Oh give thanks to the Lᴏʀᴅ, for he is good;
for his steadfast love endures forever!
(Psalm 107:1)

Contents

Introduction / 9

Part 1: Introductory Questions

Section A: General Questions

1. What Is the Difference between "Calvinism" and the "Reformed Tradition"? / 17
2. What Are the Five Points of Calvinism? / 25
3. What Truths Is Calvinism Trying to Protect? / 33
4. How Should We Respond to God's Revelation? / 39

Section B: Questions about God's Character

5. Does God Love All People? / 47
6. What Is God's Grace? / 53
7. Is the Arminian Doctrine of Prevenient Grace Biblical? / 59

Section C: Questions about Human Responsibility

8. What Is Human Freedom according to Arminianism? / 67
9. What Is Human Freedom according to Calvinism? / 75
10. What Is Compatibilism? / 83
11. Does the Bible Teach Compatibilism? (Part 1) / 89
12. Does the Bible Teach Compatibilism? (Part 2) / 95

Section D: Historical Questions

13. Who Was John Calvin and What Did He Believe? / 103
14. Were There "Calvinists" before Calvin? / 109
15. Who Was Jacob Arminius and What Did He Believe? / 115
16. What Did the Synod of Dort Teach? (Part 1) / 123
17. What Did the Synod of Dort Teach? (Part 2) / 129

Part 2: Questions about Salvation

Section A: Humanity's Sin and the Necessity of Divine Intervention

18. How Sinful Are People? / 137
19. What Is Predestination according to Calvinism? / 143
20. What Does the Bible Teach about Election and Predestination? / 151
21. Is Election Unconditional? / 157
22. Is Predestination Fair? / 163

Section B: The Extent of Christ's Atonement
    23. Did Jesus Die for the Sins of the Whole World? / 173
    24. Does the Bible Teach Definite Atonement? (Part 1) / 181
    25. Does the Bible Teach Definite Atonement? (Part 2) / 187
    26. Does Substitutionary Atonement Imply Particular Redemption? / 195

Section C: God's Powerful Grace and His Preservation of His People
    27. Is God's Grace Effective? / 205
    28. Can People Resist the Holy Spirit? / 211
    29. What Is Regeneration? / 217
    30. Will Christians Persevere in the Faith? / 223

Part 3: Additional Theological Questions

    31. What Is Hyper-Calvinism? / 231
    32. If God Is Sovereign, Is He Responsible for Evil? / 237
    33. What Is the "Order of the Decrees"? / 243
    34. Does God Have Two "Wills"? / 251

Part 4: Practical Questions

    35. Why Pray If God Has Ordained All Things? / 261
    36. Do Calvinists Practice Evangelism and Missions? / 267
    37. Can Calvinists Freely and Genuinely Offer the Gospel to All People? / 273
    38. Do Calvinists Pursue Personal Holiness? / 279
    39. Does Calvinism Lead to Doubts about Assurance of Salvation? / 285
    40. Do the Questions in This Book Matter? / 291

Select Bibliography / 297
Scripture Index / 299

Introduction

"Calvinism" is a hot topic in many conservative Christian contexts in our day. Just mention the word, and you're likely to become entangled in an argument you weren't looking for. Let me be clear about my intentions in writing this book, then. I didn't compose it in order to pick a fight. Nor is it meant to prepare you to be a more adept theological brawler. Several better motivations are behind the book in front of you. In fact, four factors led me to write it.

One impetus was simply to explain. Since "Calvinist" is a provocative label that regularly breeds misunderstanding, I wanted to lay out the Calvinistic interpretation of key biblical doctrines for interested readers' consideration. I sought to explain the Calvinistic view of salvation to those interested in understanding it better, whether they are Calvinists, Arminians, or don't know what they are or why the different labels matter. My goal has not been to win an argument with Arminians, let alone to take cheap shots at their system of doctrine. As one who was an Arminian for years and largely grew up within that tradition, I have great respect for many Arminians. I have no desire to add more acrimony to what often has been a heated debate between Calvinists and Arminians carried on with varying degrees of light. Of course, though, to explain Calvinism I have had to compare it with its main evangelical rival, Arminianism. I hope that I have represented evangelical Arminianism fairly. Calvinism, I think, stands or falls based on its consistency with the Bible's own testimony of who we are, who God is, and the manner in which God saves sinners. My hope is that after reading this book, you'll be convinced that Calvinism is correct because you see its contours clearly taught throughout Scripture.

Second, I wrote this to inform those who are new to Calvinism. Many have been surprised that Calvinism has been enjoying a resurgence in our increasingly secular society.[1] There are probably several factors behind

---

1. For example, the March 23, 2009, cover story of *Time Magazine* was "10 Ideas Changing the World Right Now." The third idea noted was "The New Calvinism" by David Van Biema (http://content.time.com/time/specials/packages/article/0,28804,1884779_1884782_1884760,00.html). In addition, see Mark Oppenheimer, "Evangelicals Find Themselves in the Midst of a Calvinist Revival," *The New York Times*, Jan. 3, 2014 (https://www.nytimes.com/2014/01/04/us/a-calvinist-revival-for-evangelicals.html).

this renaissance.[2] As one who has been encouraged by the growing coterie of "young, restless, and reformed" Christians seeking to hold on to gospel convictions in our day, I want to speak to this group of men and women.[3] I want these readers to be fortified in their biblical understanding. In addition, I hope that these pages will remind you, brother and sister, that Calvinism is not fundamentally an esoteric, ivory-tower system of thought to be debated by rarified theologians. Unfortunately, it's not atypical for those new to Calvinism (we sometimes refer to this as "the cage stage" of Calvinism) to become *de facto* hyper-Calvinists for a season as they swing from Arminianism to the other end of the spectrum until they keep reading their Bibles more and see the grave errors of hyper-Calvinism. They see that they must pray. They must evangelize. Though the cage stage may be an understandable phase, we should not indulge it, because the Bible doesn't. A proud, or non-praying, or non-evangelizing, or worldly Calvinist is, at best, grossly inconsistent with his or her system of thought. My hope is that you will be provoked to humble yourself before the majesty of God more, pray more, share the gospel more, support missions more, and pursue holiness more vigorously by reading and contemplating this book. Those characteristics—not being able to dissect the intricacies of the lapsarian debates!—are what should mark biblical Calvinists.

Third, a desire that God would be glorified has fueled these pages in front of you. Throughout Scripture God's supreme desire is that he would be honored and receive the glory that is his due. As sinners, we regularly fail to do this and erect all sorts of idols to worship in the place of the one true God. As Christians our battle against indwelling sin in many ways is simply a fight to eradicate idolatry. Biblical Calvinism is the most helpful antidote to idolatry I know. At its heart, Calvinism broadcasts a God who is supreme in all ways, one who is unlimited and saves those who are unwilling and unable to save themselves.[4] The biblical heart of Calvinism is that "salvation belongs to the Lord!" (Jonah 2:9), not to us. The biblical core of Calvinism is the remarkable "but God" of Ephesians 2:4, alerting us to the fact that even though we were utterly spiritually dead, unable to save ourselves due to our willing entrapment in sin, and therefore meriting only God's righteous eternal wrath (2:1–3), God lovingly, kindly, and mercifully rescued us (2:4–6). And he did it so that he would be glorified (2:7). All of us sinners struggle to think as highly of God as we ought. Calvinism aids us to think rightly of our Lord, for it exalts the God who is absolutely sovereign. "Our God is in the heavens; he

---

2. See, for example, Mark Dever, "Where'd All These Calvinists Come From?," June 18, 2014 (https://www.9marks.org/article/whered-all-these-calvinists-come-from/).

3. Collin Hansen, *Young, Restless, Reformed: A Journalist's Journey with the New Calvinists* (Wheaton, IL: Crossway, 2008).

4. For a Bible-saturated picture of the glory of God, see John Piper, *The Pleasures of God: Meditations on God's Delight in Being God*, rev. ed. (Colorado Springs: Multnomah, 2012).

does all that he pleases" (Ps. 115:3). In this sense, I agree with B. B. Warfield's sentiments about the heart of Calvinism:

> Perhaps the simplest statement of it is the best: that it lies in a profound apprehension of God in His majesty, with the inevitably accompanying poignant realization of the exact nature of the relation sustained to Him by the creature as such, and particularly by the sinful creature. He who believes in God without reserve, and is determined that God shall be God to him in all his thinking, feeling, willing . . . is, by the force of that strictest of all logic which presides over the outworking of principles into thought and life, by the very necessity of the case, a Calvinist.[5]

My desire that we magnify God's glory has influenced the tone of this book. Although I have tried to answer common questions asked about the Calvinistic understanding of salvation, I have tried not to be fundamentally defensive. Arminians have historically expressed several grave concerns with Calvinism. I believe that each one of them is answered satisfactorily by the testimony of Scripture. And it's because of the Bible's clear witness to Calvinism that I have attempted a more positive approach in this book. Calvinism is not mainly a denial of certain things Arminianism holds to be true (such as corporate election and universal atonement). Nor is it primarily an assertion of truths that Arminians say Calvinists cannot legitimately believe (such as indiscriminate gospel proclamation, God's love for all people, and the importance of prayer). Although that is a common portrayal, the reality is much different. Calvinism asserts truths; it doesn't fundamentally deny things. And it asserts those truths based on the authority of God's self-revelation to us in Scripture. Calvinism proclaims, "God saves!" Because of that, "All glory belongs to him!"

Fourth, I have been motivated by a desire that we rightly understand the gospel, the good news of reconciliation that God effects between sinners and himself.[6] Evangelicals are gospel-people. Calvinist or Arminian, we believe that people are sinners who must be born again (John 3:3). Calvinists rejoice that our non-Calvinistic brothers and sisters believe these truths and tell them to non-Christians. How effective, though, is the gospel to save?

Calvinism believes that in the gospel of Jesus Christ God actually accomplishes the salvation of his chosen people. It rejoices in these truths because

---

5. B. B. Warfield, "Calvinism," in *Calvin and Augustine* (Phillipsburg, NJ: P&R, 1980), 288–89.
6. Two helpful books on the gospel are Greg Gilbert, *What Is the Gospel?* (Wheaton, IL: Crossway, 2010) and Will Metzger, *Tell the Truth: The Whole Gospel to the Whole Person by Whole People* (Downers Grove, IL: InterVarsity, 1984).

the gospel teaches us that "Christ Jesus came into the world to save sinners" (1 Tim. 1:15). He completed his mission. Indeed, his name is Jesus "for he will save his people from their sins" (Matt. 1:21). Calvinism rejoices in the fact that God in Christ accomplished all that he determined to do in saving his people from their sins. It's only by God's particular grace that anyone—Calvinist, Arminian, or anyone else—believes the gospel and receives salvation. Praise his name! Calvinism stresses that God in the gospel actually saves his chosen ones by the power of his Spirit (John 3:8).

This is the "Amazing Grace" gospel of John Newton that actually saves wretches like you and me. And it's the "And Can it Be?" gospel that Charles Wesley lauded when he sang,

> Long my imprisoned spirit lay
> Fast bound in sin and nature's night;
> Thine eye diffused a quickening ray,
> I woke, the dungeon flamed with light;
> My chains fell off, my heart was free.

Calvinism is not the gospel. But it is a clearer expression of the biblical gospel than any of its evangelical rivals. I hope readers will be encouraged to trust in, and share, the gospel of Jesus Christ by reading these pages.

These four reasons motivated me to write this book. There's not much, if anything, new in it. I have benefited from reading many authors who have helped me to understand Calvinism better. You will see many of their names in the footnotes. However, the format of the 40 Questions series makes it uniquely helpful both in displaying the contours of Calvinism and in answering the typical concerns people have about it. Patient readers who work through the book in its entirety will understand the Calvinistic understanding of salvation in its totality. Yet its format will also enable readers to find answers to the questions they have by turning directly to the pertinent questions. For those who would like to quickly understand the argument of this book, I would suggest starting with five questions: 2, 3, 6, 10, and 40. The answers to these five questions get to the biblical essence of Calvinism, I think. The seventeen questions of Part 1 introduce the subject. Here you will understand what I mean by "Calvinism," what the answers to three of the most prevalent Arminian arguments against Calvinism (God's love, prevenient grace, and human free will) are, and what the most pertinent historical background issues are in the differences between Calvinism and Arminianism. Part 2 explains the significance of TULIP, or "the five points of Calvinism," showing their importance and the biblical justification for them. In Part 3, I deal with four additional theological issues related to Calvinism that are not part of the "five points." Finally, Part 4 attempts to encourage Calvinists to be practical—i.e., biblical!—in their doctrine. If you think that Calvinism has no bearing on real life, you might want to begin your reading here.

I could not have written this book on my own. I owe a fundamental debt to my father, Robert Wright (1933–2010), who taught me to love Jesus and trust the Bible. Though he never agreed with all of my Calvinism, he loved his Bible. I hope he would appreciate the biblical character and irenic tone of this book. One of the hardest parts of writing this book was narrowing down my initial list of well over sixty questions to the forty you now have in front of you. Several friends helped me to arrive at these forty. My thanks in this regard to Andrew Ballitch, David Dykes, Joshua Greever, Steve Matteucci, John Morrison, Matthew Robbins, Tom Rogstad, Tom Schreiner, and Gary Steward. My dear wife, Gretchen, read most of the penultimate draft of the book and asked many good questions and made many astute observations of it that, I hope, made the final version much clearer. Two friends at Clifton Baptist Church, Ken Billings and Tom Rogstad, kindly read the entire book and made helpful suggestions about both style and content. Ben Merkle, the book's editor, encouraged both lucidity and brevity. I hope I heeded his advice. I also thank the trustees of The Southern Baptist Theological Seminary for granting me a half-sabbatical to work on this book, and its president, R. Albert Mohler Jr., and my dean, Gregory A. Wills, for supporting my efforts. Thank you, dear friends. Of course, I alone bear responsibility for the final contents of this book in front of you.

Finally, I dedicate this book to my son, Jonathan, and his wife, Madison. From a young age Jonathan regularly asked insightful questions about Scripture and theology as we worked our way through a catechism, read the Bible together, dialogued about our Muslim neighbors in Central Asia, and discussed numerous books and sermons. He continues to be one of my regular and trusted conversation partners. Madison grew up in Papua New Guinea in a family fueled by the beliefs expressed in this book and out of a desire to bring the gospel to a people who never before heard of Christ. She exemplifies the reality that biblical Calvinists are evangelists and missionaries. I pray that Jonathan and Madison will delight even more in the God of their salvation as they revel in the biblical truths Calvinism trumpets.

PART 1

Introductory Questions

General Questions

What Is the Difference between "Calvinism" and the "Reformed Tradition"?

Since "Calvinism" is an easily misunderstood term, we need to define it carefully, especially distinguishing it from "Reformed," a word with broader connotations than "Calvinism." Calvinism is a movement set on recovering the Bible's understanding of the relationship between a sovereign God and responsible sinners. It spans many centuries and has been affirmed by pastors and theologians from a variety of church backgrounds.

"Reformed" vs. "Calvinist"

We need to clarify two essential words: "Reformed" and "Calvinist." Philip Benedict notes that the followers of John Calvin did not prefer the latter term. Instead, they styled "themselves variously the evangelical, reformed, evangelical reformed, or reformed Catholic church, the term *reformed* emerging as the most common label" in the latter part of the sixteenth century.[1] "Reformed," then, has a historically rooted genesis. These churchmen sought to distinguish themselves from both Catholics and Lutherans.

"Reformed" often has connotations that are beyond the debate between Calvinism and Arminianism over soteriology.[2] John R. de Witt, for example, identifies seven key distinctive markers of the Reformed tradition.[3] First, it stresses not only the truthfulness of Scripture but also that the Bible must be followed in its entirety. Second, God is completely sovereign. The

---

1. Philip Benedict, *Christ's Churches Purely Reformed: A Social History of Calvinism* (New Haven, CT: Yale University Press, 2002), xxiii (italics original).
2. "Soteriology" refers to the doctrine of salvation.
3. John Richard de Witt, *What Is the Reformed Faith?* (Edinburgh: Banner of Truth, 1981).

Reformed tradition insists that "nothing can stop or retard the progress of the gathering of his elect people, the building of his church, the coming of his kingdom."[4] Third, God's grace towards his elect children is invincible. Fourth, Christians must submit to Jesus as Lord, not just hold on to him as Savior. We can't have the latter apart from the former. Fifth, there is a distinction between biblical law and gospel. Fundamentally, the law teaches us how God desires for his children to live. Sixth, God has given his people the "cultural mandate" so that the church would impact society for God's glory (see Gen. 1:28). Seventh, the Reformed tradition has a distinct view of pastoral ministry "and of the life of the church in relation to it," which is marked by a particular form of church order.[5]

I. John Hesselink similarly offers five "characteristics and distinctive emphases" of the Reformed tradition.[6] First, it is God-centered, especially in its emphasis that God has to sovereignly make sinners willing to come to Christ. Second, it bases life and ministry on Scripture. Third, it teaches that doctrine must impact how one lives. Fourth, it develops a particular view of the individual Christian's relationship to the surrounding culture such that the believer should seek to glorify God in every facet of his or her life, whether he or she is called to be a bricklayer or a missionary. Finally, it has a particular view of the church, most commonly seen in Presbyterian ecclesiology, with its emphasis on both teaching elders and ruling elders and their particular relationship to the congregation.[7]

Both de Witt and Hesselink alert us to the fact that "Reformed" is about more than just how one comes to be saved by Jesus. It involves worldview distinctives and the cultural mandate (which we will not address in this book). It also has much to do with a particular vision of what the church is. According to Benedict, "At its core was the conviction that God's holy word made clear the form of worship expected from his children. . . . The gratitude they owed [God] in return should inspire them to serve him in all their deeds, to worship in the manner he had decreed, and to shun all false devotion and idolatry."[8] In other words, part of "being Reformed" is that one follows the "regulative principle," which is simply the belief that God in Scripture has regulated both how the church is to be organized and how the church is to worship him. In this way, the Reformed were different from Lutherans who assumed that as long as their worship practices were not clearly prohibited biblically, it was

---

4. Ibid., 9.

5. Ibid., 17.

6. I. John Hesselink, *On Being Reformed: Distinctive Characteristics and Common Misunderstandings* (Ann Arbor, MI: Servant, 1983), 95.

7. Ibid., 104–5.

8. Benedict, *Christ's Churches Purely Reformed*, xv–xvi.

fine to use them in their liturgy. "Reformed," in part then, has to do with one's vision of the church and worship.[9]

Richard Muller made a similar point in critiquing the notion of a "Reformed Baptist." Even though such a Baptist's soteriology might be orthodox, that individual fails to see it as part of a larger complex of ideas that are antithetical to his or her Baptist identity. Reformed Baptists are out of line, for example, with the Reformed confessions, which

> are carefully embodied patterns of teaching, drawn from Scripture and brought to bear on the life of the church. They are, in short, interpretations of the whole of Christian existence that cohere in all of their points. If some of the less-famous points of Reformed theology, like the baptism of infants, justification by grace alone through faith, the necessity of a thankful obedience consequent upon our faith and justification (the "third use of the law"), the identification of the sacraments as means of grace, the so-called amillennial view of the end of the world, and so forth, are stripped away or forgotten, the remaining famous five [i.e., the five points of Calvinism] make very little sense.[10]

De Witt, Hesselink, and Muller rightly emphasize that "Reformed" has much broader connotations than "Calvinism," avenues of the Reformed tradition that we are not going to travel in our study. For this reason, throughout the rest of the book I will forego the term "Reformed" and use "Calvinism" to identify the distinctive doctrinal position this book is intended to explain and endorse.

Why "Calvinism"?

I still need to answer the question, Why are you using a label to define a doctrinal viewpoint based on one particular person? Later, we will see just how important John Calvin is for the tradition that takes his name.[11] For now, we can note that Calvin's formulation of essential doctrines regarding salvation was so clearly manifested and beautifully articulated in his magnum opus, *The Institutes of the Christian Religion* (1559), and he was so active in defending his views from the Bible against Catholic, Lutheran, and Anabaptist opponents

---

9. On the "regulative principle of worship," see J. Ligon Duncan III, "Does God Care How We Worship?" and "Foundations for Biblically Directed Worship," in *Give Praise to God: A Vision for Reforming Worship*, ed. Philip Graham Ryken, Derek W. H. Thomas, and J. Ligon Duncan III (Phillipsburg, NJ: P&R, 2003), 17–73.
10. Richard A. Muller, "How Many Points?" *Calvin Theological Journal* 28 (1993): 428.
11. See Question 13.

that his way of understanding God's relationship to sinful humanity quickly came to be called by the shorthand name, "Calvinism."[12]

The next two chapters will define what I intend to communicate when I speak of "Calvinism." Much of the rest of the book attempts to explain and defend it. For now, though, I can say with B. B. Warfield, a nineteenth- and twentieth-century Calvinist theologian, that

> Whoever believes in God; whoever recognizes in the re-
> cesses of his soul his utter dependence on God; whoever in
> all his thought of salvation hears in his heart of hearts the
> echo of the *soli Deo gloria*[13] of the evangelical profession—by
> whatever name he may call himself, or by whatever intellec-
> tual puzzles his logical understanding may be confused—
> Calvinism recognizes as implicitly a Calvinist, and as only
> requiring to permit these fundamental principles—which
> underlie and give its body to all true religion—to work them-
> selves freely and fully out in thought and feeling and action,
> to become explicitly a Calvinist.[14]

"Calvinism," then, is a particular way of understanding how a sinner is saved that differs from Catholicism, Lutheranism, and Arminianism. Arminians, especially, forced the followers of Calvin to search the Scripture to answer the question of the relationship between a sovereign God and sinful humans in an individual's salvation.[15] J. I. Packer stresses that the two systems are antithetical to one another. Calvinism preaches a God who sovereignly saves his elect, whereas Arminianism teaches that God gives all fallen people the ability to do what they need to do in order to coop-erate with God in their salvation.[16] Calvinism proclaims that in salvation the three Persons of the Trinity are united in their saving acts towards the same people ("election by the Father, redemption by the Son, and calling by the Holy Spirit") which secures the elect's salvation; Arminianism divides the objects of affection of the three Persons ("the objects of redemption being all mankind; of calling, all who hear the gospel; of election, those who respond"). Packer's summary is apt:

---

12. Benedict, *Christ's Churches Purely Reformed*, xxii–xxiii.
13. *soli Deo gloria* means "to God alone belongs the glory."
14. B. B. Warfield, "Calvinism," in *Calvin and Augustine* (Phillipsburg, NJ: P&R, 1980), 290.
15. See Question 15.
16. Calvinism "holds that God saves sinners without their assistance, while synergism ('working together') [the Arminian view] teaches that salvation depends on our coopera-tion. In all its varieties, synergism teaches that God's grace makes everything possible, but our response makes everything actual" (Michael Horton, *Pilgrim Theology: Core Doctrines for Christian Disciples* [Grand Rapids: Zondervan, 2012], 251).

> The two theologies thus conceive the plan of salvation in quite different terms. One makes salvation depend on the work of God, the other on a work of man; one regards faith as part of God's gift of salvation, the other as man's own contribution to salvation; one gives all the glory of saving believers to God, the other divides the praise between God, who, so to speak, built the machinery of salvation, and man, who by believing operated it.[17]

Arminianism asserts "synergism," the idea that human salvation is the result of the cooperation between the gracious, sovereign God and renewed human freedom. Calvinism, alternatively, affirms "monergism," the biblical reality that God alone acts to save spiritually dead people whom he's elected to be his own. Calvinism, in other words, is just shorthand expressing the biblical reality that God saves his people, the ones he has eternally chosen to belong to him, the ones for whom his Son died. It's the life-giving truth of Ephesians 2:4: "but God." It's the soul-comforting reality of Romans 8:28: "we know that for those who love God all things work together for good, for those who are called according to his purpose," and of Romans 8:39 that nothing "will be able to separate us from the love of God in Christ Jesus our Lord." It's the praise-inspiring, hope-giving certainty of Galatians 2:20: "I have been crucified with Christ. It is no longer I who live, but Christ who lives in me. And the life I now live in the flesh I live by faith in the Son of God, who loved me and gave himself for me." This is what the rest of this book means by "Calvinism."

It is the same poetic theology of hymns such as "A Debtor to Mercy Alone" by Augustus Toplady (1740–1778):

> A debtor to mercy alone,
> Of covenant mercy I sing;
> Nor fear, with Thy righteousness on,
> My person and off'ring to bring.
> The terrors of law and of God
> With me can have nothing to do;
> My Savior's obedience and blood
> Hide all my transgressions from view
>
> The work which His goodness began,
> The arm of His strength will complete;
> His promise is Yea and Amen,

---

17. J. I. Packer, "'Saved by His Precious Blood': An Introduction to John Owen's *The Death of Death in the Death of Christ*," in *A Quest for Godliness: The Puritan Vision of the Christian Life* (Wheaton, IL: Crossway, 1990), 128–29.

And never was forfeited yet.
Things future, nor things that are now,
Nor all things below or above,
Can make Him His purpose forgo,
Or sever my soul from His love.

My name from the palms of His hands
Eternity will not erase;
Impressed on His heart it remains
In marks of indelible grace.
Yes, I to the end shall endure,
As sure as the earnest is giv'n;
More happy, but not more secure,
The glorified spirits in heav'n.

The "Calvinism" of This Book

In researching and writing this book, I have employed numerous sources from soteriological Calvinists. If you peruse the footnotes, you will notice that most of them span in time from the sixteenth to the twenty-first century. I didn't intentionally try to have sources from each of these periods, but you'll notice, for example, John Calvin from the sixteenth century, Francis Turretin from the seventeenth, Jonathan Edwards from the eighteenth, Robert Dabney from the nineteenth, J. I. Packer from the twentieth, and Roger Nicole from the twenty-first. Beyond that, I refer to "Calvinists" who predated Calvin in the sixth century up to the Reformation of the sixteenth century.[18] You'll also see that some of them are Presbyterian or Reformed, some Congregationalist, some Baptist, some Anglican, and others are non-denominational in orientation. In fact, Augustine and others referenced in Question 14 were Catholics! In other words, I have intentionally tried to support my biblical case with a variety of sources to guard myself from presenting a minority position within Calvinism.

Additionally, I have often used two Calvinistic confessional documents that have garnered broad support among Calvinists. The first, the *Canons of the Synod of Dort* (1618–19), were written directly to controvert the new movement of Arminianism.[19] It has confessional status in the Dutch Reformed tradition. The second, the *Westminster Confession of Faith* (1646), was a product of English Puritans (primarily Presbyterians, but some others too) during an unusual period of Puritan control in England.[20] The Westminster Confession, which has confessional status in Presbyterian churches, is probably the most

---

18. See Question 14.
19. See Questions 16 and 17.
20. See, for example, Chad Van Dixhoorn, *Confessing the Faith: A Reader's Guide to the Westminster Confession of Faith* (Edinburgh: Banner of Truth, 2014).

significant confessional document in English-speaking churches because of its broad influence. Twelve years after its production, in 1658, English Congregationalists led by John Owen revised it slightly and released it as the Savoy Declaration. Eager to show that they were similar to their Presbyterian and Congregationalist brethren, English Baptists used both Westminster and Savoy as the basis for their Second London Baptist Confession, often referred to as the 1689 Confession because of its year of public release.[21] The Westminster–Savoy–1689 tradition agrees on almost all matters of soteriological significance. Given its influence in the English-speaking world, I have used the Westminster Confession frequently as an expression of Calvinistic thought in this book.

REFLECTION QUESTIONS

1. Do you think the distinction between "Reformed" and "Calvinistic" is important? Why?

2. How would you define a "Reformed" Christian in your own words?

3. Do you think Warfield is correct in his quotation above, or is he a bit arrogant? Why?

4. How do you think that your own history with Calvinism will impact your interaction with the material in the rest of the book? Are there particular aspects of your own journey you especially need to be aware of as you consider Calvinism?

5. Have you read the Westminster Confession of Faith (or its Congregationalist or Baptist derivatives)? If not, it might be helpful to read a copy.

---

21. Released in 1689, it had actually been composed in 1677.

What Are the Five Points of Calvinism?

The "five points of Calvinism" are a summary of Calvinists' response to the Arminian view of the manner in which sinners are saved. They are not the gospel, but they are important for how we understand the gospel, how we think of God, how we navigate the difficulties of life, and how we worship our Lord. The five points supremely remind us that from beginning to end "salvation belongs to the LORD" (Jonah 2:9). God chose his people for salvation (1) out of the helpless state of their sin (2) simply because he desired to save them and not due to anything he saw in them. (3) He sent his Son to atone for all their sins. (4) He calls them to himself in the gospel and overcomes their sinful resistance. (5) And he preserves them in the faith until he brings them to be with him eternally in heaven. These are the five points.

The Ironies of the Five Points of Calvinism

Ironies abound in labeling these truths the "five points of Calvinism." First, even though I think the five points are all found in John Calvin's writings, he never summarized his beliefs using these categories. Second, when Calvinists came up with the "five points" they were not intending to summarize everything about Calvinistic theology. Instead, they were responding to five attacks on their faith from a group of Arminians. Arminians are, in a sense, responsible for the five points of Calvinism. Third, even though many students remember the five points by the TULIP mnemonic (total depravity, unconditional election, limited atonement, irresistible grace, and the perseverance of the saints), that was not originally a summary of Calvinism. The tulip as a memory device (which would have been very fitting since the Dutch are known for their beautiful tulips and the Synod of Dort took place in the Netherlands) would not have worked in Latin, which was the language in which the five points were originally written. TULIP was developed later, and it is probably not the most helpful way to summarize the five points, as our exposition below will show.

TULIP, then, is prone to misunderstanding. Timothy Paul Jones and Daniel Montgomery suggest that its genesis dates to 1905 when Cleland McAfee first summarized Calvinism's five points using this TULIP acrostic:

T	T̲otal depravity
U	U̲niversal sovereignty
L	L̲imited atonement
I	I̲rresistible grace
P	P̲erseverance of the saints[1]

In fact, Calvinists had summarized Dort's findings differently for generations.[2] In 1895, prominent Calvinist theologian Robert L. Dabney published a booklet on the five points of Calvinism. He was not willing to truncate the doctrine into a simple mnemonic but often provided several summary points. Dabney, first of all, spoke of "original sin, total depravity, and inability of the will." Not denying human agency, he denied the fallen sinner's ability to do any good on his own.[3] Second, he considered "the nature and agency of the moral revolution, named effectual calling and regeneration." Such a divine intervention is essential to reverse "the original dispositions which hitherto prompted the soul to choose sin and reject godliness."[4] Third, he noted "God's election" of individuals to salvation which Scripture teaches is both "unconditioned and sovereign."[5] Fourth, Dabney discussed "particular redemption" while, fifth, he summarized the "perseverance of the saints."[6] TULIP was not sacrosanct.

The Five Points of Calvinism

These truths matter. They matter because they are central to our understanding of the gospel. The five points of Calvinism are all about God and his grace—how planned it is, how effective it is, how much we contribute to it, how lasting it is. For this reason, some Calvinists prefer to call these truths

---

1. Daniel Montgomery and Timothy Paul Jones, *Proof: Finding Freedom through the Intoxicating Joy of Irresistible Grace* (Grand Rapids: Zondervan, 2014), 132. The article in which this date is given is an appendix in Kenneth J. Stewart, *Ten Myths about Calvinism: Recovering the Breadth of the Reformed Tradition* (Downers Grove, IL: InterVarsity Press, 2011), 291–92.
2. In 1913 William Vail recorded the opinions of several Reformed thinkers prior to this date. He notes four different options for categorizing and labeling the "five points" (William H. Vail, "The Reader's View," in *The Outlook* [June 21, 1913], in Stewart, *Ten Myths*, 291–92).
3. Robert L. Dabney, *The Five Points of Calvinism* (1895; Harrisonburg, VA: Sprinkle, 1992), 8.
4. Ibid., 25.
5. Ibid., 38, 41.
6. Ibid., 60, 66.

"the doctrines of grace."[7] As our exposition of each of the five points will now demonstrate, they are all about God's grace.

T: Total (or Radical) Depravity[8]

Sin is our rebellion against our Creator and Lord. Selfishly, we have made ourselves gods and have tried to overturn the rightful rule of Almighty God. Adam represented us all and so plunged each one of us into an existence of sinfulness and guilt. We are born as sinners, and everything we do in life is affected by our sin. Because of our depravity, none of us seeks after God or can obey him.[9]

The "T" of TULIP, "total," is meant to portray how pervasive sin is in fallen humanity. Sin affects every part of us, as Roger Nicole reminds us:

> Evil is at the very heart and root of man. It is at the very foundation, at the deepest level of human life. This evil does not corrupt merely one or two or certain particular avenues of the life of man but is pervasive in that it spreads into all aspects of the life of man. It darkens his mind, corrupts his feelings, warps his will, moves his affections in wrong directions, blinds his conscience, burdens his subconscious, afflicts his body.[10]

In this regard then—since our minds, affections, and volition are penetrated by the devastating effects of sin—Nicole suggests that "radical" or "pervasive" depravity are what we intend rather than the sweeping "total."[11] The moniker "total depravity" claims too much, for "it suggests that there is no good whatsoever in human beings, that we are always as wicked as we might possibly be."[12] This is not what Calvinism claims. Rather, "Sin is *radical* in the sense that it touches the root (*radix*) of our lives," according to R. C. Sproul.[13] Every part of what we are as humans is affected by our sin. Every part. Sproul is right: if people "really accepted the biblical view of human corruption, the debate about predestination" would already be decided.[14] The

---

7. E.g., Roger Nicole, *Our Sovereign Saviour: The Essence of the Reformed Faith* (Fearn, UK: Christian Focus, 2002), 75–89; Thomas J. Nettles, *By His Grace and for His Glory: A Historical, Theological, and Practical Study of the Doctrines of Grace in Baptist Life* (Lake Charles, LA: Cor Meum Tibi, 2002).

8. See Question 16.

9. Scripture proof for each of the five points will be given in subsequent chapters.

10. Nicole, *Our Sovereign Saviour*, 48.

11. Ibid., 49.

12. Timothy George, *Amazing Grace: God's Pursuit, Our Response*, 2nd ed. (Wheaton, IL: Crossway, 2011), 84.

13. R. C. Sproul, *Chosen by God*, rev. ed. (Carol Stream, IL: Tyndale, 1986), 80 (italics original).

14. Ibid., 81.

pervasive, radical nature of our sinfulness necessitates a divinely initiated salvation outside of ourselves.

U: Unconditional (Sovereign) Election[15]

Before the creation of the world, and apart from viewing anything that we would do regarding salvation, God chose (or elected) a particular group of people to be his own. He set his affections on this group because he loved them. In love he gave them everything that they would need for salvation—a Savior, saving faith, the regenerating and sustaining grace of his Spirit, redemption, adoption, and sanctification. The central point emphasized here, according to Nicole, is that "it is God who takes the initiative. There is no previous merit or condition in the creature, either present or foreseen, which determines the divine choice." In other words, "God in his own sovereign wisdom chooses, for reasons that are sufficient unto himself, those who shall be saved." Thus, Nicole prefers "sovereign election" to "unconditional election."[16]

L: Limited (or Definite) Atonement[17]

The saving effects of Christ's death are limited to the elect. In other words, Jesus died specifically for those whom the Father had given him and for the ones to whom the Spirit would grant faith. The substitutionary death of Christ on the cross was purposeful and definite.

For this reason, many Calvinists have taken issue with the term "limited" when applied to the atonement. Nicole, for instance, notes that Calvinists and Arminians both "limit" the atonement, the former in terms of its breadth (to the elect alone), the latter in terms of its depth (it is ineffective in itself to save people, who must add something to it to make it effective). The real question, he insists, is, What was Christ's purpose in dying? It was definite, hence Nicole's favored term, "definite atonement." Christ's substitutionary work "was not a blanket substitution. It was a substitution that was oriented specifically for the purpose for which he came into this world, namely, to save and redeem those whom the Father has given him." One could also call it "particular redemption" since Jesus's death "is planned for particular people and accomplished what it purposed."[18] The purposive nature of Christ's death leads Michael Horton to note that God's verdict of Christ's death was "mission accomplished."[19]

---

15. See Questions 18–22.
16. Nicole, *Our Sovereign Saviour*, 49–50. Timothy George also prefers "sovereign election" to "unconditional election" (*Amazing Grace*, 87).
17. See Questions 22–25.
18. Nicole, *Our Sovereign Saviour*, 51.
19. Michael Horton, *Putting Amazing Back Into Grace: Embracing the Heart of the Gospel*, rev ed. (Grand Rapids: Baker, 2011), 105–25.

I: Irresistible (or Effective) Grace[20]

God's saving grace is always effective to save the ones whom he has chosen and for whom Christ died and to whom the Spirit has granted faith. In this sense, then, it is irresistible. It accomplishes God's purpose, which is the salvation of his people. However, "irresistible" can be misunderstood, as Timothy George points out,

> because it seems to suggest that sinners come to God in a mechanical, impersonal way, as a piece of metal is drawn to a magnet. . . . In the Bible, not only *can* grace be resisted, but it invariably is. . . . Like wayward sheep, we have all resisted and gone astray (see Isa. 53:6). I like the term *overcoming grace* because it conveys the truth witnessed to by so many Christians: despite their stubbornness and rebellion, they say, God did not give up on them. Like a persistent lover, he kept on wooing until, at last, his persistence won the day. His love and mercy overcame their rebellious resistance.[21]

God's grace cannot finally be resisted if he has determined to save the person. At some point, he will overcome their resistance. His grace will be effective (or, to use the older word, "effectual") to save his chosen people.

P: Perseverance (or Preservation) of the Saints[22]

Christians will forever remain Christians. They can't and won't "lose their salvation," for God eternally chose them for salvation, Christ paid for all their sins, and the Spirit will sustain them in their faith. They will, by God's grace, persevere in the faith until they go to be with the Lord. Saying "perseverance" stresses our role in keeping ourselves in the faith, which is certainly a biblical emphasis. Thus, Peter tells us that Christians "by God's power are being guarded through faith for a salvation ready to be revealed in the last time" (1 Peter 1:5). They truly exercise faith. The greater emphasis, though, is that God will keep his people because "those who have been won by the grace of God will not lose out but will be preserved by God's grace to ultimate salvation." Nicole avers, "The key to perseverance is the preservation by God of his saints, that is, the stability of his purpose and the fixity of his design."[23] Because God has sovereignly saved his people, he will keep them for all eternity as his beloved children.

---

20. See Questions 26–28.
21. George, *Amazing Grace*, 86 (italics original).
22. See Question 30.
23. Nicole, *Our Sovereign Saviour*, 53–54.

Do the Points Matter?

The five points are not Scripture. But for several reasons, they are important. First, Calvinism is not a logical system per se. It is an attempt to understand what God has revealed in Scripture about himself, his ways, and us. We are bound to the word of God, and we see these truths revealed there. Second, non-Calvinists regularly question the legitimacy of these biblical truths. There are aspects of Calvinism that strike humans as unfair or utterly incomprehensible. The temptation is to deny them because they do not sit well with us. Since there are continual attacks on these precious gospel truths, there is a need for regular defenses of them. Third, Calvinism is an attempt to delight in what God delights in, namely, his sovereign glory. Paul exclaims, "Oh the depth of the riches and wisdom and knowledge of God! How unsearchable are his judgments and how inscrutable his ways! . . . For from him and through him and to him are all things. To him be glory forever" (Rom. 11:33, 36). Calvinism emphasizes God's rights as the King who reigns over all, who always accomplishes exactly what he wills (Ps. 115:3). Fourth, Calvinism revels in the fact that the gospel is a gospel of grace. All other -isms add something as a necessary component to our salvation. But Dabney was right to note that "the Bible system of grace" is what "men call Calvinism." He suggests that Calvinism's

> grand evidence is that it corresponds with Scripture. "Let God be true, and every man a liar." This doctrine exalts God, his power, his sovereign, unbought love and mercy. They are entitled to be supremely exalted. This doctrine humbles man in the dust. He ought to be humbled; he is a guilty, lost sinner, the sole yet the certain architect of his own ruin. Helpless, yet guilty of all that makes him helpless, he ought to take his place in the deepest contrition, and gives all the glory of his redemption to God. This doctrine, while it lays man's pride low, gives him an anchor of hope, sure and steadfast, drawing him to heaven; for his hope is founded not in the weakness, folly, and fickleness of his human will, but in the eternal love, wisdom, and power of almighty God.[24]

Finally, only the truths of Calvinism can ultimately comfort Christians through the hardships of life. The truth that God in his grace set his affection on us and promises to keep us as his own will sustain us as we sojourn through this world to heaven.

---

24. Dabney, *Five Points of Calvinism*, 79–80.

REFLECTION QUESTIONS

1. Do you think TULIP is a helpful way to summarize Calvinism? Why?

2. What are other acrostics for summarizing Calvinism's five points that you know?

3. Are there particular points of the five that you disagree with? Why?

4. Would you add other points to explain the heart of Calvinism? What are they?

5. Do you agree with Dabney's quote at the end of this chapter? Why?

What Truths Is Calvinism Trying to Protect?

Every theological system has a core principle, or principles, it is unwilling to compromise. The last chapter showed that Calvinism's five points are not its core principle. Rather, they guard the biblical truth that God saves his people. The five points, instead, are part of a nexus of beliefs that revolve around and protect Calvinism's understanding of God. Calvinism teaches that God is the sovereign Lord who is free, glorious, and particular in his affections.

Arminianism's Core Principles

Before looking at Calvinism's core principles, we should examine those of Arminianism so that we can understand Calvinism's perspective better. One apologist for Arminianism argues that, as opposed to Calvinism, Arminianism "exults in the free offer of grace and bears joyous testimony to God's loving kindness."[1] God's love, he says, and the corresponding freeness of grace define Arminianism. In Arminianism, the "universality of grace" is fundamental, leading to the basic presupposition of the system: "that God is good in an unqualified manner, and that he desires the salvation of all sinners."[2] Calvinism, by contrast, stumbles over these biblical realities in three ways, he argues: "Exegetically, it stumbles over the great universal texts of Scripture. Theologically, it impugns the goodness of God and casts a dark shadow over the gospel. Morally, far from glorifying his justice, it calls it into question and raises very serious doubts about it."[3]

---

1. John Wagner, "Foreword," in *Grace for All: The Arminian Dynamics of Salvation* (Eugene, OR: Wipf and Stock, 2015), xviii.
2. Ibid., xv.
3. Ibid., xviii.

Jerry Walls and Joseph Dongell also charge Calvinism with distorting who God is. They argue that

> the truly fundamental dispute is not over power but rather over God's character. . . . The fundamental issue here is which theological paradigm does a better job of representing the biblical picture of God's character: which theological system gives a more adequate account of the biblical God whose nature is holy love?

In failing to emphasize God's "holy love," they contend, Calvinism "distorts the biblical picture of God."[4] Instead, they focus on God's holy love which stresses the Lord's goodness as a means of freeing God from any responsibility for the sin and evil rampant in this world.

Roger Olson is equally explicit: "Real Arminianism has always believed in human freedom for one main reason—to protect the goodness of God and thus God's reputation in a world filled with evil."[5] Arminianism, then, is an apologetic scheme which stresses human free will for two reasons: "First, to protect and defend God's goodness; second to make clear human responsibility for sin and evil."[6] Since Arminianism centers on defending God's goodness from any involvement in or approval of evil, it judges Calvinism as a grave error. Olson charges that Calvinism's "theology may be God-centered but the God at its center is unworthy of being the center. Better a man-centered theology than one that revolves around a being hardly distinguishable from the devil."[7]

Thankfully, Olson is unusual among contemporary Arminians for his scathing opinion of Calvinism's vision of God. Nonetheless, he and the other Arminians we noted identified the chief issue as the vision each system has of God. It remains for us to examine Calvinism's view of the Lord.

Calvinism's Chief Principle: God Is God

"As Calvinists," Joel Beeke writes, "we are enamored with God. We are overwhelmed by His majesty, His beauty, His holiness, and His grace. We seek His glory, desire His presence, and model our lives after Him."[8] "Calvinists,"

---

4. Jerry L. Walls and Joseph R. Dongell, *Why I Am Not a Calvinist* (Downers Grove, IL: InterVarsity Press, 2004), 8. For a Calvinistic treatment of God's holy love, see David F. Wells, *God in the Whirlwind: How the Holy-love of God Reorients Our World* (Wheaton, IL: Crossway, 2014).
5. Roger Olson, "Arminianism Is God-Centered Theology," in *Grace for All: The Arminian Dynamics of Salvation* (Eugene, OR: Wipf and Stock, 2015), 6.
6. Ibid.
7. Ibid.
8. Joel R. Beeke, *Living for God's Glory: An Introduction to Calvinism* (Orlando: Reformation Trust, 2008), 42.

he says, "are people whose theology is dominated by the idea of God."[9] He's right. Calvinists' chief principle is the idea that all of history and life is dominated by one reigning, personal being—God. "In the beginning God" (Gen. 1:1); "by [Christ] all things were created, in heaven and on earth, visible and invisible, whether thrones or dominions or rulers or authorities—all things were created through him and for him" (Col. 1:16); "from [God] and through him and to him are all things. To him be glory forever. Amen" (Rom. 11:36).

The Westminster Confession defines God as "infinite in being and perfection." He is "immutable, immense, eternal, incomprehensible, almighty, most wise, most holy, most free, most absolute." He is "most loving, gracious, merciful, long-suffering, abundant in goodness and truth, forgiving iniquity, transgression, and sin" (2.1). God has "all life, glory, goodness, blessedness, in and of Himself; and is alone in and unto Himself all-sufficient." "He is the alone fountain of all being, of whom, through whom, and to whom are all things; and hath most sovereign dominion over them, to do by them, for them, or upon them whatsoever Himself pleaseth" (2.2). Westminster, largely using the language of Scripture, sketches out some of the God-ness of God.

B. B. Warfield agrees with the Confession. He argues that Calvinism's heart "lies in a profound apprehension of God in His majesty."

In Calvinism, he observes, "theism comes to its rights" because Calvinism trumpets God as majestic.[10] He not only knows and plans all that comes to pass in human history, but he actively works his great will so that it is accomplished. In this, he is distinctly unlike us. Indeed, in this, he shows himself to be God.

God Is Sovereignly Free

Flowing from his deity, God is sovereign over all his creation and he is free to do within it whatever he chooses to do. No one and nothing has the right or the power to oppose him or question his actions. His sovereignty is an aspect of his deity, for if he could not control all aspects of his creation and even left a small part of it up to chance, he would not be the King. Warfield is correct that

> A God who could or would make a creature whom he could not or would not control, is no God. . . . He would have ceased to be a moral being. It is an immoral act to make a thing that we cannot or will not control. . . . To suppose that God has made a universe—or even a single being—the control of which he renounces, is to accuse him of similar immorality.[11]

---

9. Ibid., 40.
10. B. B. Warfield, "Calvinism," in *Calvin and Augustine* (Phillipsburg, NJ: P&R, 1980), 288, 289.
11. B. B. Warfield, *Selected Shorter Writings* (Phillipsburg, NJ: P&R, 2001), 1:104.

Fortunately, though, the God of the Bible is in complete and minute control of all that goes on in his creation. He is sovereign. Beeke reminds us that "God's sovereignty is His supremacy, His kingship, and His deity. His sovereignty declares Him to be God. . . . God is the Lord of life and the Sovereign of the universe, whose will is the key to history."[12] God's royal supremacy and almighty power are not bare exercises of his strength to demonstrate his authority. He providentially rules over all things for his name's sake to be sure, but he also graciously loves and saves his people and cares for them impeccably. He can only do so because he is sovereign. "In Christ, the warm and fatherly sovereignty of the God of the Scriptures is vastly different from the cold and capricious sovereignty of other 'gods.' . . . God's fatherly sovereignty in Christ is the essence of who God is."[13]

The Lord's supremacy (i.e., his sovereignty) is not merely a characteristic that God chooses to display some times more than others. He is always sovereign because he is always God. Daniel Montgomery and Timothy Paul Jones helpfully note that "sovereignty is essential to God's nature. God cannot relinquish his sovereignty over human history any more than God can commit suicide."[14] Calvinists believe that God is the great Sovereign of all the universe he's created who freely and always works his will.

Sovereignty Leads to God's Glory

Two realities flow from the fact that God is completely sovereign. The first is that everything God does in the universe he does for his glory. Thomas Schreiner describes God's glory as "the beauty, majesty, and greatness of who he is; therefore, in all he does, whether in salvation or in judgment, the greatness of his being is demonstrated."[15] God's glory is intricately related to the fact that he is great, or sovereign. In all things—including the creation of the universe, the rebellion that ensues with the Fall and human wickedness that issues from it, and in his judgment against rebellious creatures—God shows his glory.[16] Consider some of the evidences of God's glory. Creation is entirely his work (Job 38:4–11; Isa. 44:24; Rev. 4:11). Providence is a work of his hand alone (Ps. 135:6; Matt. 10:29; Rom. 11:36). Judgment is a work reserved for him alone (Acts 17:31; Rom. 2:5–11, 16; Rev. 20:11–13). Supremely, though, Schreiner notes that God demonstrates his glorious nature in rescuing his people from the consequences of their sin. As Exodus 34:6–7 and Psalm 106:8

---

12. Beeke, *Living for God's Glory*, 39.
13. Ibid., 40.
14. Daniel Montgomery and Timothy Paul Jones, *Proof: Finding Freedom through the Intoxicating Joy of Irresistible Grace* (Grand Rapids: Zondervan, 2014), 29.
15. Thomas R. Schreiner, "A Biblical Theology of the Glory of God," in *For the Fame of God's Name: Essays in Honor of John Piper*, eds. Sam Storms and Justin Taylor (Wheaton, IL: Crossway, 2010), 216.
16. See Ibid., 216–21.

show, to be sure "God manifests his glory in judgment, but the emphasis here shows that he demonstrates his glory particularly in pouring his mercy and grace and forgiveness upon his people."[17] As Warfield observes, Calvinism's concern for God's glory results in "the absolute exclusion of the creaturely element in the initiation of the saving process, that so the pure grace of God may be magnified."[18] A Calvinist is one who removes

> the evil leaven of Synergism by which, as he clearly sees, God is robbed of His glory and man is encouraged to think that he owes to some power, some act of choice, some initiative of his own, his participation in that salvation which is in reality all of grace. There is accordingly nothing against which Calvinism sets its face with more firmness than every form and degree of autosoterism.[19]

John Piper, echoing Jonathan Edwards, has shown that from beginning to end, the message of the Bible is that everything God does he does for his name's sake, or "for his glory."[20] It would be idolatry for God to do anything other than for his own glory. God chose his people for his glory (Eph. 1:4–6). He created us for his glory (Isa. 43:6–7). He called Israel for his glory (Isa. 49:3; Jer. 13:11). He restored Israel from exile for the glory of his name (Ezek. 36:22–23, 32). Jesus receives us into his fellowship for the glory of God (Rom. 15:7). We are to do everything for God's glory (1 Cor. 10:31). Jesus's supreme aim is that we would see and enjoy his glory (John 17:24).[21] God's glory, his supremacy, is one result of his sovereignty.[22]

Sovereignty Leads to Particularity
The second result of his sovereignty is that God delights to set his affection on particular persons simply because he loves them (Deut. 7:7–8; Eph. 1:4–5). It is an aspect of God's sovereignty, of his deity, his otherness, that he has the prerogative to decide whom to love savingly. As King, the Lord sovereignly sets his affection on particular persons. This particular, sovereign love of God for his elect means that his chosen ones can draw confidence from the

---

17. Ibid., 221.
18. Warfield, "Calvinism," 293.
19. Ibid., 293–94. "Autosoterism" is "self-salvation." "Synergism" is the view that human beings and God must cooperate to make salvation effective.
20. See John Piper, *God's Passion for His Glory: Living with the Vision of Jonathan Edwards* (Wheaton, IL: Crossway, 1998).
21. These references, and others, are in John Piper, *Let the Nations Be Glad!: The Supremacy of God in Missions* (Grand Rapids: Baker, 1993), 17–21.
22. This motivation would be reprehensible for us, God's creatures. Yet it is appropriate and even desirable for God since he is holy, perfect, and all-good.

fact that his special love for them ensures that he will do all that is necessary to bring them to him finally and forever.

Summary

Calvinism's core principle—its view of God—affects the gospel. Michael Horton reminds us that the debate between Arminianism and Calvinism

> goes to the heart of the gospel itself. That does not mean that those with whom we differ don't really believe the gospel. We are justified through faith in Christ, not through doctrinal precision. However, are our doctrinal assumptions and convictions consistent with that profession of faith? Much of the debate comes down to one basic difference: Arminians affirm *synergism* (i.e., "working together," or cooperation between God's grace and human willing and activity), while Calvinists affirm *monergism* (i.e., "one-working," or God's grace as the effectual source of election, redemption, faith, and perseverance).[23]

For the sake of God's glory, as well as for the integrity of the gospel itself, Calvinists seek to protect the aspects of God's character highlighted in this chapter.

REFLECTION QUESTIONS

1. Do you think that Calvinism's desire to let God be God seems arrogant? Or do you think this accurately reflects the Bible's message?

2. How sovereign do you think the Bible presents God to be? Can you think of anything the Lord is not ruling over? What?

3. Do you think that Warfield was correct in arguing that God would be immoral if he created something he could not control? Why?

4. Do you think God is egotistical for doing everything for his own glory? Why?

5. Do you think it is right for God to set his saving affection on particular persons and not others? Why?

---

23. Michael Horton, *For Calvinism* (Grand Rapids: Zondervan, 2011), 16.

How Should We Respond to God's Revelation?

B efore we get into discussions of complicated doctrines such as predestina- tion, evil, and definite atonement, we need to pause and check our hearts because Calvinism deals with significant and awe-inspiring truths. Are we willing to let God direct our thinking about him, us, and how we are brought into a relationship with him? Five statements encapsulate how we should re- spond to God.

1. Let God Be God

We must allow God to decide who he is and how he will interact with us. Because of our on-going struggle with sin, we all struggle to do this in different ways. There are aspects of God's revelation of himself in the Bible that we especially like, and there are characteristics we think he should, or should not, possess. And in our minds we start to make these things *the* central defining point of who we think God is. Any time someone says (or thinks), "I like to think of God as . . ." that individual is on dangerous ground. John Calvin was correct when he charged that each of us is a "per- petual factory of idols."[1] When we substitute an idea of who God should be for who he really is, we're idolaters. At the end of the day, putting it as kindly as I can, it is irrelevant whether or not you or I "like to think of God" in particular ways.

God—the one who created all that exists and reigns over it, the one who providentially guides every facet of his creation, including us, the one "in [whom] we live and move and have our being" (Acts 17:28)—has the right to

---

1. John Calvin, *Institutes of the Christian Religion*, Library of Christian Classics, 2 volumes, ed. John T. McNeill, trans. Ford Lewis Battles (Philadelphia: Westminster, 1960), 1.11.8. See Question 13.

be God. He tells us who he is, what he is like, who we are, and how he will be in relationship with us. It's not up to us to conjure up what we think he should be like. We, like Isaiah, are "people of unclean lips." Our attitude towards the Lord must be one of awe and reverence, for "Holy, holy, holy is the Lord of hosts" (Isa. 6:3, 5). God is God; we are not. As John Frame notes, while discussing both God's interaction with Job and his declaration of absolute divine sovereignty in Romans 9, "Because God is who he is, the covenant Lord, he is not required to defend himself against charges of injustice. He is the judge, not we."[2] We must let God be God.[3]

2. Submit to the Bible

God didn't have to reveal himself to us. He could have left us in our ignorance to try to figure out our way in life and into eternity. Think about those around the world right now who don't have access to the Bible or who are trapped in false religions. That is where we would be today if it were not for God's gracious revelation of himself and his ways to us in holy Scripture. Even the fact that we have the Bible is evidence of God's extreme kindness to us.

The Bible is the very breathed-out revelation of God to us (2 Tim. 3:16), a remarkable and exact product of God as incredible as the creation of the universe by the Spirit of God (Gen. 1:1–2). Since it is God's word, the Bible comes to us with absolute divine authority. It is without error. More than that, this word is given to us to be useful in shaping our thinking and living. It sits in judgment over us. We must never determine what aspects of it we admire or dislike, as we might decide between two items on a menu. No, Scripture is always true whether or not we like what it says. And when we find ourselves repulsed by its truth, we need to be honest with God, confess our sin, and ask him to give us affection for every part of who he is.

Isaiah 66 gives us a remarkable glimpse into the heart of our majestic God:

> Thus says the Lord: "Heaven is my throne, and the earth is my footstool; what is the house that you would build for me, and what is the place of my rest? All these things my hand has made, and so all these things came to be, declares the Lord. But this is the one to whom I will look: he who is humble and contrite in spirit and trembles at my word." (vv. 1–2)

Our responsibility is to tremble at God's word, to submit to it, to let it fashion our thinking about God and ourselves.

---

2. John M. Frame, *The Doctrine of God* (Phillipsburg, NJ: P&R, 2002), 180.
3. See Philip S. Watson, *Let God Be God: An Interpretation of the Theology of Martin Luther* (London: Epworth, 1947).

3. Humble Yourself before God

From beginning to end, the Bible is insistent that God is not like us. He is high and lifted up, majestic in his glory, different from us.

> The LORD is a great God,
>   and a great King above all gods.
> In his hand are the depths of the earth;
>   the heights of the mountains are his also.
> The sea is his, for he made it,
>   and his hands formed the dry land.
>
> Oh come, let us worship and bow down;
>   let us kneel before the LORD, our Maker! (Ps. 95:3–6)

How great is God? Consider Psalm 139 where the psalmist exults in God's knowledge of him (vv. 1–6), in God's omnipresence (vv. 7–12), as well as in God's intricate craftsmanship (vv. 13–16). Consequently, J. I. Packer exhorts us, "Here, then, is the first step in apprehending the greatness of God: to realize how unlimited are His wisdom, and His presence, and His power."[4]

Nothing is greater than God. Nothing. No one has done the things he has done. "Who has measured the waters in the hollow of his hand and marked off the heavens with a span, enclosed the dust of the earth in a measure and weighed the mountains in scales and the hills in a balance?" (Isa. 40:12). Even the great nations of the earth "are like a drop from a bucket, and are accounted as dust on the scales" to the Lord (40:15). God is sovereign over his creation, over the great rulers of the world (for he "brings princes to nothing, and makes the rulers of the earth as emptiness" [40:23]). Therefore, "Behold your God!"[5]

God is majestic and transcendent; we are pitiful and minute by comparison. God is the Creator—all-knowing, all-powerful, perfect in every way, not bound by anything or anyone. We are creatures. We have multiple limits—in our knowledge, in our strength, in our perspective, in our integrity. "But who are you, O man, to answer back to God? Will what is molded say to its molder, 'Why have you made me like this?' Has the potter no right over the clay, to make out of the same lump one vessel for honored use and another for dishonorable use?" (Rom. 9:20–21). Because of our creaturely limitations, there will be many things that we don't have the capacity to understand. In addition, God has not revealed everything to us either: "The secret things belong to the LORD our God" (Deut. 29:29). We do not have the right as God's creatures to attempt to pry into his hidden wisdom. Rather, our obligation is to sit humbly before his word: "but the things that

---

4. J. I. Packer, *Knowing God* (Downers Grove, IL: InterVarsity Press, 1973), 76.
5. Ibid., 77–78.

are revealed belong to us and to our children forever, that we may do all the words of this law" (Deut. 29:29).

The reality is that God is starkly different than we are. Wayne Grudem writes, "Because God is infinite and we are finite and limited, we can never fully understand God."[6] We will never completely understand our Lord. Referencing biblical texts such as Job 37:5; Psalm 147:5; Jeremiah 33:3; and 1 Corinthians 2:7, Daniel Montgomery and Timothy Paul Jones observe, "We must approach God with awareness that he is beyond us and that we will never *fully* understand him." They helpfully point out, "Like children, we are called to accept things that perhaps don't make logical sense to us when we first encounter them. Maybe they won't make logical sense to us this side of heaven."[7]

They are correct. As our Creator, God is majestic and beyond our understanding in his fullness and perfection:

> Oh, the depth of the riches and wisdom and knowledge of God!
> How unsearchable are his judgments and how inscrutable his ways!
> For who has known the mind of the Lord,
> Or who has been his counselor?
> Or who has given a gift to him that he might be repaid?
> For from him and through him and to him are all things.
> To him be glory forever. Amen. (Rom. 11:33–36)

As one of his creatures, be humble before your Creator. Don't question his right to do as he chooses.

4. Worship God Reverently

From beginning to end the Bible calls us to worship God because of his perfect, awe-inspiring character and for the wondrous deeds he has accomplished for his people. Note these two New Testament texts:

> Blessed be the God and Father of our Lord Jesus Christ, who has blessed us in Christ with every spiritual blessing in the heavenly places, even as he chose us in him before the foundation of the world, that we should be holy and blameless before him. In love he predestined us for adoption to himself as sons through Jesus Christ, according to the purpose of his will, to the praise of his glorious grace, with which he has

---

6. Wayne Grudem, *Systematic Theology: An Introduction to Biblical Doctrine* (Grand Rapids: Zondervan, 1994), 149.

7. Daniel Montgomery and Timothy Paul Jones, *Proof: Finding Freedom through the Intoxicating Joy of Irresistible Grace* (Grand Rapids: Zondervan, 2014), 141 (italics original).

blessed us in the Beloved. . . . to the praise of his glory. . . . to the praise of his glory. (Eph. 1:3–6, 12, 14)

To those who are elect exiles of the Dispersion in Pontus, Galatia, Cappadocia, Asia, and Bithynia, according to the foreknowledge of God the Father, in the sanctification of the Spirit, for obedience to Jesus Christ and for sprinkling with his blood: May grace and peace be multiplied to you. Blessed be the God and Father of our Lord Jesus Christ! According to his great mercy, he has caused us to be born again to a living hope through the resurrection of Jesus Christ from the dead, to an inheritance that is imperishable, undefiled, and unfading, kept in heaven for you, who by God's power are being guarded through faith for a salvation ready to be revealed in the last time. (1 Peter 1:1–5)

One temptation for those who are engaging with the truths of Bible as expressed in Calvinism is to become intoxicated with the wonderful ideas they're seeing—sometimes for the first time, sometimes for the thousandth. Because these are glorious, heart-pounding, intoxicating truths! But if we allow them to remain ethereal ideas, we will have done both God and ourselves a disservice. God declares, "I am the LORD; that is my name; my glory I give to no other, nor my praise to carved idols" (Isa. 42:8). If we are not moved to praise God for his sovereignty over everything, if we are not brought to our knees in worship since the Creator has delighted in weak, sinful clay like us, if we do not sing out to the one who in his sovereign freedom predestined us to be his children before the creation of the world—then we are failing to engage properly with the truths Calvinism holds dear. The truths of Calvinism should lead us to worship God.

5. Trust God

Related to the necessity of our worshiping God, we must trust the Lord. Faith, of course, is one of the great themes of the Bible. God has uniformly called on his people to throw themselves upon his mercy and compassion and to follow him in the nitty-gritty, difficult parts of life. Trust involves an awareness of our poverty, a recognition that God is able to meet our need, and then a conscious giving of that concern to the Lord with an awareness that he is the only one who can accomplish what we would like to happen. It is doing what Peter exhorts us, in "casting all your anxieties on him, because he cares for you" (1 Peter 5:7).

Faith is essential to the Christian life. Indeed, "without faith it is impossible to please him, for whoever would draw near to God must believe that he exists and that he rewards those who seek him" (Heb. 11:6). We don't put our faith in an idea. We don't trust an abstraction. No, just like young children learning to trust their parents, we run to our heavenly Father and give our lives, our hopes, our concerns, our everything over to him. We do this because he is a Person!

Trust, then, is essential as we consider the truths of Calvinism. We're not trusting that our "system" is better than some other intellectual construct. No, we're believing that the glorious God revealed in Scripture is real. We want to know him as a Person and to tangibly rely on him.[8] Trust the Lord.

REFLECTION QUESTIONS

1. Do you struggle with doing any of the five suggestions in this chapter? Why?

2. In which of the five areas have you seen the most consistency in your own life?

3. Do you have a consistent plan and time for your Bible reading? If not, what can you do to make sure you're regularly reading Scripture?

4. How does it make you feel that you're a creature crafted by Almighty God?

5. Are you moved to worship God as you consider who he is? What aspects of his character call out for your praise? Sinclair Ferguson has noted that Calvinists have always been tremendous singers. How's your singing?[9]

---

8. See J. I. Packer's *Knowing God* for help doing this.
9. Sinclair Ferguson, "Doxology," in Joel R. Beeke, *Living for God's Glory: An Introduction to Calvinism* (Grand Rapids: Reformation Trust, 2008), 387–96.

Questions about God's Character

Does God Love All People?

The Bible proclaims twice that "God is love" (1 John 4:8, 16). His very nature is to love because he is love. From eternity past, the Father, Son, and Holy Spirit have loved one another. In this sense, love is a more integral attribute to God's character than are justice and wrath, which are only necessitated after sin entered into God's creation. Calvinists delight that God loves all his creation, including unbelievers who are in a state of rebellion to him—indeed including those whom he did not eternally predestine to be his adopted children. God loves everyone. But he reserves his saving, eternal, life-giving love for his elect.

Arminian Conceptions of God's Love

Christians get into trouble when they assume the nature of God's love is exactly like their own experience of love. J. I. Packer perceptively notes that "many theological mistakes have been made through likening the God of infinite power, holiness, goodness, and wisdom to finite and fallen humanity."[1] Humans seem prone to hold God to our standards when we try to conceptualize the reality that "God is love" since we think we know what that should mean.

Arminians sometimes charge Calvinists with denying God's love since a loving God would not elect only some people for salvation. John Wesley, for example, taught that due to predestination, Calvinism "represent[s] God as worse than the devil—more false, more cruel, more unjust." He exclaims, "No Scripture can mean that God is not love. . . . [W]hatever it prove beside, no Scripture can prove predestination."[2] The heat of Wesley's diatribe

---

1. J. I. Packer, "The Love of God: Universal and Particular," in *Still Sovereign: Contemporary Perspectives on Election, Foreknowledge, and Grace*, eds. Thomas R. Schreiner and Bruce A. Ware (1995; Grand Rapids: Baker, 2000), 277.
2. John Wesley, "Free Grace," in *John Wesley's Sermons: An Anthology*, ed. Albert Cook Outler and Richard P. Heitzenrater (Nashville: Abingdon, 1991), 57–58.

is comparable to Roger Olson's invective. Olson asserts that Calvinism's "so-called double predestination of individuals by God is inconsistent with his love, and the teaching makes it difficult to tell the difference between God and the devil." If God acts the way Calvinists say he does, "then God's 'goodness,' God's 'love,' God's 'justice' are mere words with no ascertainable meaning."[3] There we have it: "God is love" rules out Calvinism. These people wrongly hold the infinite God to standards of human conceptions of what "love" is.

What Is Love?

The Bible—not our emotions—must define our understanding of God's love. Hebrew and Greek words for "love" are used hundreds of times in the Bible. Combine those with words for "mercy," "kindness," and "covenant faithfulness" and you have hundreds of more occurrences that teach us of God's love for all that he has created. Jack Cottrell clearly defines God's love as "his self-giving affection for his image-bearing creatures and his unselfish concern for their well-being, that leads him to act on their behalf and for their happiness and welfare."[4] The Lord, for example, says in Hosea, "My heart recoils within me; my compassion grows warm and tender. I will not execute my burning anger; I will not again destroy Ephraim; for I am God and not a man, the Holy One in your midst, and I will not come in wrath" (Hos. 11:8–9). Nothing commends sinners to God. Instead, "God loves people because he has chosen to love them . . . and no reason for his love can be given except his own sovereign good pleasure."[5] God's love is similar to the best of human loving, but it is not identical to our love. Exactly what "God is love" means must be learned from "the teaching about God that the Bible gives."[6]

The Objects of God's Love

To understand what it means that "God is love" we need to ask whom God loves. God is love, and God loves. But—just as a husband loves his wife and the female members of his church differently—God does not love all persons the same way.

The simplest way to see this is to notice the difference between God's love for all persons and his love for the elect. Packer observes that "God loves all in some ways (everyone whom he creates, sinners though they are, receive many underserved good gifts in daily providence)" while "he loves some in all ways (that is, in addition to the gifts of daily providence he brings them to faith, to new life, and to glory according to his predestinating purpose)."[7] God loves

3. Roger E. Olson, *Against Calvinism* (Grand Rapids: Zondervan, 2011), 104, 109.
4. Jack Cottrell, *What the Bible Says about God the Redeemer* (Joplin, MO: College Press, 1987), 336; quoted in John M. Frame, *The Doctrine of God* (Phillipsburg, NJ: P&R, 2002), 414.
5. J. I. Packer, *Knowing God* (Downers Grove, IL: InterVarsity Press, 1973), 112.
6. Packer, "The Love of God," 279–81.
7. Ibid., 283–84.

two sets of people (the non-elect and the elect). He loves them truly. But he loves them differently.

Notice what Scripture teaches us on this score. In the first place, then, God loves all people. The fact that the Lord created them in his image expresses God's love for them. God "gives to all mankind life and breath and everything" (Acts 20:25). Everything we have that allows us to live—oxygen and water, minds, emotions, wills, bodies that can process food—all of these are expressions of God's love to human beings. Our Father in heaven "makes his sun rise on the evil and on the good, and sends rain on the just and on the unjust" (Matt. 5:45). All these things evidence God's love for all persons because he did not have to create the world as he did. He gave us these good gifts because he loves us all.

More than that, he expresses "kindness and forbearance and patience" to people so that they will repent (Rom. 2:4). Even our consciences that convict all of us of wrongdoing are evidence of God's love for his creatures (Rom. 2:12–16). The supreme evidence of God's love for all persons is that he sent his one and only Son into the world. "Though he was in the form of God, [Christ] did not count equality with God a thing to be grasped, but made himself nothing, taking the form of a servant, being born in the likeness of men" (Phil. 2:6–7). And we see that God's love for a lost world (he "so loved the world") was his motivation in sending "his only Son, that whoever believes in him should not perish but have eternal life" (John 3:16). He desired the salvation of the world, because he "did not send his Son into the world to condemn the world, but in order that the world might be saved through him" (3:17). Therefore, the loving cry of God goes out: "Whoever believes in the Son has eternal life; whoever does not obey the Son shall not see life" (3:36). This is real love, and it is directed towards all persons. It is, as Geerhardus Vos notes, "the love of compassion which God retains for every lost sinner."[8] Since God loves all his creatures, we can and should say "God loves you" to unbelievers, as John Frame observes:

> On the basis of John 3:16, we can also say, "God loves you, because you are his handiwork, his image. God sent his Son to die, to redeem a people from this fallen world. So he gave you a priceless opportunity: if you believe, you will be saved. If you do believe, you will enjoy the fullness of God's blessing. If you do not, you only have yourself to blame."[9]

---

8. Geerhardus Vos, "The Scriptural Doctrine of the Love of God," in *Redemptive History and Biblical Interpretation: The Shorter Writings of Geerhardus Vos*, ed. Richard B. Gaffin, Jr. (Phillipsburg, NJ: P&R, 1980), 443.
9. Frame, *The Doctrine of God*, 419.

Yet, God loves his chosen people with a different type of love—or a different intensity or degree of love—a raising-them-from-death-to-life love (Eph. 2:4–7). This is the "higher love which not merely desires, but purposes and works out the salvation of some."[10] Both "loves" are real. Yet, they have different objects and different effects. This observation goes a long way to understanding the difference between Calvinism and Arminianism on the crucial issue of God's love. Packer's words are direct, but they are accurate:

> Arminianism gives Christians much to thank God for, but Calvinism gives them more. . . . The Arminian idea is simpler, for it does not involve so full or radical an acknowledgement of the mystery of God's ways, and it assimilates God more closely to the image of man, making him appear like a gentle giant who is also a great persuader and a resourceful maneuverer, although he is sometimes frustrated and disappointed. But if the measure of love is what it really gives to the really needy and undeserving, then the love of God as Calvinists know it is a much greater thing than the Arminians imagine, and is much diminished by the Arminian model of God and his ways with mankind.[11]

It is crucial that we understand that God's love is not monolithic. In this regard, D. A. Carson has helpfully noted that Scripture points out five different objects of his love. First, God the Father has a unique love for his Son. For example, Jesus teaches us that "the Father loves the Son and has given all things into his hand" (John 3:35). There is a unique love between the Father and the Son. Second, God loves his creation. He created it good, because he loves it (Gen. 1–2), and he continues to love it in his sovereign providence, bringing good to his creation (e.g., Matt. 10:29). Third, God loves all people and desires their salvation (e.g., John 3:16). Ezekiel 33:11 demonstrates this: "As I live, declares the Lord God, I have no pleasure in the death of the wicked, but that the wicked turn from his way and live; turn back, turn back from your evil ways, for why will you die, O house of Israel?" God truly loves all people and wants them to be saved.

Fourth, God has a "particular, effective, and selecting love towards his elect."[12] Although the Lord desires all to be saved, for his own reasons he chooses not to act on that desire in regards to all people. Rather, he loves certain individuals particularly; these he actually saves. Scripture is replete with this truth. Moses reminds Israel that, "to the Lord your God belong heaven

---

10. Vos, "The Scriptural Doctrine of the Love of God," 444.
11. Packer, "The Love of God," 286.
12. D. A. Carson, *The Difficult Doctrine of the Love of God* (Wheaton: Crossway, 2000), 18.

and the heaven of heavens, the earth with all that is in it. Yet the LORD set his heart in love on your fathers and chose their offspring after them, you above all peoples, as you are this day" (Deut. 10:14–15). He did this simply because he loved them, not on account of anything they had done or would do (Deut. 7:7–8). Paul praises God for the particularity of his love for the elect: "In love he predestined us for adoption as sons through Jesus Christ" (Eph. 1:4). He exhorts husbands to "love your wives, as Christ love the church and gave himself up for her" (Eph. 5:25). John also speaks of God's special love for the elect:

> Anyone who does not love does not know God, because God is love. In this the love of God was made manifest among us, that God sent his only Son into the world, so that we might live through him. In this is love, not that we have loved God but that he loved us and sent his Son to be the propitiation for our sins. (1 John 4:8–10)

Fifth, the Lord also loves his "own people in a provisional or conditional way," the condition being their obedience.[13] Obedience is not the condition of salvation (for salvation is what the fourth sort of love has resulted in). Rather, it is the condition of the strength and comfort of God's people's relationship with him. For example, Jesus speaks of the condition of obedience to experience God's love: "If you keep my commandments, you will abide in my love, just as I have kept my Father's commandments and abide in his love" (John 15:10).[14]

Calvinists revel in the love of God that we see taught in Scripture and that we have experienced in our lives. We believe that God loves everyone. But we also want to heed Carson's warning, "If you absolutize any one of these ways in which the Bible speaks of the love of God, you will generate a false system that squeezes out other important things the Bible says, thus finally distorting your vision of God."[15]

Summary

We must let the Bible, not our emotions or opinions, determine what it means that "God is love." And we must be willing to submit to that definition. God's very nature is to love. He loves all persons, some more intensely than others. Calvinists believe God's love is the only reason any of us are believers in Jesus Christ. And this love that showed itself in the sending of God's Son into the world is what we should proclaim to unbelievers so that they will be drawn to Christ. We need to hold tenaciously to, revel in, worship God for,

---

13. Ibid., 19.
14. These five different orientations of God's love are found in ibid., 16–21.
15. Ibid., 75.

and indiscriminately proclaim, "God is love"—because he is. We also need to remember that our God loves different objects with different sorts of love.

REFLECTION QUESTIONS

1. In your own words, how would you define God's love?

2. Where do you think the analogy between God's love and human love breaks down?

3. How would you respond to Wesley's and Olson's critiques of Calvinists' beliefs about God's love that were noted in this chapter?

4. Does the fact that "God so loved the world" (John 3:16) motivate you to share the gospel with unbelievers? Why?

5. How do you think it can be loving of God to choose some for salvation (Eph. 1:4) while at the same time not setting his saving affection on everyone (Rom. 9:13)?

What Is God's Grace?

The God of the Bible is infinitely relational (since Father, Son, and Spirit exist eternally in a loving relationship) and infinitely powerful. His grace is his loving power bringing sinful creatures into relationship with him. Although sinful people deserve only God's eternal condemnation, he is gracious towards his chosen ones and grants them the opposite of their just deserts—eternal life through a relationship with him. Grace, then, is not an impersonal force. Grace manifests God's remarkable love.

The Elements of Grace

Timothy George correctly notes that "grace is the great theme of the Bible."[1] He observes, "The very last verse in the Bible summarizes the message of Holy Scripture from Genesis to Revelation: 'The grace of the Lord Jesus be with all' (Rev. 22:21)." Indeed, "The word *grace* is found some 150 times in the New Testament alone."[2] More than just using the word "grace," Scripture abounds with statements of God's steadfast love and covenant faithfulness, his mercy, his love, his rescuing of his people from their sin. Who is God? He is "The LORD, the LORD, a God merciful and gracious, slow to anger, and abounding in steadfast love and faithfulness" (Exod. 34:6).

Grace, then, is a—perhaps *the*—major biblical theme. John Frame succinctly defines it as God's "sovereign, unmerited favor, given to those who deserve his wrath."[3] More expansively, it is a sovereign, life-giving expression of God's love to certain underserving sinners. Grace has four elements. God's grace is relational, sovereign, salvific, and particular. We will notice each of these elements in turn.

---

1. Timothy George, *Amazing Grace: God's Pursuit, Our Response*, 2nd ed. (Wheaton, IL: Crossway, 2011), 16.
2. Ibid., 15 (italics original).
3. John M. Frame, *The Doctrine of God* (Phillipsburg, NJ: P&R, 2002), 426.

First, *God's grace is relational* in the sense that his goal is to bring people into a saving relationship with himself. Grace brings God's love to his chosen people, just as Moses wrote of the motivation the Lord had in choosing his people Israel to be his own: "It was not because you were more in number than any other people that the LORD set his love on you and chose you, for you were the fewest of all peoples, but it is because the LORD loves you" (Deut. 7:7–8). God's love was his motive for choosing his people. He desired them to be in relationship with him. Later, through Jeremiah, the Lord said,

> Let not the wise man boast in his wisdom, let not the mighty man boast in his might, let not the rich man boast in his riches, but let him who boasts boast in this, that he understands and knows me, that I am the LORD who practices steadfast love, justice, and righteousness in the earth. (Jer. 9:23–24)

God graciously allows his people to have an intimate knowledge of him, which is the promise of the new covenant:

> For this is the covenant that I will make with the house of Israel after those days, declares the LORD: I will put my law within them, and I will write it on their hearts. And I will be their God, and they shall be my people. And no longer shall each one teach his neighbor and each his brother, saying, "Know the LORD," for they shall all know me, from the least of them to the greatest, declares the LORD. For I will forgive their iniquity, and I will remember their sin no more. (Jer. 31:33–34)

This covenant is purely gracious. God is the actor (notice that "I" is the subject, the one who does these glorious things), and his people are the grateful recipients. And it is relational at its core, for the result of this grace is a relationship with God ("they shall all know me"). Inaugurated by Jesus (Luke 22:20), this new and better covenant (Heb. 8:6), ushers God's people into an intimate, personal relationship with him. J. I. Packer is thus correct to note that in grace "the thought is always of the gift of God's personal bestowal, given as a proof of his affection towards the individual recipient."[4] God's grace is relational.

Second, *God's grace is sovereign* in the sense that it is almighty and always accomplishes its goal. God's grace is not potential, waiting on something outside of himself to activate it. Nor is his grace stymied by others' intransigence. It always accomplishes its purpose, which should not surprise us given that

---

4. J. I. Packer, *God's Words: Studies in Key Bible Themes* (1981; Grand Rapids: Baker, 1988), 98.

the Lord is a covenant-making and covenant-keeping God. He sovereignly accomplishes his goal in grace.

The source of grace in a sinner's life is God's sovereign election. And his election is purely of grace, as Paul reminds us. "At the present time there is a remnant, chosen by grace. But if it is by grace, it is no longer on the basis of works; otherwise grace would no longer be grace" (Rom. 11:5–6). The remnant of the elect people exists because God sovereignly chose them in his grace. God "saved us and called us to a holy calling, not because of our works but because of his own purpose and grace, which he gave us in Christ Jesus before the ages began" (2 Tim. 1:9). Paul doesn't wish that hopefully God's people will be saved some day. Rather, because of God's grace, which he determined to give them from eternity past, they were already saved. God's grace is sovereign.

Third, *God's grace is salvific*. It accomplishes the salvation of those whom the Lord loves and chooses to be his own. This should not surprise us since "grace," John tells us, "came through Jesus Christ" (John 1:17). The saving gospel message, in fact, can be called "grace," as when Paul testified "to the gospel of the grace of God" (Acts 20:24). For this reason Paul and Barnabas urged the early church "to continue in the grace of God" (Acts 13:43), which meant "keep trusting the gospel." Packer's extensive definition of grace rightly emphasizes its salvific component:

> The word "grace" thus comes to express the thought of God acting in spontaneous goodness to save sinners: God loving the unlovely, making covenant with them, pardoning their sins, accepting their persons, revealing himself to them, moving them to response, leading them ultimately into full knowledge and enjoyment of himself, and overcoming all obstacles to the fulfilment of this purpose that at each stage arise. Grace is election-love plus covenant-love, a free choice issuing in a sovereign work. Grace saves from sin and all evil; grace brings ungodly men to true happiness in the knowledge of their Maker.[5]

Grace is God's unmerited favor towards sinners which brings salvation to them. God's grace saves.

Fourth, *God's grace is particular*. Since it is sovereign, his grace accomplishes his end, which is a saving relationship with the objects of his mercy. If he had intended the salvation of all persons, everyone would go to heaven. That, though, is not God's intention. His saving grace is not directed to everyone.

---

5. Ibid., 97–98.

Though God's saving grace is focused on the elect, he has "common grace" for all his creation, including all sinful persons. John Murray defines common grace as *"every favour of whatever kind or degree, falling short of salvation, which this undeserving and sin-cursed world enjoys at the hand of God."*[6] In this non-salvific sense, God's grace has a universal focus. It is common in that it benefits all creation. For instance, the Lord restrains sin from its full expression; it never exerts itself farther than the Lord allows. He holds back his wrath, because he is patient and desires people's salvation. He gives every person temporal blessings, things like rain, sunshine, food, and governments to restrain evil.[7] This is the sense, then, and the only sense in which God's grace has a universal focus.[8]

Particularity, for instance, pervades Ephesians 1:1–14. God has blessed only "us" because we are "in Christ" (v. 3). He "chose" (v. 4) and "predestined us for adoption" (v. 5). We are recipients of redemption and forgiveness (v. 7), we have a wonderful inheritance awaiting us (v. 11), and we have been sealed with the Spirit (v. 13). All of these blessings are directed not to all humanity but to the "saints," believers in Jesus Christ (v. 1). All of these blessings which have been poured out on us are ours because God has chosen to be gracious to us. Thus, God's electing and predestining of us is "to the praise of his glorious grace" (v. 6). The magnificent forgiveness we have received is "according to the riches of his grace" (v. 7). God's grace is particular.

Three Adversatives

We sometimes see a thing most clearly when we contrast it with its opposite. The New Testament does this frequently regarding the awe-inspiring experience of grace that Christians have received. We will notice three passages specifically, each revolving around adversative conjunctions. They demonstrate that a Christian's status has changed dramatically from what it was prior to salvation. Each passage highlights the fact that God's grace is defined as his powerful disposition to bring about the salvation of his elect.

First, we note Romans 3:21–26. Paul sets out the issue that faces all of humanity in the previous chapters. Our sin (spelled out in glaring detail in 1:18–32) makes us all guilty and unwilling to seek after God's forgiveness (3:11–12). Jew and Gentile alike are in this sad state of sin and rebellion and hopelessness (2:1–3:10). All that any person deserves, then, is the wrath of God (1:18; 2:5, 8; 3:5). No one can do anything to gain his or her salvation. No one seeks God. No one does good. God does it all, as we see in the adversative

---

6. John Murray, "Common Grace," in *Collected Writings of John Murray* (Edinburgh: Banner of Truth, 1977), 2:96 (italics original).

7. These aspects of God's common grace, and more, are discussed in Frame, *Doctrine of God*, 429–37.

8. As we will see in the next question, Arminianism wrongly believes that God's saving grace is equally disseminated to each individual.

that starts 3:21: "but now." The Lord provides righteousness for guilty, wrath-deserving sinners who are unable to save themselves. He does it by sending his only Son, Jesus, to be the wrath-bearer (this is the meaning of "propitiation" in 3:25) who dies for his elect. In this way God is just (for he punishes sin by pouring out his wrath), and he can justify sinners (who turn from their evil rebellion and trust in Christ; 3:26). Faith, rather than our attempt to do good works, is what unites a sinner to Jesus (3:22, 25–31). And this faith, Paul asserts, has its origin in God's "grace as a gift" (3:24). The sinner deserved God's wrath. "But now" God saved the unrighteous person by uniting him or her with Christ by faith.

Second, we observe the same pattern in Titus 3:4–7. Outside of Christ, unbelievers are disobedient and in slavery to "various passions and pleasures" (3:3). They are unable to save themselves. But in his "mercy" and "grace" (3:5, 7), God moves. God saves. The motivation is the Lord's kindness (3:4) because it is certain that sinners can do nothing to contribute to their rescue. Due to God's grace, believers relish the "but when."

> But when the goodness and loving kindness of God our Savior appeared, he saved us, not because of works done by us in righteousness, but according to his own mercy, by the washing of regeneration and renewal of the Holy Spirit, whom he poured out on us richly through Jesus Christ our Savior, so that being justified by his grace we might become heirs according to the hope of eternal life. (Titus 3:4–7)

Third, Ephesians 2:4 also highlights the adversative nature of grace. The conjunction in verse 4 ("but God") follows on the heels of one of the starkest expositions of sin in the New Testament. Paul says that those who are outside of Christ are dead with respect to their sins and trespasses (2:1); there is nothing in them but spiritual death. That death doesn't make them completely passive, for they actively pursue their own desires. Paul's description of their acting and following and living in 2:1–3 is an awful portrait of the walking dead. They purposefully and energetically pursue evil and their own sinful desires. Their entire nature is opposed to God. They deserve only his wrath (2:3). This makes God's act of salvation astounding. It is this very nature of salvation (God's love expressed in his doing what they don't deserve and can't do themselves) that is grace. This is Paul's way of defining grace in 2:5, 7, and 8.

> But God, being rich in mercy, because of the great love with which he loved us, even when we were dead in our trespasses, made us alive together with Christ—by grace you have been saved—and raised us up with him and seated us with him in the heavenly places in Christ Jesus, so that in the coming ages

he might show the immeasurable riches of his grace in kindness toward us in Christ Jesus. For by grace you have been saved through faith. And this is not your own doing; it is the gift of God. (Eph. 2:4–8)

Grace is God's disposition of love and mercy (2:4) making dead sinners (note his repetition of their deadness in 2:5) alive. God makes them alive (2:5); he raises them with Christ (2:6); he seats them in the heavenlies together with Christ (2:6). This is monergism, God being the sole force responsible for salvation. This is grace. "But God."

Summary

God's grace is one of his glorious attributes. It exemplifies his love for sinners and results in his life-giving act of bringing sinners like us into an intimate relationship with himself. It is sovereign, done by him alone, guided by his wisdom alone. It saves. And it is specifically directed towards his chosen ones. May we always marvel at "but God"!

REFLECTION QUESTIONS

1. How would you define grace in your own words? Would you add other elements than the four noted in this chapter?

2. Can you think of other biblical texts that highlight the character of God's grace? What are they?

3. Timothy George writes that 1 Corinthians 4:7 ("What do you have that you did not receive? If then you received it, why do you boast as if you did not receive it?") "shatters the myth of self-reliance and points us to the reality of salvation by grace better than any other text I know."[9] Do you agree with him? Is God's grace leading you to be humble?

4. How do you anticipate that an Arminian would respond to what we saw in this chapter? Why?

5. Do you regularly thank God for his grace?

---

9. George, *Amazing Grace*, 58.

Is the Arminian Doctrine of Prevenient Grace Biblical?

Prevenient grace is one of Arminianism's central doctrines. Calvinists stress that God's grace (since, biblically, it is sovereign, particular, and effective) will absolutely result in the salvation of the elect. Arminians, however, redefine grace in order to guard the integrity of human "free will" and to protect God from being liable for anyone's condemnation. Rather than being a divine power that absolutely saves (Calvinism), Arminians conceive of prevenient grace as merely a sufficient divine empowerment which enables sinners—by the right use of their "free will"—to trust in Christ.[1] Prevenient grace provides for a universal opportunity of salvation, but it saves no one unless the individual cooperates with it.

Prevenient Grace Defined

"Prevenient" is an archaic word meaning, "anticipating, going before, preceding."[2] Prevenient is "going-before" grace. It precedes one's conversion to Christ and is universal in its scope so that all persons have an equal opportunity to be saved. Three central ideas related to prevenient grace in Arminianism are "sufficient," "enabling," and "conscience."

Prevenient grace is both sufficient and enabling grace because the Holy Spirit gives an individual sufficient grace "to consent, believe, and be converted" if the person so chooses. Thus, according to Jacob Arminius, "when God knocks, it is certain that the man can open, and consequently he has sufficient grace." Unbelievers possess "sufficient grace to enable them not to resist and even to yield to the Holy Spirit."[3] Prevenient grace is sufficient grace.

---

1. See Question 8.
2. Robert E. Picirilli, *Grace, Faith, Free Will: Contrasting Views of Salvation: Calvinism and Arminianism* (Nashville: Randall House, 2002), 153 (italics removed).
3. Arminius, *Works*, 3:520, 521; quoted in Picirilli, *Grace, Faith, Free Will*, 157.

Prevenient grace also empowers a sinner to respond to the gospel. Robert Picirilli maintains it "is that work of the Holy Spirit that 'opens the heart' of the unregenerate . . . to the truth of the gospel and enables them to respond positively in faith."[4] R. G. Tuttle insists that for John Wesley this grace is "the universal work of the Holy Spirit in the hearts and lives of people" in which they "experience the gentle wooing of the Holy Spirit, which prevents them from moving so far from 'the way' that when they finally understand the claims of the gospel upon their lives, he guarantees their freedom to say yes."[5] Another Arminian states, "Grace is not an arbitrary divine cause but the free gift of God's enablement."[6] Prevenient grace, then, enables everyone to respond to Christ.

Wesley located the gift of this enabling sufficient grace in God's gift of conscience, the notion of what's right and what's wrong, that all persons possess. Conscience, he averred, "is not natural, but a supernatural gift of God, above all his natural endowments." Conscience, in fact, is "the Son of God, that is 'the true light, which enlighteneth every man that cometh into the world.' So that we may say to every human creature, 'He,' not nature, 'hath showed thee, O man, what is good.'"[7]

Picirilli argues that prevenient grace is a process of three divine works in an individual—conviction, persuasion, and enablement. First, the Spirit convicts the sinner "of his sins and guilt, of his condemnation, of the fact that God's way is right, and of the fact that God has provided redemption for him if he will but accept the gift of God in faith."[8] Second, the Spirit persuades him, making "the truth appealing to the sinner. It draws him, woos him, puts the 'bite into conviction.'"[9] Third, "the Spirit enables the otherwise unable person to receive Christ by faith."[10] Exactly how this enablement works is mysterious, for "we cannot fully explain all the mysterious workings of God's Spirit on the heart, for we do not understand all that well just how the understanding and the will operate. Whatever is required, the Spirit makes saving faith possible."[11] For Wesley, this was equated with "a graciously restored free will." In other words, "a certain measure of free will is supernaturally restored by the Holy

---

4. Picirilli, *Grace, Faith, Free Will*, 154.

5. R. G. Tuttle, "Prevenient Grace," in *Evangelical Dictionary of Theology*, ed. Walter A. Elwell (Grand Rapids: Baker, 1984), 1164. For John Wesley's view of prevenient grace, see Kenneth J. Collins, *The Theology of John Wesley: Holy Love and the Shape of Grace* (Nashville: Abingdon, 2007), 73–82.

6. Mildred Bangs Wynkoop, *Foundations of Wesleyan-Arminian Theology* (Kansas City, MO: Beacon Hill, 1967), 57.

7. John Wesley, "On Conscience," in *The Works of the Rev. John Wesley, A.M.*, ed. John Emory (New York: Waugh and Mason, 1835), 2:378.

8. Picirilli, *Grace, Faith, Free Will*, 155.

9. Ibid.

10. Ibid.

11 Ibid.

Spirit (based upon the work of Christ), to all people who, apart from such a restoration, are not free, soteriologically speaking."[12] In his grace, God convicts, persuades, and enables one to have faith if the sinner chooses to do so.

Prevenient Grace and Arminianism

Prevenient grace is essential to evangelical Arminianism. This system believes in total depravity (so that the sinner is unable to turn to Christ on his or her own), human accountability to God, God's desire for everyone's salvation, and God's justice (conceived in such a way that people are never condemned for what they could not do). In a sense, all these doctrines cohere in prevenient grace, for it is "the key distinctive doctrine of Arminianism," as Roger Olson affirms.[13] Tuttle argues it "constitutes the heart of Wesley's Arminianism."[14]

Because of its belief in prevenient grace, Arminianism espouses "cooperation" or "synergism." Given the reality of prevenient grace, the only reason why people go to hell is their refusal to come to Jesus, which they were enabled by the Holy Spirit to do. They failed to cooperate with God's grace. John Collins reports that Wesley's view of prevenient grace seen "in terms of the priority of divine action with respect to all grace, issues in divine/human cooperation, a genuine 'working with,' . . . a synergism."[15] Olson maintains that Arminius's "is an evangelical synergism that reserves all the power, ability and efficacy in salvation to grace, but allows humans the God-granted ability to resist or not resist it. The only 'contribution' humans make is non-resistance to grace. This is the same thing as accepting a gift."[16]

"Cooperation" and "synergism" thus characterize prevenient grace, which distinguishes Arminianism from Calvinism, as Picirilli maintains,

> the point of departure between Calvinists and Arminians here is simply this: Calvinists believe this work is performed only for the elect and that it is necessarily effectual; Arminians believe that this gracious work is performed for the elect and non-elect alike. Some who experience this pre-regenerating [i.e., prevenient] grace believe and are saved; others are brought to exactly the same point of possibility but reject the gospel and perish forever.[17]

---

12. Collins, *Theology of John Wesley*, 79, 78.
13. Roger E. Olson, *Arminian Theology: Myths and Realities* (Downers Grove, IL: InterVarsity Press, 2006), 159.
14. Tuttle, "Prevenient Grace," 1164.
15. Collins, *Theology of John Wesley*, 75–76. "Synergism" is the belief that God's grace and human freedom cooperate in salvation.
16. Olson, *Arminian Theology*, 165.
17. Picirilli, *Grace, Faith, Free Will*, 156–57.

Biblical Support

Here is the heart of Picirilli's apology for prevenient grace:

> [prevenient grace] is intended to express the truth found in passages like John 6:44: "No man can come to me, except the Father which hath sent me draw him." In this light, pre-regenerating [i.e., prevenient] grace may be called *drawing*. Or Acts 16:14: "Lydia . . . whose heart the Lord opened, that she attended unto the things which were spoken of Paul"; pre-regenerating grace may therefore be called *opening the heart*. Or John 16:8: "When [the Spirit] is come, he will reprove the world of sin, and of righteousness, and of judgment." In this sense, pre-regenerating grace may be called *conviction*.[18]

Collins maintains that Wesley's justification for prevenient grace rested almost wholly on John 1:9—"the true light, which gives light to everyone, was coming into the world."[19] Olson doesn't need to offer much support for prevenient grace, since it "is a biblical concept assumed everywhere in Scripture." The only support he records is this: "It is the powerful but resistible drawing of God that Jesus spoke about in John 6. Contrary to what some Calvinist commentators argue, the Greek word *elkō* (e.g., John 6:44) does not have to mean 'drag' or 'compel.' . . . According to various Greek lexicons it can mean draw or attract."[20]

It seems the main reason Arminians trumpet prevenient grace is human experience and their own perceptions of what God's justice is. Prevenient grace appears to make sense of the fact that God commands people to do things and holds them accountable for their actions. "Why would God give commands unless people were given some ability to obey them?"[21] The logic (and it fits with our experience too) is cogent: God commands; we are held responsible for our choices and actions; since God is just and will not arbitrarily punish people, he must give all persons the ability that they need to make these choices; otherwise God shows himself to be a tyrant. Since Scripture shows us that God holds people accountable for their actions and since Arminius's objective, in Carl Bangs's words, was "a theology of grace which does not leave man a 'stock or a stone,'" prevenient grace therefore has to be a reality.[22] Picirilli agrees: "Since God and men are both personal, this means that God deals with men in the mode of influence and response,

---

18. Ibid., 154–55 (italics original).
19. Collins, *Theology of John Wesley*, 74.
20. Olson, *Arminian Theology*, 159.
21. Millard J. Erickson, *Christian Theology* (Grand Rapids: Baker, 1985), 925.
22. Carl Bangs, *Arminius* (Grand Rapids: Zondervan, 1985), 195; quoted in Olson, *Arminian Theology*, 164.

not cause and effect. The latter is the mode of operation of machines, not persons."[23] Prevenient grace protects human autonomy and accountability as well as God's justice.

Biblical Critique

The biblical support offered for prevenient grace is meager. We begin with John 1:9 ("The true light, which gives light to everyone, was coming into the world"), probably the key biblical text for the doctrine of prevenient grace. Against the Arminian interpretation, Thomas Schreiner observes that "gives light" here "refers not to inward illumination [as Wesley assumed] but to the exposure that comes when light is shed upon something." The context demonstrates this conclusion: "Some are shown to be evil because they did not know or receive Jesus (John 1:10–11), while others are revealed to be righteous because they have received Jesus and have been born of God (John 1:12–13)." The broader context of John 3 confirms this way of understanding the light's work. "Those who are evil shrink from coming to the light because they do not want their works to be exposed (v. 20). But those who practice the truth gladly come to the light so that it might be manifest that their works are wrought in God (v. 21)." Schreiner concludes that "the light exposes and reveals the moral and spiritual state of one's heart." It shows "where people are in their relationship to God."[24] The context will not allow for an Arminian interpretation which asserts that God inwardly illumines all persons with the gospel, if only they will respond to the Lord's overtures.

Similarly, Schreiner notes that John 6:44 ("No one can come to me unless the Father who sent me draws him.") must be read in the context of 6:37 ("All that the Father gives me will come to me, and whoever comes to me I will never drive away"). He refers to D. A. Carson's discussion of these verses in which Carson notes, "this 'drawing' activity of the Father cannot be reduced to what theologians sometimes call 'prevenient grace' dispensed to every individual, but this 'drawing' is selective, or else the negative note of v[erse] 44 is meaningless."[25] Schreiner insists, "The Johannine conception of drawing is not that it makes salvation possible, but that it makes salvation effectual. Those who are drawn will come to Jesus and believe."[26]

Schreiner and Carson are correct in their critique of this key Arminian text. Given the dearth of biblical support for prevenient grace, Millard Erickson's critique is cogent: "The problem is that there is no clear and adequate basis

---

23. Picirilli, *Grace, Faith, Free Will*, 156.
24. Thomas R. Schreiner, "Does Scripture Teach Prevenient Grace in the Wesleyan Sense?," in *The Grace of God, the Bondage of the Will, Vol. 2: Historical and Theological Perspectives on Calvinism*, ed. Thomas R. Schreiner and Bruce A. Ware (Grand Rapids: Baker, 1995), 376.
25. D. A. Carson, *The Gospel According to John* (Grand Rapids: Eerdmans, 1991), 293; quoted in Schreiner, "Prevenient Grace," 377–78.
26. Schreiner, "Prevenient Grace," 378.

in Scripture for this concept of a universal enablement. The theory, appealing though it is in many ways, simply is not taught explicitly in the Bible."[27]

Arminianism has to jettison the biblical conception of sovereign, saving, particular grace in order to protect human free will. In asserting synergism, or cooperation, Arminians do not teach that salvation is by grace alone (*sola gratia*). God's grace is redefined as a power which can save, as long as the human agent employs it properly. Olson tellingly admits that to Arminians, "grace *brings* God's undeserved and unmerited favor to humans *who exercise* faith with repentance and trust in Christ alone for salvation."[28] Notice the words "brings," and "who exercise." Olson has redefined the biblical concept of grace to meet his preconceptions of what grace must be (remember, he said prevenient grace is assumed everywhere in the Bible) to fit his understanding of human agency. Collins similarly forthrightly admits that "although the continental reformers and Wesley all assented to a doctrine of total depravity, the basic contours of their theologies remain distinct, due to different conceptions of grace."[29] He is correct. Arminianism—even of the "classical" or "Reformation" type, which is undoubtedly much better than other sorts of Arminianisms—must redefine God's grace. Biblically, grace does not wait for a human response. Grace is God's sovereign favor to individual sinners which accomplishes his goal of saving them. Truly, it is because of God's kind, particular, and effective grace that we are saved.

REFLECTION QUESTIONS

1. Can you define "prevenient grace" in your own words?

2. Do you think Calvinists can say they believe in prevenient grace? Why? How do you think they would define it differently?

3. Do you think "evangelical synergism" is a biblical idea? Why?

4. Look at John 1 and 3. Do you think they teach the Arminian doctrine of prevenient grace?

5. Why do you think Arminians believe that prevenient grace is biblical?

---

27. Erickson, *Christian Theology*, 925.
28. Olson, *Arminian Theology*, 161 (italics added).
29. Collins, *Theology of John Wesley*, 82.

Questions about Human Responsibility

What Is Human Freedom according to Arminianism?

Arminians believe in "libertarian free will" in salvation, which means the unaided human will can equally decide to receive Jesus or to reject him. At the point of decision, nothing in the person's past, present, or future, and no divine influence, impinge upon the will to such a degree that they influence it to make its decision. The person's will is autonomous in its decision making. Although this might seem to cohere with human experience, libertarian freedom does not accord with the Bible's teaching that fallen humans are profoundly affected by their sin, circumstances, and aspirations and that nothing short of God's gracious intervention can lead them to receive Jesus.

General Consideration

Even though Arminian and Calvinistic theologians define human freedom differently, they agree on a great deal. They believe that human beings possess a level of personal freedom that separates them from the rest of the created order. Being created in the image of God implies that persons can and do make countless important choices. People are not mindless lemmings. They are not automatons, driven by forces outside their control. They make significant decisions that affect them, others, and the rest of creation.

However, significant differences exist between Arminians and Calvinists over the question of the extent of human freedom. To Arminians, in order for humans to be free, their freedom must be exercised apart from God's sovereign intervention. God limits his sovereignty with regard to a person's deciding whether or not to trust in Christ for salvation. In this realm, then, people have so-called "libertarian freedom," a freedom often called "free will." Since God created us in his image, since the Bible is filled with commands for us to do all sorts of things, since God holds people accountable for their actions, and since God chooses not to violate our personhood, all persons have freedom to decide to trust Christ or not. Such is the Arminian notion of freedom.

The Arminian notion of libertarian freedom, though, is not found in the Bible. Agreeing that people experience significant freedom when they make decisions and that God does indeed hold people accountable for their actions, Calvinists believe that Arminians fundamentally fail to take into account the Bible's teaching on the devastating effects of the fall into sin on our ability to choose. Arminian free will cannot stand in light of the Scripture's teaching that people are in significant bondage to sin. People choose. But, apart from God's intervening grace, they choose sin based on their sinful predispositions.

Arminian "Libertarian Freedom"

We want to let Arminians themselves tell us what they mean by "libertarian freedom." We shall do so by examining three expositions of Arminian freedom. First, Jerry Walls and Joseph Dongell defend "libertarian freedom" in this manner: "The essence of this view is that a free action is one that does not have a sufficient condition or cause prior to its occurrence; it also holds that some human actions are free in this sense."[1] Several realities ground the appropriateness of this view. "First, the common experience of deliberation assumes that our choices are undetermined." The entire process of deliberation "assumes that it really is up to us how we will decide."[2] In the second place, "it seems intuitively and immediately evident that many of our actions are up to us in the sense that when faced with a decision, both (or more) options are within our power to choose." This "immediate sense of power to choose between alternative courses of action" is more real than any Calvinistic theory that says our wills are determined.[3] Additionally, only this notion of freedom makes sense of the reality that we're morally accountable beings. Walls and Dongell offer this syllogism to make their point:

> *Premise 1*: "If we are morally responsible for our actions, we must be free."

> *Premise 2*: "We are morally responsible for our actions."

> *Conclusion*: "Therefore, we must be free."[4]

1. Jerry L. Walls and Joseph R. Dongell, *Why I Am Not a Calvinist* (Downers Grove, IL: InterVarsity Press, 2004), 103.
2. Ibid.
3. Ibid., 104.
4. Ibid.

Their entire argument is founded on human experience and purported logic. The meaning of "free" in the first premise is assumed, which, of course, wins the argument (they think).

Second, noting that "the nature of free will" is a "point where Calvinism and Arminianism diverge and where no middle ground seems possible," Roger Olson defines the Arminian notion of "libertarian free will" in this way:

> When an agent (a human or God) acts freely in the libertarian sense, nothing outside the self (including physical realities within the body) is causing it; the intellect or character alone rules over the will and turns it one way or another. Deliberation and then choice are the only determining factors, although factors such as nature and nurture, and divine influence come into play. Arminians do not believe in absolute free will; the will is always influenced and situated in a context. Even God is guided by his nature and character when making decisions. But Arminians deny that creaturely decisions and actions are controlled by God or any force outside the self.[5]

Olson is correct that God is guided in his actions by his holiness ("his nature and character") when he chooses. But Olson gets tangled up when he considers human choosing and its relationship to human nature. On the one hand, he says the human will is sovereign in the realm of choosing, for he says "deliberation and then choice are the only determining factors." So, deciding and choosing—both of which are functions of the will—are deterministic. God may "come into play," but he can't do it in any way that will impinge upon human sovereignty. On the other hand, though, he says the human will may be influenced in its decision-making by things like its context and its nature. Yet, at the end of the day, "the self" is sovereign, not controlled by anything outside itself, including God.

Olson asserts that in Adam, humanity lost all free will. Yet, God in his mercy restored this freedom through his prevenient grace so "sinners under the influence of prevenient grace have genuine free will as a gift of God; for the first time they can freely say yes or no to God. Nothing outside the self determines how they will respond."[6] This is a gift of God to all persons.

Two things make free will essential, Olson argues. "Arminians believe in free will because they see it everywhere assumed in the Bible, and because it is necessary to protect God's reputation."[7] The first is grounded in human

---

5. Roger Olson, *Arminian Theology: Myths and Realities* (Downers Grove, IL: InterVarsity Press, 2006), 75.
6. Ibid., 76.
7. Ibid., 98.

experience. The second, though, is crucial: "The real reason Arminians reject divine control of every human choice and action is that this would make God the author of sin and evil. For Arminians this makes God at least morally ambiguous and at worst the *only* sinner."[8] His logic is simple, though unconvincing. He maintains, "Arminianism is all about protecting the reputation of God by protecting his character as revealed in Jesus Christ and Scripture. Arminians are not concerned about some humanly derived fascination with fairness. . . . But love and justice are necessary to goodness, and both exclude [divine] willing determination of sin, evil or eternal suffering."[9] Our experience combined with apologetic enterprise of exonerating God from charges that he is in any way unjust or responsible for the sin we see and experience in the world proves libertarian free will.

Third, theologian Jack Cottrell echoes Olson's contentions with some different nuances. He asserts that "the kind of world [God] chose to create is able to operate and progress in such a way that God does not need to be the direct cause of all things. In fact, most specific things that happen in the world are not caused by God." Essential to this world is "the existence of beings who possess a significantly free will. This kind of free will (which is the only kind that is genuinely free) is sometimes called the power of opposite choice." He approvingly quotes Norman Geisler's definition of the power of opposite choice: "At a minimum, freedom means the power of contrary choice; that is, an agent is free only if he could have done otherwise."[10] Cottrell's fuller explanation is significant:

> a will is significantly free only if the choices it makes are not caused or determined, either directly or indirectly, by an outside force. Thus we can say that truly free will is the ability to choose between opposites without that choice's being fixed or determined by some power outside the person's own will. This applies especially to the sinner's ability either to believe or to reject the gospel. As Forlines says, "In Arminianism there is agreement that human beings have freedom of choice. This includes the freedom to place their faith in Christ upon hearing the gospel, or conversely they can refuse to place their faith in Christ."[11]

---

8. Ibid., 99 (italics original).
9. Ibid., 100.
10. Norman Geisler, *Chosen But Free* (Minneapolis: Bethany, 1989), 44; quoted in Jack Cottrell, "The Classical Arminian View of Election," in *Perspectives on Election: Five Views*, ed. Chad Owen Brand (Nashville: B&H, 2006), 100.
11. Cottrell, "Classical Arminian View," 100, quoting F. Leroy Forlines, *The Quest for Truth: Answering Life's Inescapable Questions* (Nashville: Randall House, 2001), 322.

As we did with Olson's, we need to pay attention to Cottrell's logic. The will has to be absolutely contingent (that is, it is undetermined or uncaused and therefore unpredictable) at the time of choosing. The will, whatever it is (Cottrell assumes its meaning but doesn't define it), is free from any influence, even of an indirect nature. Presumably it is also free from the influence of that person him- or herself when they make their independent decision. Otherwise, Cottrell argues, the will cannot be free in any real sense.

Cottrell combats the Calvinistic notion of compatibilistic free will, claiming that Calvinists eschew true freedom in their misplaced quest for divine control. They believe, he says, that God places in us "the specific motives and desires that will inevitably cause us to make only the choices that God has determined we shall make." This might feel like freedom from our perspective, but it is spurious. "The psychological feeling of freedom cannot replace the true inward ability to make a genuine choice between opposites."[12] Additionally, Cottrell argues, Calvinists often misrepresent Arminian conceptions of free will by asserting that it must include "the so-called 'liberty of indifference,' according to which all choices are seen as arbitrary, unpredictable, capricious, and random." This is a faulty representation, though, for "the ability of the will to choose between opposites does not require equal influence toward both sides; sometimes the will opts for a certain choice against overwhelming influences in the opposite direction."[13]

Whether they reject the Calvinistic doctrine of "total depravity" or believe that "God through a universal preparatory grace mitigates the depravity and restores a measure of freedom," which is prevenient grace, Arminians believe that the person is free from any controlling constraint outside his will when he is confronted with the claims of the gospel.[14] According to Cottrell, "When the gospel message reaches the sinner, he is *not* in a state of unremedied total depravity and thus of total inability to believe in Jesus without an unconditional, selective, irresistible act of the Spirit. Rather, every sinner is able to make his own decision of whether to believe or not."[15]

Summary

Arminian conceptions of human "free will" in matters of salvation have two sources. In the first place, their notion of human freedom is fundamentally rooted in *apparent* logic. Arminians argue that God couldn't justly hold people accountable for their actions if they didn't have the corresponding ability to do the opposite thing. In the second place, they rely on human experience. That is, when we make choices, we feel like we're doing what we

---

12. Cottrell, "The Classical Arminian View," 100–101.
13. Ibid., 101.
14. Ibid., 121.
15. Ibid. (italics original).

want to do apart from anything other than our will determining what we will choose. Their definition of freedom and their experience of making choices—along with a general sense of right and wrong—is paramount.

In fact, the problem with Arminian libertarian freedom is fundamentally biblical. Scripture teaches that the persons who make choices are sinners. Their sinful state radically influences the choices they can make. Calvinist theologian Robert Reymond's lengthy rejoinder to Cottrell is noteworthy in this regard:

> [People's] moral choices are also determined by the total complexion of who they are. And the Bible informs us that men are not only finite but are now also sinners to boot, who by nature *cannot* bring forth good fruit (Matt. 7:18), by nature *cannot* hear Christ's word that they might have life (John 8:43), by nature *cannot* accept the Spirit of truth (John 14:17), by nature *cannot* be subject to the law of God (Rom. 8:7), by nature *cannot* discern truths of the Spirit of God (1 Cor. 2:14), by nature *cannot* confess from the heart Jesus as Lord (1 Cor. 12:3), by nature *cannot* inherit the kingdom of God (1 Cor. 15:50), by nature *cannot* control the tongue (James 3:8), and by nature *cannot* come to Christ (John 6:44–45, 66). In order to do any of these things, they must receive powerful aid coming to them *ab extra* [i.e., from outside themselves]. So there simply is no such thing among men as a free will that can always choose the right if it wants to.[16]

Reymond is correct (as we shall see in the next question). People's choices are greatly influenced by who they are. Arminian "free will" does not do justice to the scope of the biblical witness because of its insistence that libertarian choices be uncaused, indifferent, and unnecessary. In Arminianism, the "will" of the person, not the person himself, is what chooses. Nowhere, though, does the Bible ascribe our decisions to a component of who we are (the will). Everywhere in Scripture, the entire person chooses. For this reason, persons are responsible for the choices they make.

---

16. Robert L. Reymond, "Responses to Jack W. Cottrell," in *Perspectives on Election: Five Views*, ed. Chad Owen Brand (Nashville: B&H, 2006), 136–37 (italics original).

REFLECTION QUESTIONS

1. Have you ever considered the extent of a fallen person's freedom in matters related to salvation? Before reading this chapter, how would you have described it?

2. Do you think the Bible teaches "free will"? If so, how would you define it?

3. What do you think are other alternatives to Arminian notions of libertarian free will?

4. Arminian theologian Robert Picirilli surmises that "man is free, as possessing a true will, to make real choices and decisions between two (or more) courses of action. . . . A choice that actually can go but one way is not a choice, and without this 'freedom' there is not personality."[17] Do you agree with Picirilli? Why?

5. Look at the biblical citations in the quotation from Robert Reymond. How do you think Arminians would respond to his use of these texts?

---

17. Robert E. Picirilli, *Grace, Faith, Free Will: Contrasting Views of Salvation: Calvinism and Arminianism* (Nashville: Randall House, 2002), 41.

What Is Human Freedom according to Calvinism?

Calvinism teaches that human beings possess real freedom. We always do what we want to do, choosing from all sorts of options. The Bible often asserts that we make real, significant choices. Yet Scripture also insists that our choices are affected by our nature. Who we are bounds our choices. We cannot choose to do something that is inconsistent with who we are. Created in the image of God, human beings are free agents who have real freedom and express it regularly in the choices they make.

"Compatibilist," not "Libertarian" Freedom

As we noted in the previous chapter, Arminian conceptions of "libertarian freedom" wrongly assume that an individual's character does not impact the choices he or she makes. Libertarian freedom also denies that God can determine a free choice we make. Arminians believe that when persons act, they must act independently of God. The Bible, however, never speaks in this way. Scripture assumes and asserts compatibilism.[1] Calvinism asserts "compatibilist freedom: the freedom to do what you want to do."[2] This human freedom is consistent with God's determination of all things that will happen. In short, "compatibilist freedom means that even if every act we perform is caused by something outside ourselves (such as natural causes or God), we are still free, for we can still act according to our character and desires."[3]

---

1. See Questions 10–12.
2. John M. Frame, *The Doctrine of God* (Phillipsburg, NJ: P&R, 2002), 136.
3. Ibid. It's fair to ask, I think, whether Arminians can say the same thing given their view of libertarian freedom. One wonders how they can legitimately hold persons accountable for their choices since decisions don't ultimately reflect people's character.

Calvinism—with its view of compatibilist freedom—teaches that persons are truly free to do what we want to do. For that reason, we are responsible before the Lord for the choices we make. We are confronted in Scripture with commands given to persons. "Repent." "Believe." "Return to me." "Trust in the Lord." These biblical commands, and so many others, remind us that we are responsible individuals, constantly making choices. And we will be held accountable for the choices we make. Eternally. Scripture is clear: "Whoever believes in him is not condemned, but whoever does not believe is condemned already, because he has not believed in the name of the only Son of God" (John 3:18). Our free decisions truly matter. Persons will go to heaven or hell eternally based on the choices they freely have made regarding the gospel. These commands require freedom to obey and will result in punishment if not heeded. This is the case because God created us free agents. As John Murray confirms, "We are responsible for our acts because they are the result of our volition."[4]

Our Nature and Our Choices

Although we know instinctively that we are free, we also know that our freedom has limitations. I might feel "free" to breathe underwater, but I will drown. I might want to express my "freedom" to jump over a two story building, but I will not be able to do so. My nature affects my ability to do all sorts of things. More seriously, consider God. The Lord is the freest of all beings, never frustrated in his choices. Yet, in his freedom our God will never do certain things. He won't lie or sin, for example. More importantly, God *cannot* lie. But why not, if he is completely free? The answer is that God will always act according to his nature. Since he is completely holy, he will always act perfectly in line with his character. His perfect freedom is bounded by his perfect nature.

The same reality holds for humans. We act in a manner consistent with our nature; in other words, a person's "moral choices are also determined by the total complexion of who they are."[5] We don't make choices apart from who we are. The biblical justification for such a view is plentiful. Jesus taught that we will know people's characters, or natures, by observing the fruits of their lives (Matt. 7:20). Good persons yield good fruit, and bad persons produce bad results because "every healthy tree bears good fruit, but the diseased tree bears bad fruit. A healthy tree cannot bear bad fruit, nor can a diseased tree bear good fruit" (Matt. 7:17–18). Moral agents' actions occur in the soil of who they are, from their natures. In other words, we act in line with our

---

4. John Murray, "Free Agency," in *Collected Writings of John Murray* (Edinburgh: Banner of Truth, 1977), 2:61.
5. Robert L. Reymond, "Responses to Jack W. Cottrell," in *Perspectives on Election: Five Views*, ed. Chad Owen Brand (Nashville: B&H, 2006), 136.

character. Murray reminds us that "the whole complex of desires, of motives" and of "principles" make up "the distinguishing moral and religious bent, aim, purpose" of a person, what "Scripture calls the heart."[6]

Thus, unbelievers sin because they are sinners. People do not become sinners because they choose to sin. The problem is much deeper than that, rooted in who we are, not merely in our decisions. Non-Christians are unable to perform spiritually good actions. Indeed, Jesus affirmed that "everyone who commits sin is a slave to sin" (John 6:34). They do what they want to do. The problem is that their natures are sinful, so all that they do is sin. Even the "good" actions they perform are done with wrong motivations. For this reason, Jesus said that people had to be born again, born from above (John 3:3, 5). "No one," our Lord says, "can come to me unless the Father who sent me draws him." Indeed, "no one can come to me unless it is granted to him by the Father" (John 6:44, 65).

The New Testament authors consistently teach that people are in bondage to sin in such a manner that they are unable to do anything spiritually good. Paul's lengthiest exposition of this point comes in his epistle to the Romans. He says there that because of our rebellion, all people are "under sin" (Rom. 1:18–32). This means, among other things, that "none is righteous, no, not one; no one understands; no one seeks God. All have turned aside; together they have become worthless; no one does good, not even one." The result of this is that "the whole world may be held accountable to God" (Rom. 3:10–12, 19). We should not quickly skirt over these shocking statements of fact. No one does good (Rom. 3:12). No one seeks God (Rom. 3:11). Everyone hates God (Rom. 1:30).

For these reasons the apostle observes that "the mind that is set on the flesh is hostile to God, for it does not submit to God's law; indeed, it cannot. Those who are in the flesh cannot please God" (Rom. 8:7–8). Paul's "cannot"s matter! It is not just that most people don't obey and please the Lord. It's not merely that many haven't found the means of doing the right thing apart from God's intervention. Rather, non-Christians will not do the right thing because they cannot. "We not only sin, but cannot do otherwise."[7] Unbelieving persons do not have "free will" to choose Jesus. The sinful nature they have in Adam—the reality that defines who they are—means that they both can't and won't obey God by submitting to the gospel. They will do exactly what they want to do, so in that sense they are free. But their freedom is constrained by who they are. Because of our union with Adam, all persons are born condemned; we are disobedient people; we are sinners (Rom. 5:18–19). As such, we sin.

Paul teaches the same thing in Ephesians 2. Outside of Christ, people are spiritually "dead." They are extremely active in their deadness (Eph. 2:1–3).

---

6. Murray, "Free Agency," 61.
7. Frame, *Doctrine of God*, 131.

But they are just what the apostle calls them: "dead." The only hope for such dead people is "but God" (Eph. 2:4). They must be acted upon in grace by the sovereign God.

When the Jewish leaders protested against Jesus's charge that they were slaves to sin, our Lord charged them: "Why do you not understand what I say? It is because you cannot bear to hear my word. You are of your father the devil, and your will is to do your father's desires" (John 8:43–44). They "cannot" hear Jesus's word because they "are not of God" (v. 47). Their sin makes them unable to receive and follow Jesus's commands.[8]

Moral Inability and Natural Ability

In an ironic manner (since they are usually seen as being polar opposites of each other), Arminians and hyper-Calvinists reason similarly to each other regarding human freedom. They both aver that responsibility before the Lord is limited by ability.[9] The Arminian argues that in order for non-Christians to be held accountable by the Lord for their sin, they must be able (apart from specific divine intervention) to respond to the gospel. Conversely, the hyper-Calvinist believes that the sinner's deadness in sin and subsequent inability means he or she is not responsible to respond to the gospel in faith and repentance. Biblical Calvinists hold to compatibilism, though, and believe both Arminians and hyper-Calvinists are letting their logic and experience—rather than the Bible—determine their theology.

No Calvinist has spent as much time discussing human freedom as Jonathan Edwards in his *The Freedom of the Will* published in 1754.[10] In this tightly argued apology for Calvinism, Edwards seeks to make a simple point against the charges of the Arminians: people (and God) are free agents who make decisions that accord with their nature. The fundamental error of Arminians, he asserts, is to make the human will its own entity. To them, the will is completely self-determining. Nothing affects the will at the point of decision—nothing about the person making the choice and nothing in his past or perceived future. This Arminian definition of a will is contrary to what is assumed by all people, that is, that the will consists "in opportunity to do as one pleases." Over against this obvious meaning of will, Arminians "have introduced a new strange liberty, consisting in indifference, contingence, and self-determination; by which they involve themselves and others in great obscurity, and manifold gross inconsistence."[11] Their inconsistency can be proved in three ways.

---

8. Also see 1 Corinthians 2:14.
9. See Question 31.
10. The complete title is *A Careful and Strict Enquiry into the Modern Prevailing Notions of that Freedom of Will, Which Is Supposed to Be Essential to Moral Agency, Vertue and Vice, Reward and Punishment, Praise and Blame.*
11. Jonathan Edwards, *Freedom of the Will*, ed. Paul Ramsey, *The Works of Jonathan Edwards*, vol. 1 (New Haven, CT: Yale University Press, 1957), 429.

First of all, Edwards charges the Arminians with assuming what the will is but never defining it. So he does. "The will," he observes, is "that by which the mind chooses anything. . . . in every act of will whatsoever, the mind chooses one thing rather than another."[12] The will of a person is determined by "that motive, which, as it stands in view of the mind, is the strongest" at the moment of choice.[13] The will is not an independent, autonomous agent. It is intimately related to the rest of the person, especially the person's affections. Later Calvinists agree with Edwards's point. James Montgomery Boice explains, "Our choices are determined by what we think is the most desirable course of action."[14] Biblically, our hearts are the center of our being, determining what we love and hate, what we hope for, and what we decide. Mark Talbot is right:

> In Scripture, our hearts are the core of our personal beings. They are thus central to every crucial aspect of our humanity: our inner life and character (1 Sam. 16:7; Matt. 15:19; 1 Pet. 3:4), our feelings and emotions (Pss. 4:7; 13:2; 25:17; 2 Cor. 6:11), our intellectual faculties and activities (Pss. 49:3; 53:1; Prov. 2:2; Mark 2:6; Luke 1:51; 2:51), and our desires and will and purposes (Pss. 27:8; 37:4; 57:7; John 13:2; Acts 5:3f.).[15]

We choose what we want to choose. And what we want to choose is a function of who we are and what motivates us at the moment.

Second, following this, Edwards carefully defines freedom. His preferred term is "liberty." Liberty is not a component of the will. Rather, liberty identifies one who has the power of volition (or, will). So persons are free—notwithstanding the motives they have at the moment of choice, the causes that precede their choices, and the future they anticipate—as long as nothing constrains them to act in a way they do not want to act or restrains them from doing what they want. A person is free when he does what he wants to do. This is "free" will.[16] People possess this freedom because God has created us as moral, free agents.

Third, Edwards speaks of persons' ability. It is best, he teaches, to divide ability into two types, moral and natural. An individual can have "natural ability"—that is, all the stuff required to do something, but if he or she is morally "unable," he or she will not do the thing. This is because moral inability

---

12. Ibid., 137.
13. Ibid., 141. See R. C. Sproul, *Chosen by God*, rev. ed. (Carol Stream, IL: Tyndale, 1986), 40.
14. James Montgomery Boice, *Foundations of the Christian Faith: A Comprehensive and Readable Theology*, rev. ed. (Downers Grove, IL: InterVarsity Press, 1986), 212.
15. Mark R. Talbot, "When All Hope Has Died: Meditation on Profound Christian Suffering," in *For the Fame of God's Name: Essays in Honor of John Piper*, eds. Sam Storms and Justin Taylor (Wheaton, IL: Crossway, 2010), 85–86.
16. Edwards, *Freedom of the Will*, 163–64.

("the opposition or want of inclination to do something") provides the motives the person has.[17] And, remember, motives are essential when a person makes a free choice. If one despises God, for example, one will inevitably choose to reject his summons to come to him in repentance and faith. Left to him- or herself, the unbeliever will invariably choose to act in accord with his or her very being, which is set in opposition to the Lord.

Consider an unbelieving person who hears the gospel command to repent and trust in Jesus. Is he or she able to respond to the gospel summons? Edwards would answer "yes and no." The person is naturally able in the sense that he or she has ears to hear the message, a brain to understand the simple gospel summons, and a capacity to choose things based on motives. The individual is not lacking any of the "stuff" necessary to repent and believe. But—apart from sovereign divine intervention to make him or her be born again—he or she is morally unable. He hates the God whose message it is and the fact that this Lord tells him what to do and teaches that he has sinned and is not able to save himself. Biblically, his heart is opposed to God; he is dead in trespasses and sin; he cannot and will not obey God.

Summary

Murray summarizes the Calvinist position well:

> We are not free because the will or power of volition is in a state of indifference or indeterminancy. It is not an autonomous power or agent that can register any series of volitions. . . . Volition is causally determined by what the person most characteristically is. The liberty or freedom consists in the fact that the series of volitions is determined by the self; in the sense relevant to our topic, volition is self-determined. Action is self-action, volition is self-volition, determined by what the person is, and not by any compulsion or coercion extraneous to the person.[18]

Calvinists teach that people have real freedom, a freedom to do exactly what they want to do. But their "wants" are always determined by who they are and by their motives at the time of their choosing. Scripture, not our sense of freedom, must determine how we interpret and understand our freedom as well as the freedom of unbelievers.

---

17. Ibid., 159.
18. Murray, "Free Agency," 62.

REFLECTION QUESTIONS

1. How would you explain the Calvinistic understanding of human freedom?

2. Can you think of other biblical texts that indicate that people act according to their natures and according to their motives?

3. Do you agree with Edwards's definition of the "will"? Why?

4. Do you agree that non-Christians are morally unable to trust in Jesus? Why?

5. Do you think Edwards's distinction between "natural" and "moral" ability is a helpful delineation? If so, do you think it has any practical implications for how we preach the gospel?

What Is Compatibilism?

Compatibilism is the belief that these two seemingly contradictory truths are in fact compatible with each other:

1. God is absolutely sovereign, but his sovereignty never functions in such a way that human responsibility is curtailed, minimized, or mitigated.

2. Human beings are morally responsible creatures—they significantly choose, rebel, obey, believe, defy, make decisions, and so forth, and they are rightly held accountable for such actions; but this characteristic never functions so as to make God absolutely contingent [i.e., dependent on something outside himself].[1]

Compatibilism is either assumed or taught on throughout the Bible. It is the heart of the biblical Calvinism I am advocating. Compatibilism simply asserts that God is absolutely sovereign, and at the same time, people are truly responsible for their actions and choices. It allows us to believe both of the truths Jesus taught in John 6: "I am the bread of life; whoever comes to me shall not hunger, and whoever believes in me shall never thirst. . . . All that the Father gives me will come to me, and whoever comes to me I will never cast out" (John 6:35, 37). Humans are responsible. God is sovereign.[2]

---

1. D. A. Carson, *How Long, O Lord? Reflections on Suffering and Evil* (Grand Rapids: Baker, 1990), 201.
2. This is also how such Calvinistic luminaries as John Calvin and Jonathan Edwards understood the relationship of sovereignty and responsibility. See Paul Helm, "Calvin the Compatibilist," in his *Calvin at the Centre* (New York: Oxford University Press, 2010), 227–72.

Compatibilism and Its Rivals

Relating God's absolute sovereignty and true human responsibility is difficult. Different theological systems go awry because they negate or limit one or the other of these truths. We will note how four theories relate these truths before we survey the Calvinistic position.

Theologically, the two positions on the extreme ends of the spectrum are fatalism and Pelagianism. Fatalism so emphasizes the divine will that it leaves no place for human willing. *Que sera, sera* ("whatever will be, will be") is its mantra. Fatalists don't believe in a personal, loving, feeling God, but in an impersonal force that accomplishes its will irrespective of human willing. Pelagianism, on the opposite end of the spectrum, puts all of the stress on human choice. God was gracious, Pelagians teach, in giving humans his law and complete free will to obey it. If a person chooses to do so, he can follow the Lord perfectly. Fatalism and Pelagianism are both heretical, espousing unbiblical and gospel-negating views.

Closer to the middle of the spectrum are hyper-Calvinism and Arminianism. Hyper-Calvinists so overemphasize divine sovereignty that they wrongly limit human responsibility, to the point that they teach that an unconverted person is not accountable to respond to the gospel summons.[3] They also maintain that Christians are not responsible to share the gospel with unbelievers. God's sovereignty and human responsibility cannot fit together in hyper-Calvinists' minds, so they jettison responsibility. Arminians do the opposite. They overemphasize the ability of fallen sinners to respond to the gospel. In response to the overwhelming number of commands given to people throughout the Bible, Arminians teach that God limits his sovereignty. Here's the logic of Arminianism: since God requires a thing of a person and holds him or her accountable for doing it, God had to limit his intervention in that action and give the individual all the requisite ability to accomplish it. Otherwise, it would be unjust for God to hold the person accountable for doing something that he or she did not have the complete means of accomplishing. The logic is quite simple. It is just wrong. Hyper-Calvinism and Arminianism are both logical attempts at understanding the relationship of God's complete sovereignty to human responsibility.

Biblical Calvinists eschew the errors of fatalism and Pelagianism. They also shun the wrongheadedness of both hyper-Calvinism and Arminianism. Instead, Calvinists attempt to hold together what the Bible asserts from beginning to end: God is completely sovereign, and at the same time people are truly responsible for their choices and actions. Since the Bible teaches both, we must hold on to them tenaciously.

---

3. This view is sometimes called "hard determinism," whereas compatibilism is sometimes labeled "soft determinism." See Question 31.

Definitions

Compatibilism is sometimes labelled an "antinomy" or a "paradox." J. I. Packer prefers antinomy. An antinomy, he argues, theologically is "an *apparent* incompatibility between two apparent truths. . . . There are cogent reasons for believing each of them; each rests on clear and solid evidence; but it is a mystery to you how they can be squared with each other."[4] An antinomy, though, is not the same as a nonsensical statement or verbal sleight of hand. Packer distinguishes an antinomy from a paradox, which is a play on words in which "what creates the appearance of contradiction is not the facts, but the words. The contradiction is verbal, but not real."[5] Concerning God's sovereignty and human responsibility, we must

> [r]efuse to regard the apparent inconsistency as real; put down the semblance of contradiction to the deficiency of your own understanding; think of the two principles as, not rival alternatives, but, in some way that at present you do not grasp, complementary to each other. Be careful, therefore, not to set them at loggerheads, nor to make deductions from either that would cut across the other (such deductions would, for that very reason, be certainly unsound).[6]

He concludes, "Man is a responsible moral agent, though he is *also* divinely controlled; man is divinely controlled, though he is *also* a responsible moral agent. God's sovereignty is a reality, and man's responsibility is a reality too."[7] Such is the antinomy.

Anthony Hoekema prefers paradox. His conclusion is that "God is totally sovereign over our lives, directing them in accordance with his will, but that nevertheless we are required to make our own decisions and are held totally responsible for them," for "the Bible teaches both." On the one hand, texts like Proverbs 21:1 ("The king's heart is in the hand of the LORD; he directs it like a watercourse wherever he pleases") and Ephesians 1:11 ("In him we were also chosen, having been predestined according to the plan of him who works out everything in conformity with the purpose of his will") mandate our belief in God's absolute sovereignty. But texts such as John 3:36 ("Whoever believes in the Son has eternal life, but whoever rejects the Son will not see life, for God's wrath remains on him") and Revelation 22:12 ("Behold, I am coming soon! My reward is with me, and I will give to everyone according to what he

---

4. J. I. Packer, *Evangelism and the Sovereignty of God* (Downers Grove, IL: InterVarsity Press, 1961), 18–19 (italics original).
5. Ibid., 19–20.
6. Ibid., 21.
7. Ibid., 23 (italics original).

has done") force us to acknowledge human responsibility.[8] The "paradox" in speaking of these two truths, then, equals an apparent contradiction one must hold on the basis of biblical revelation.

Bruce Ware's favored term for the relation of these two truths is "compatibilism."[9] By this he means that "*God's determination* of what people do is compatible with their carrying out those determined actions with *genuine human freedom and responsibility*."[10] Among other texts, he highlights Acts 2:23 and 4:27–28. Note Luke's recounting of the agents responsible for Christ's death:

> This Jesus, delivered up according to the definite plan and foreknowledge of God, you crucified and killed by the hands of lawless men. (Acts 2:23)

> For truly in this city there were gathered together against your holy servant Jesus, whom you anointed, both Herod and Pontius Pilate, along with the Gentiles and the peoples of Israel, to do whatever your hand and your plan had predestined to take place. (Acts 4:27–28)

So, who put Jesus to death? "Peter gives us two, not just one, answers, both of which are necessary for a full accounting, and only together are they sufficient to explain who put Jesus on the cross."[11] Wicked people killed Jesus on the cross; God also put him there. The first "clearly involves the plans and actions of free moral agents." The second "involves God's determination of what He would do, a determination carried out precisely through and not apart from free moral agents."[12] So compatibilism means "that God determines what someone does, and yet they are held responsible for their actions."[13] God acts. They act.

"Antinomy." "Paradox." "Compatibilism." We might quibble over which word is better to speak of this biblical reality, even though they are close to each other.[14] I prefer "compatibilism" because it highlights that there is no logical or moral discontinuity between these two truths. Paul Helm is correct to note

8. Anthony A. Hoekema, *Saved by Grace* (Grand Rapids: Eerdmans, 1989), 5–6.

9. Bruce A. Ware, *God's Greater Glory: The Exalted God of Scripture and the Christian Faith* (Wheaton, IL: Crossway, 2004), 61–160; idem, "The Compatibility of Determinism and Human Freedom," in *Whomever He Wills: A Surprising Display of Sovereign Mercy*, ed. Matthew Barrett and Thomas J. Nettles (Cape Coral, FL: Founders, 2012), 212–30.

10. Ware, "Compatibility of Determinism and Human Freedom," 213 (italics original).

11. Ibid., 219.

12. Ibid., 220.

13. Ibid., 221.

14. Timothy George argues, "We believe that God is absolutely sovereign over all that he has made. And we also believe that he has given free moral agency and responsibility to the men and women created in his image." Four words have been used to show the relationship: "contradiction," "antinomy," "paradox," and "mystery." He prefers "mystery": "In theology, a mystery is an

the danger of the "antinomy" position is that it is so vague as to leave room, in theory at least, for saying that Arminian libertarian freedom and divine sovereignty are both true even if we can't reconcile them.[15] The same criticism could be assigned to "paradox." "Compatibilism" is better, for it reminds us that both these truths are true and are reconcilable, even if we don't grasp exactly how.

Parameters of Compatibilism

D. A. Carson usefully demonstrates that passage after passage from the Bible assumes compatibilism.[16] God is absolutely sovereign, including over the human will. Yet, his sovereignty does not alleviate true human responsibility, for people are created morally responsible. Nevertheless, their responsibility does not make God contingent; that is, he is not dependent on the choices people make. The sovereign God is perfectly good in all he does.[17]

Carson insists that five truths must circumscribe our thinking about compatibilism. First, no one completely understands how these truths fit together. We must leave room for mystery. Second, there is an asymmetry in relationship to God's interaction with good and evil. God stands behind evil in such a way that not even evil takes place outside the bounds of his sovereignty, yet he is not liable for the evil that occurs. Other agents are always responsible for the evil and wrongdoing. On the other hand, God stands behind good in such a way that it not only takes place within the bounds of his sovereignty, but it is always credited to him, and only derivatively to secondary agents.[18]

Third, human responsibility is not immediately the same as human freedom. People often have incorrect notions of human freedom, so discussions of freedom must be bound by two constraints. On the one hand, "human freedom cannot involve absolute power to contrary; that is, it cannot include such liberal power that God himself becomes contingent." God's hands are not tied by our choices. He is not dependent on us. Instead, human freedom is related to "voluntarism." People "do what we want to do, and that is why we are held accountable for what we do." On the other hand, human freedom is decisively affected by our fallen condition. "Our wills, then, are not truly free; they are enslaved by sin."[19]

Fourth, the God of the Bible is a supremely personal being, for he is personal by nature. God is a "he," not an "it." He thinks, feels, and relates. He does

    assumed truth that the human mind cannot comprehend but must accept by faith" (*Amazing Grace: God's Pursuit, Our Response*, 2nd ed. [Wheaton, IL: Crossway, 2011], 36–37).

15. Paul Helm, *The Providence of God, Contours of Christian Theology* (Downers Grove, IL: InterVarsity Press, 1993), 62–66.

16. Carson, *How Long, O Lord?*, 202–12. Carson's more extensive treatment of this subject can be found in D. A. Carson, *Divine Sovereignty and Human Responsibility: Biblical Perspectives in Tension* (Atlanta: John Knox, 1981).

17. Ibid., 202–205.

18. Ibid., 213.

19. Ibid., 214–15.

whatever is necessary to do to be personal. At the same time, though, God is different from us. He is transcendent, not subject to us or to any of his creation. He is the sovereign one. Fifth, many of our problems with compatibilism are related to things we do not understand about the very nature of God. How can a transcendent God also be personal? How is God (the good God who hates all evil) sovereign over evil? Carson's conclusion is apropos: "The mystery of providence is in the first instance not located in debates about decrees, free will, the place of Satan, and the like. It is located in the doctrine of God."[20] It should not surprise us that we cannot fathom how the truths of God's sovereignty and human responsibility cohere. God is above us, reigning as the transcendent sovereign of the universe. Yet, we can trust that he is good and will always do right.

Summary

Compatibilism is the best way to relate God's sovereignty and human responsibility without downplaying either of them. Arminianism asserts human freedom in such a way that God's sovereignty is lessened. Hyper-Calvinism asserts God's sovereignty in such a way that humans are not responsible. Both may make sense to the human mind. But neither one is biblical. Only biblical compatibilism (i.e., Calvinism) takes enough account of the Bible's dual emphasis on God's absolute sovereignty and true human responsibility. The irony is that often Calvinism is disparaged as being logical but not biblical. The reality is that Calvinists are the ones who are willing to hold together the full scope of the Bible's teaching.

REFLECTION QUESTIONS

1. How would you define "compatibilism" in your own words?

2. What places in the Bible teach that God is completely sovereign?

3. Where does Scripture assert that humans are truly responsible?

4. Do you have problems logically relating God's sovereignty to human responsibility?

5. Do you have problems emotionally relating God's sovereignty to human responsibility?

---

20. Ibid., 218.

Does the Bible Teach Compatibilism? (Part 1)

The previous chapter asserted that compatibilism is the framework the Bible assumes. God is truly sovereign; his will be done in heaven and on earth; nothing and no one can thwart his intention. Ever. And at the same time, human beings are truly accountable to God for their thoughts, attitudes, and actions; we are responsible for what we do. Always. Since this is not only the framework of the Bible but also the structure of biblical Calvinism, this chapter and the next one will use several examples to prove that compatibilism is central to the Bible's message. We cannot make sense of the Bible's clear teaching that God is sovereign over every detail of his universe and that people are held accountable for the choices they make apart from a concept like compatibilism. These two chapters are not going to solve the challenge of how to reconcile these two truths. Apparently, the biblical authors did not think there was a problem to solve. We need to hold to both truths tenaciously—and simultaneously.

Foundation 1: God's Sovereignty

The reality of our Lord's complete control over everything (in his willing and carrying out that will into completion in history) lies at the heart of the Bible. God controls because he is the King. He is sovereign. This truth is one of the dual tenets of compatibilism. The message of the Bible from the first chapter ("In the beginning God created the heavens and the earth" [Gen. 1:1]) to the last ("the angel showed me the river of the water of life, bright as crystal, flowing from the throne of God and of the Lamb" [Rev. 22:1]) is that God sovereignly reigns over everything. Not one thing—be that the most inconsequential human decision or the smallest drop of rain—occurs apart from his will. The Bible trumpets the truth that our God reigns completely over his creation. Consider these texts.

- See now that I, even I, am he, and there is no god beside me; I kill and I make alive; I wound and I heal; and there is none that can deliver out of my hand. (Deut. 32:39)
- Our God is in heaven; he does whatever pleases Him. (Ps. 115:3)
- The Lord does whatever pleases him, in the heavens and on the earth, in the seas and all their depths. (Ps. 135:6)
- Your eyes saw my unformed substance; in your book were written, every one of them, the days that were formed for me, when as yet there were none of them. (Ps. 139:16)
- I form light and create darkness, I make well-being and create calamity, I am the LORD, who does all these things. (Isa. 45:7)
- Who has spoken and it came to pass, unless the Lord has commanded it? Is it not from the mouth of the Most High that good and bad come? (Lam. 3:37–38)
- At the end of the days I, Nebuchadnezzar, lifted my eyes to heaven, and my reason returned to me, and I blessed the Most High, and praised and honored him who lives forever, for his dominion is an everlasting dominion, and his kingdom endures from generation to generation; all the inhabitants of the earth are accounted as nothing, and he does according to his will among the host of heaven and among the inhabitants of the earth; and none can stay his hand or say to him, "What have you done?" (Dan. 4:34–35)
- Are not two sparrows sold for a penny? And not one of them will fall to the ground apart from your Father. (Matt. 10:29)
- [God] works all things according to the counsel of his will. (Eph. 1:11)
- Oh, the depth of the riches and wisdom and knowledge of God! How unsearchable are his judgments and how inscrutable his ways! . . . For from him and through him and to him are all things. To him be glory forever. Amen. (Rom. 11:33, 36)

Everything that occurs in this world happens according to our God's counsel. He wills everything that comes to pass. Charles Hodge is correct, then, in maintaining

> (1.) That the sovereignty of God is universal. It extends over all his creatures from the highest to the lowest. (2.) That it is absolute. There is no limit to be placed to his authority. He doeth his pleasure in the armies of heaven and among the inhabitants of the earth. (3.) It is immutable. It can neither be ignored nor rejected. It binds all creatures, as inexorably as physical laws bind the material universe. . . . Although this sovereignty is thus universal and absolute, it is the sovereignty of wisdom, holiness, and love. The authority of God is limited by nothing

out of Himself, but it is controlled, in all its manifestations, by his infinite perfections. . . . Infinite wisdom, love, and power, belong to Him, our great God and Saviour, into whose hands all power in heaven and earth has been committed.[1]

Foundation 2: Human Responsibility

At the same time that God is completely sovereign over all things, people are responsible for the choices they make—from the most inconsequential to the greatest. As those uniquely created in the image of God, people are assigned responsibilities. The Lord holds them accountable for their actions, including the ultimate accountability of sending to hell those who fail to repent and trust in Jesus. The Bible is replete with this truth. Consider these examples.

- And the LORD God commanded the man, saying, "You may surely eat of every tree of the garden, but of the tree of the knowledge of good and evil you shall not eat, for in the day that you eat of it you shall surely die." (Gen. 3:16–17)
- Now therefore fear the LORD and serve him in sincerity and in faithfulness. Put away the gods that your fathers served beyond the River and in Egypt, and serve the LORD. (Josh. 24:14)
- Blessed is the man who walks not in the counsel of the wicked, nor stands in the way of sinners, nor sits in the seat of scoffers. (Ps. 1:1)
- Come, everyone who thirsts, come to the waters; and he who has no money, come, buy and eat! Come, buy wine and milk without money and without price. . . . Incline your ear, and come to me; hear, that your soul may live. (Isa. 55:1, 3)
- But I say to you, Love your enemies and pray for those who persecute you. (Matt. 5:44)
- "Repent and be baptized every one of you in the name of Jesus Christ for the forgiveness of your sins, and you will receive the gift of the Holy Spirit." . . . And with many other words he bore witness and continued to exhort them, saying, "Save yourselves from this crooked generation." (Acts 2:38, 40)
- Now this I say and testify in the Lord, that you must no longer walk as the Gentiles do, in the futility of their minds. (Eph. 4:17)
- Wives, submit to your own husbands, as to the Lord. (Eph. 5:22)
- Husbands, love your wives as Christ loved the church and give himself up for her. (Eph. 5:25)
- Children, obey your parents in the Lord, for this is right. (Eph. 6:1)
- Fathers, do not provoke your children to anger, but bring them up in the discipline and instruction of the Lord. (Eph. 6:4)

---

1. Charles Hodge, *Systematic Theology* (1871; Grand Rapids: Eerdmans, 1986), 1:440–41.

The Bible, we see, is filled with commands for people to obey—with both blessings and curses attached. God gives people directives that they must comply with. Real human responsibility is part of the very fabric of Scripture. Created in the image of God, we make decisions that have huge ramifications. John Hammett's observation is correct:

> We are asked to participate responsibly and voluntarily in God's purposes for us. That is what we mean by the term *person*. Other creatures fulfill God's purposes for them involuntarily. They have no choice. . . . the influences we receive from our physical frame, our psychological makeup, our environmental conditioning, and our genetic inheritance do not rise to the level of determinism, for God holds us responsible for how we play the hand we are dealt.[2]

From cover to cover the Bible explicitly teaches and everywhere assumes that human beings are responsible to God.

Two Biblical Examples of Compatibilism

In the previous chapter, we noticed that the only way to understand who was responsible for Jesus's death on the cross is by employing a compatibilistic framework. We need the rubric of compatibilism to understand human decision-making and a Christian's responsibility to grow in Christlikeness. First, compatibilism explains human decision-making. I decided today to make coffee and not tea to wake up in the wee hours of the morning. I really did. (And it was dark roast, my favorite.) Yet, I decided what the Lord sovereignly ordained I would choose. Scripture is clear on this. The king's choices, for instance, are his own. "Every way of a man is right in his own eyes" (Prov. 21:2). He does what he wants to do (just as the kings throughout Israel's history are held accountable for their choices; see 1 Kings–2 Chronicles). Yet, he does exactly what the Lord decided he would do: "The king's heart is a stream of water in the hand of the Lord; he turns it wherever he will" (Prov. 21:1).

The same is true of larger choices, such as Assyria's decision to invade Israel. God is sovereign in this. Indeed, he says that Assyria is his agent in this destruction. He wields the Assyrians as a man might swing a rod; God expresses his anger through their actions: "Ah, Assyria, the rod of my anger; the staff in their hands is my fury!" (Isa. 10:5). The Lord sent the Assyrians and commanded them to destroy his people (10:6). He calls the havoc they worked against Israel his own work (10:12). God is sovereign in all this (even, mysteriously, in the heartache and destruction the Assyrians caused). Yet, at

---

2. John S. Hammett, "Human Nature," in *A Theology for the Church*, rev. ed., eds. Daniel L. Akin, Bruce Riley Ashford, and Kenneth Keathley (Nashville: B&H, 2014), 316–17 (italics original).

the very same time, the Assyrians are held accountable for their actions. They are responsible—responsible for their arrogance and boastfulness in their actions (10:12), responsible for their bloodthirstiness in their military conquests (10:7). To say that this was either God or the Assyrians at work would be to miss the Scripture's point. Both are active in the same event. Both—in unique ways—are responsible for the same event.

Second, compatibilism interprets a Christian's sanctification. Believers are, Paul commands, to "work out your own salvation with fear and trembling" (Phil. 2:12). Here he emphasizes our responsibility. It is real. But that's not all Paul says. We are to do this, "for it is God who works in you, both to will and to work for his good pleasure" (Phil. 2:13). God's work grounds ours. So who works? Both God and us. God works in us, and we are to work, too. To deny either one would be to misunderstand Paul's intention here.[3]

Compatibilism and the Nature of Scripture

As evangelicals we believe in the inerrancy of the Bible. The biblical doctrine of the authority and inerrancy of Scripture, in fact, is grounded in compatibilism. The Bible is both God's word ("breathed out" as an act of divine creation reminiscent of the original act of creation in Genesis 1, as Paul writes in 2 Timothy 3:16) and a work of human composition. We see the latter all over the Bible. Human authors wrote in three different languages (Hebrew, Aramaic, and Greek), and their writing styles, vocabulary, and use of different genres were as different as other human authors' styles. Just as you and I write differently from each other, and indeed just as we might compose different types of literature on varied occasions, so they wrote in distinct manners. Some of them researched their work (e.g., Eccl. 1:13; Luke 1:1–4). Some were aware of other works that gave a fuller description of the material they were describing (how many times does the author of 2 Kings write something like "the rest of the account of so and so is written in the Chronicles of the kings of Judah and Israel"?). Yet, what they wrote were the very words of God, the "breathed out" creation of the Lord.

This is why the Bible has authority and claims that authority for itself. No one gives it authority; it is authoritative. And it is also why B. B. Warfield was correct in his classic essay to note that what Scripture says, God says; what God says, Scripture says. The two are correlative.[4] The true, trustworthy, and authoritative voice of God is heard in the Bible. And yet this Bible was written by men who thought, researched, and used their own unique styles while

---

3. See Question 38.
4. Benjamin B. Warfield, "'It Says:' 'Scripture Says:' 'God Says:'," in *The Inspiration and Authority of the Bible*, ed. Samuel G. Craig (Phillipsburg, NJ: P&R, 1948), 299–348. Also see J. I. Packer, *"Fundamentalism" and the Word of God: Some Evangelical Principles* (Grand Rapids: Eerdmans, 1958), 85–91.

composing it. Peter's contention that "men spoke from God as they were carried along by the Holy Spirit" (2 Peter 1:21) suggests something akin to compatibilism. Men spoke. And they said what the Holy Spirit wanted them to say. Both truths—though we might not understand exactly how both God and the human authors were active in the same event—are just that. They are true. Compatibilism allows us to maintain the dual authorship of the Bible, human and divine.[5]

Summary

The entire structure of Scripture assumes compatibilism because (1) God is really sovereign and accomplishes his will and (2) human beings are really responsible for our actions. Both truths are explicitly taught and everywhere assumed in the Bible. Compatibilism allows us to make sense of the way human decisions are made, who is the responsible agent in our sanctification, and the nature of Scripture.

REFLECTION QUESTIONS

1. Has reading this chapter helped you to understand compatibilism better? How?

2. What other texts in Scripture can you think of that teach that God is utterly sovereign?

3. Can you imagine God being truly sovereign while also limiting his sovereignty so that it did not interfere with human "free will"? Would God still be truly sovereign if he acted in this manner?

4. What other biblical texts teach or assume real human responsibility?

5. How do you think believing in compatibilism should impact your evangelism? Your prayer life? Your worship of God?

---

5. See Stephen J. Wellum, "The Inerrancy of Scripture," in *Beyond the Bounds: Open Theism and the Undermining of Biblical Christianity*, ed. John Piper, Justin Taylor, and Paul Kjoss Helseth (Wheaton, IL: Crossway, 2003), 237–74.

Does the Bible Teach Compatibilism? (Part 2)

Compatibilism—the truth that God is completely sovereign and at the same time humans are truly responsible—is taught and assumed throughout Scripture. This framework is the only way in which we can hold to both of these truths at the same time. We will see this, first, through a sampling of biblical texts that assume compatibilism; second, by noting several texts having to do with salvation that are compatibilistic; and, third, by observing how the Gospel of John assumes compatibilism.

Compatibilism Assumed in Scripture

Without using the term "compatibilism," the Bible does not flinch from asserting in the same context that God is utterly sovereign and people are still responsible. I have no intention of recounting every instance of this in Scripture, for this notion is assumed so often in the Bible. The following examples of different instances of compatibilism will show, though, that compatibilism is the framework of Scripture.[1]

In the first place, decisions—from the smallest to the greatest—occur within a compatibilistic framework. Solomon tells us, "Many are the plans in the mind of a man, but it is the purpose of the LORD that will stand" (Prov. 19:21; see 16:33). The person truly thinks and determines a course of action. What he decides is what the Lord purposed. Both are true.

Even more momentous decisions only make sense when we have the category of compatibilism. Notice these two instances dealing with Joseph's brothers' decision to sell their younger brother into slavery:

---

1. These instances of compatibilism are ones that I have noticed in my own Bible reading. For more examples, see John M. Frame, *Systematic Theology: An Introduction to Christian Belief* (Phillipsburg, NJ: P&R, 2013), 155–68.

> And now do not be distressed or angry with yourselves because you sold me here, for God sent me before you to preserve life. . . . So it was not you who sent me here, but God. (Gen 45:5, 8)

> As for you, you meant evil against me, but God meant it for good, to bring it about that many people should be kept alive, as they are today. (Gen. 50:20)

Who is responsible for this act, the brothers or the Lord? Both! Timothy George, then, is correct in his comments on Genesis 50:20:

> Note carefully: not only did God permit what occurred, but he actually *intended* it. He "meant" it, as the KJV and several other versions have it. What Joseph's brothers did, of course, was wicked in every respect. They were not absolved of responsibility for their treachery. But God in his sovereignty was also at work even in that horrible circumstance to accomplish something marvelous.[2]

Still other decisions, such as the one of Eli's sons, are also compatibilistic. "But they would not listen to the voice of their father, for it was the will of the LORD to put them to death" (1 Sam. 2:25). We can ask, Who is responsible for these two men's deaths? In a real sense, the sons were, for they were wicked and foolish. And in a real sense, God was, for he willed to kill them. Both are true, and we cannot negate either one.[3] "You have caused my beloved and my friend to shun me," the psalmist laments (Ps. 88:18). The friend really turned away; at the same time, his turning was caused by God. Both are true.

Second, a person's ability to understand should also be interpreted compatibilistically. Luke tells us of the disciples, "But they did not understand this saying, and it was concealed from them, so that they might not perceive it. And they were afraid to ask him about this saying" (Luke 9:45). The disciples thought and considered, but they did not grasp Jesus's words. They were responsible for their ignorance. But they also did not grasp it because the Lord had decided to conceal the meaning from them. Both are true.

Third, even human emotions should be understood compatibilistically. People feel joy. God makes them joyful. "And they kept the Feast of Unleavened Bread seven days with joy, for the LORD had made them joyful and had turned the heart of the king of Assyria to them, so that he aided them in the work

---

2. Timothy George, *Amazing Grace: God's Pursuit, Our Response*, 2nd ed. (Wheaton, IL: Crossway, 2011), 51 (italics original).
3. For similar instances, see 2 Samuel 17:14; 2 Chronicles 10:15 and 25:20.

of the house of God, the God of Israel" (Ezra 6:22). We never feel less than human when we experience deep emotions like joy. But these are not removed from the Lord's sovereign control. We *are* joyful. God *makes us* joyful. Both are true.[4] Similarly, Paul writes, "May the Lord direct your hearts to the love of God and to the steadfastness of Christ" (2 Thess. 3:5). The Thessalonian believers were responsible to love God with all their hearts (see Matt. 22:37). And God would work in their hearts so that they would love him. Both realities are true.[5]

Fourth, the growth of the church in evangelism and discipleship should be understood through the framework of compatibilism. Paul told the Corinthians, "I planted, Apollos watered, but God gave the growth. . . . According to the grace of God given to me, like a skilled master builder I laid a foundation, and someone else is building upon it. Let each one take care how he builds upon it" (1 Cor. 3:6, 10). Paul was responsible as the apostle to the Gentiles to take the gospel to the unreached, and then Apollos came and taught and built on that foundation. Both were responsible for using their gifts to do this. But growth in grace occurred when the Lord gave it. Both the human actions and God's action were real and necessary.

Compatibilism and Salvation

Even more significant than the plethora of texts noted above, though, are texts which communicate compatibilism in the most important of all choices. We see in the following texts that—in the decision to turn to the Lord for forgiveness and repentance from a life of sin—both God is sovereign and people are responsible for their decisions. The following three examples from the Old Testament assume compatibilism.

In the first instance, we notice the hardening of Pharaoh's heart. God hardens it so that the king does not submit to the Lord. "I will harden Pharaoh's heart" (Exod. 7:3). And at the very same time, the monarch stubbornly refuses to listen to and obey God: "Still Pharaoh's heart was hardened, and he would not listen to them, as the LORD had said" (Exod. 7:13; see 7:22–23; 8:15). We must not say only one agent was involved in the hardening. Both—Pharaoh and God—were. At the same time.

A second occurrence happens in God's interaction with Israel. Moses highlights God's sovereignty in not giving the people the heart, that is, the desire and inclination, to obey the Lord. "But to this day the LORD has not given you a heart to understand or eyes to see or ears to hear" (Deut. 29:4). And in the same context, Moses warns the people of their responsibility to obey God so they won't be punished:

---

4. Also see Ezekiel 3:7, 18.
5. Also see Jude 1, 20–21, 24–25.

> Beware lest there be among you a man or woman or clan
> or tribe whose heart is turning away today from the LORD
> our God to go and serve the gods of those nations. . . . The
> LORD will not be willing to forgive him, but rather the anger
> of the LORD and his jealousy will smoke against that man,
> and the curses written in this book will settle upon him,
> and the LORD will blot out his name from under heaven.
> (Deut. 29:18, 20)

The Lord sovereignly chooses not to act, and the people are held accountable for not following him.

A third episode followed soon after and was quite similar. The Lord in his sovereignty promises that he would work mightily to change his people: "And the LORD your God will circumcise your heart and the heart of your off-spring," and at the very same moment they would do something "so that you will love the LORD your God with all your heart and with all your soul, that you may live" (Deut. 30:6, see vv. 19–20).

Do not move on too quickly. Notice what is being said. Pharaoh and the Israelites were truly responsible for their decisions: "do not harden your heart," do not let your heart turn away from God, "choose life." And in the very same instance, God was absolutely sovereign: "I will harden Pharaoh's heart," the Lord did not give a heart to understand, "God will circumcise your heart." Both concepts are true. In a manner we do not grasp, they are compatible.

Similarly, Acts records several instances from Paul's ministry that only make sense if we assume the reality of compatibilism:

> And when the Gentiles heard this, they began rejoicing
> and glorifying the word of the Lord, and as many as were ap-
> pointed to eternal life believed. (Acts 13:48)

> One who heard us was a woman named Lydia, from the city
> of Thyatira, a seller of purple goods, who was a worshiper of
> God. The Lord opened her heart to pay attention to what was
> said by Paul. (Acts 16:14)

> When he arrived, he greatly helped those who through grace
> had believed. (Acts 18:27)

These remarkable instances of compatibilism have the same elements. God sovereignly acted to save, and in the same moment the people responsibly acted. The Lord appointed some to life; they believed. God opened Lydia's heart; she paid attention. God graciously intervened in his people's lives; they believed. We must hold both truths to be true.

We could multiply the examples by looking at more biblical texts.[6] What are we left to conclude about the relationship of divine sovereignty and human responsibility in salvation? Simply this: God is completely and definitively sovereign in regards to who experiences salvation, and at the same time, people are truly responsible for their actions.

Compatibilism in John

The Gospel of John is remarkable for its number of compatibilistic passages regarding the sovereignty of God and the responsibility of people in salvation. We shall limit our attention to a few of them.[7]

John presses on his readers their responsibility to come to Jesus for forgiveness. "But to all who did receive him, who believed in his name, he gave the right to become children of God" (John 1:12). They must receive Jesus and trust in him; no one else does it for them. Yet, the next verse reports that those who received and believed Jesus were those "who were born, not of blood nor of the will of the flesh nor of the will of man, but of God" (John 1:13). They act. God acts. This is compatibilism.

Later Jesus says, "The Son gives life to whom he will" (John 5:21), showing that his choosing—rather than the choice of the individual person—is primary in salvation. At the same time, he teaches that those who refuse him are guilty: "you refuse to come to me that you may have life. . . . I have come in my Father's name, and you do not receive me. If another comes in his own name, you will receive him" (John 5:40, 43). They could have, and should have, come to Jesus, but they did not. Yet only those Jesus willed to come to him came.

John 6 contains several compatibilistic threads. People are responsible to trust in Christ for salvation. This is the "work" God requires of men (John 6:29). Similarly, "I am the bread of life; whoever comes to me shall not hunger, and whoever believes in me shall never thirst" (John 6:35). But God must sovereignly act: "All that the Father gives me will come to me, and whoever comes I will never cast out" (John 6:37). They must come. They come because the Father has given them to the Son (John 6:38–39). The will of the Father is "that everyone who looks on the Son and believes in him should have eternal life" (John 6:40). So God's will, on the one hand, is a universal condition that anyone who believes in Jesus will be saved. This highlights human responsibility. On the other hand, God's will is also that those the Father gives to the Son will come to the Son. God's will is determinative. Both truths are compactly highlighted here.

---

6. See, among others, Matthew 11:25–30; Romans 9:11–24; 10:8–17; 2 Thessalonians 2:13–15.
7. Also see Robert W. Yarbrough, "Divine Election in the Gospel of John," in *Still Sovereign: Contemporary Perspectives on Election, Foreknowledge, and Grace*, eds. Thomas R. Schreiner and Bruce A. Ware (Grand Rapids: Baker, 2000), 47–62.

Compatibilism is reiterated later. Everyone is responsible to come to Jesus for forgiveness: "whoever believes has eternal life" (John 6:47). "I am the living bread that came down from heaven. If anyone eats of this bread, he will live forever" (John 6:51; see 6:53–57). However, only those God sovereignly chooses will come to Jesus for forgiveness. "No one can come to me unless the Father who sent me draws him" (John 6:44). "Everyone who has heard and learned from the Father comes to me" (John 6:45). John assumes compatibilism.

Summary

Compatibilism is the proper way to interpret God's interaction with people from the least to the most significant issues in a person's life. Scripture does not seek to explain how God can be completely sovereign and at the same time people can be fully responsible to the Lord in the same event. But the many texts we have examined demonstrate that this is what the Bible teaches. As the rest of this book is going to show, this is useful to remember when discussing Calvinism. God's sovereignty never functions to alleviate human beings of responsibility. Nor does our responsibility ever work so as to make God less than fully sovereign. Both are true. This is one of the keys to understanding biblical Calvinism.

REFLECTION QUESTIONS

1. How did this chapter help you to understand compatibilism better?

2. Can you think of other examples of compatibilism in Scripture?

3. What practical benefits follow if you believe in compatibilism regarding human salvation? Is God's real sovereignty protected? Is humanity's true responsibility also guarded?

4. Do texts like John 3:16 ("For God so loved the world, that he gave his only Son, that whoever believes in him should not perish but have eternal life") establish or disprove compatibilism? Why?

5. Why do you think Arminians oppose using compatibilism as a framework for interpreting the Bible?

Historical Questions

Who Was John Calvin and What Did He Believe?

John Calvin was a sixteenth-century French Protestant Reformer who drew on his study of Scripture and the Augustinian tradition within church history to formulate his doctrine in his *Institutes of the Christian Religion*. Calvin said little that was new, but he presented his ideas cogently and winsomely and thus influenced the tradition that took his name, Calvinism. After looking at Calvin's life, we will note three of his doctrines that are central to the ongoing discussion between Calvinists and Arminians.

Calvin's Life

Jean Cauvin was born July 10, 1509, in Noyon, France. He began studying in Paris to train for an ecclesiastical position but then moved to Orléans to study law. There he was influenced towards Protestantism by Melchior Wolmar. Along the way he Latinized his name to Johannes Calvinus, from which we derive John Calvin.

Fleeing France due to persecution for his Protestantism, Calvin went to Basel where the first edition of his *Institutes of the Christian Religion* was published in 1536. Later, Guillaume Farel convinced Calvin to help him reform the church in Geneva, a Swiss city across the southeastern border of France. Calvin helped initially from 1536 to 1538. From 1538–1541 Calvin lived in Strasbourg where he was mentored by Martin Bucer, began writing biblical commentaries, started translating the Psalms for corporate singing, and got married. He returned to Geneva in 1541 and remained there the rest of his life. Calvin developed his ecclesiology during this time, composed a catechism, led the pastors of the city in their pastoral duties, labored to maintain the ethical character of the city and its citizens, preached and lectured multiple times a week, engaged in controversies, and wrote tirelessly.

Even though Calvin was plagued by physical ailments, in addition to his writing, in 1559 he founded the Geneva Academy, hiring Theodore Beza (1519–1605) to lead it.[1] Calvin also oversaw church-planting efforts in France, an enterprise that entailed a good bit of danger for the young men who went out from Geneva. He lived to see the initial wars of religion in France between the Protestant Huguenots and Catholic armies in 1562, but died soon after, aged 55, on May 27, 1564. Per his request, this giant of the Protestant faith was buried in an unmarked grave.[2]

Calvin's Thought

Calvin was a prolific and gifted writer.[3] In addition to his sermons, he wrote commentaries on most of the books in the Bible, numerous polemical treatises, essays on church order, hundreds of letters, and his magnum opus, the *Institutes of the Christian Religion* ("Institutes" means "Instruction"), a handbook introducing the Christian faith that grew from its original version of 1536 over several revisions to its longer, more-detailed fifth and final 1559 edition.[4] Here we will note some of the it's significant teachings.

Providence

Calvin teaches that we won't believe God to be the supreme Creator until we acknowledge his providence (1.16.1).[5] Providence is the truth that "all events are governed by God's secret plan" (1.16.2). Referencing texts like Psalm 115:3, Calvin claims that providence is nothing less than God's active omnipotence, "not the empty, idle, and almost unconscious sort" that some imagine "but a watchful, effective, active sort, engaged in ceaseless activity." In other words, "nothing happens except what is knowingly and willingly decreed by" the Lord (1.16.3). God, by definition, is the one "who in accordance

1. Beza is sometimes wrongly blamed for deviating from Calvin's thought and initiating a novel theology called "Calvinism." See Shawn D. Wright, *Theodore Beza: The Man and the Myth* (Fearn, UK: Christian Focus, 2015).
2. Three good sources for the details of Calvin's life, from most simple to most complex, are Herman J. Selderhuis, *John Calvin: A Pilgrim's Life* (Downers Grove, IL: InterVarsity Press, 2009); T. H. L. Parker, *John Calvin: A Biography* (Louisville: Westminster, 1975); and Bruce Gordon, *Calvin* (New Haven, CT: Yale University Press, 2009). For Calvin's pastoral ministry in Geneva, see Scott M. Manetsch, *Calvin's Company of Pastors: Pastoral Care and the Emerging Reformed Church, 1536–1609* (Oxford: Oxford University Press, 2013).
3. Introductions to Calvin's thought include Timothy George, *Theology of the Reformers*, rev. ed. (Nashville: B&H, 2013), 171–264, and David W. Hall and Peter A. Lillback, eds., *A Theological Guide to Calvin's Institutes: Essays and Analysis* (Phillipsburg, NJ: P&R, 2008).
4. Wulfert de Greef, *The Writings of John Calvin: An Introductory Guide*, trans. Lyle D. Bierma (Grand Rapids: Baker, 1993).
5. The standard English translation, and the one we will use, is John Calvin, *Institutes of the Christian Religion*, Library of Christian Classics, 2 volumes, ed. John T. McNeill, trans. Ford Lewis Battles (Philadelphia: Westminster, 1960). We will reference it the standard way: "book.chapter.section." So, book 1, chapter 1, section 1 is "1.1.1."

with his wisdom has from the farthest limit of eternity decreed what he was going to do, and now by his might carries out what he has decreed" (1.16.8). So providence absolutely accomplishes God's will and is carried out by a personal God, not blind forces.

God uses instruments—sometimes good and other times evil—to accomplish his will, and these agents are accountable for the choices they make. But God commits no evil. Human deeds are real choices, even though in a mysterious way they are enveloped by the will of God (1.17.3–6, 9; 1.18.4). Nothing occurs apart from God's will. Christians should be comforted that difficulties are determined by our good, wise, and loving Father. Calvin argues that a Christian's solace "is to know that his Heavenly Father so holds all things in his power, so rules by his authority and will, so governs by his wisdom, that nothing can befall except he determine it." Indeed, "ignorance of providence is the ultimate of all miseries; the highest blessedness lies in the knowledge of it" (1.17.11).

Humanity in Sin

Central to knowing ourselves (1.1.1) and the reality that necessitates a divine work of salvation, is the fact of human sin. When Adam sinned, we all fell into a state of condemnation and guilt. "Adam, by sinning, not only took upon himself misfortune and ruin but also plunged our nature into like destruction. This was not due to the guilt of himself alone, which would not pertain to us at all, but was because he infected all his posterity with that corruption into which he had fallen" (2.1.6). In other words, "the beginning of corruption in Adam was such that it was conveyed in a perpetual stream from the ancestors into their descendants" (2.1.7). So, "Adam's sin is our sin as well."[6]

The result of Adam's sin, then, is that we're all infected at birth with original sin, a sin from which we cannot free ourselves by our own efforts. Original sin is "a hereditary depravity and corruption of our nature, diffused into all parts of the soul, which first makes us liable to God's wrath, then also brings forth in us those works which Scripture calls 'works of the flesh.' And that is properly what Paul often calls sin" (2.1.8). Due to original sin we all inevitably actually sin.

Sin infects every part of us—our reason, affections, bodies, will, everything. Calvin avers that "the whole man is overwhelmed—as by a deluge—from head to foot, so that no part is immune from sin and all that proceeds from him is to be imputed to sin" (2.1.9). Lest anyone try to blame God for his sinful condition, we must remember that we have "no reason to complain except against ourselves" (2.1.10). We do what we want, and for that reason we deserve condemnation.

---

6. George, *Theology of the Reformers*, 222.

Non-Christians are slaves to sin in Adam. "Man has now been deprived of freedom of choice and bound over to miserable servitude," Calvin estimates (2.2). Unbelievers are unable to do anything to save themselves. It is "indisputable that free will is not sufficient to enable man to do good works," Calvin claims, "unless he be helped by grace, indeed by special grace, which only the elect receive through regeneration" (2.2.6).[7]

Predestination

God's predestination is essential because those predestined are vile, guilty, helpless sinners who can do nothing to merit or gain their own salvation.[8] Divine predestination represents the only way anyone can be saved. It is that "by which God adopts some to hope of life, and sentences others to eternal death." More fully, Calvin maintains,

> We call predestination God's eternal decree, by which he compacted with himself what he willed to become of each man. For all are not created in equal condition; rather, eternal life is foreordained for some, eternal damnation for others. Therefore, as any man has been created to one or the other of these ends, we speak of him as predestined to life or to death. (3.21.5)

Six contours of Calvin's doctrine of predestination are significant. First, it is sovereign, planned by the King of the universe. It is absolute "in the sense that it is not conditioned upon any finite contingencies, but rests solely on God's immutable will."[9] Second, it is useful. Predestination is "very sweet fruit" to Christians for "we shall never be clearly persuaded, as we ought to be, that our salvation flows from the wellspring of God's free mercy until we come to know his eternal election, which illumines God's grace by this contrast: that he does not indiscriminately adopt all into the hope of salvation but gives to some what he denies to others" (3.21.1). To find assurance of salvation, look to Christ who is "the mirror wherein we must, and without self-deception may, contemplate our own election" (3.23.5). If you want to know if you're elect, trust in Jesus.

Third, predestination is "double" because it includes reprobation. Timothy George observes that for Calvin, "God to the praise of His mercy has ordained some individuals to eternal life, and to the praise of His justice has ordained

---

7. Calvin noted that "Few have defined what free will is, although it repeatedly occurs in the writings of all" (2.2.4).

8. A helpful treatment of Calvin's doctrine of predestination is Fred H. Klooster, *Calvin's Doctrine of Predestination*, 2nd ed. (Grand Rapids: Baker, 1977).

9. George, *Theology of the Reformers*, 241.

others to eternal damnation."[10] We see this in Calvin's definition noted above: "All are not created in equal condition; rather, eternal life is foreordained for some, eternal damnation for others" (3.21.5). Rather than charging God with being unjust, we must remember that God owes no one grace since all are fallen and guilty. Rather than complain against God, people should realize that in themselves they only deserve hell:

> Let the sons of Adam come forward; let them quarrel and argue with their Creator that they were by his eternal providence bound over before their begetting to everlasting calamity. What clamor can they raise against this defense when God, on the contrary, will call them to account before him? If all are drawn from a corrupt mass, no wonder they are subject to condemnation! (3.23.3)

This may be hard to accept, Calvin notes, but in Romans 9:20–21, Paul "did not look for loopholes of escape as if he were embarrassed in his argument but showed that the reason of divine righteousness is higher than man's standard can measure, or than man's slender wit can comprehend" (3.23.4).

Fourth, though, Calvin also argues that persons are all responsible to come to Christ for forgiveness. We have earlier called this holding-sovereignty-together-with-responsibility belief, "compatibilism."[11] Speaking of those reprobated, that is, predestined to death, Calvin writes, "For even though by God's eternal providence man has been created to undergo that calamity to which he is subject, it still takes its occasion from man himself, not from God, since the only reason for his ruin is that he has degenerated from God's pure creation into vicious and impure perversity" (3.23.9). The reprobate have only themselves to blame for their damnation.

Fifth, Christians are responsible to tell unbelievers the gospel so they may repent and believe. God, indeed, invites all to salvation, even though he chooses only some to be his own. Paul serves as the model here, for he both believed in free election and zealously preached the gospel (3.22.10). In the call of the gospel, "God invites all equally to himself through the outward preaching of the word" (3.24.8). For this reason, preachers are free and bold to preach God's mercy, for what do they "do but continually preach God's free call?" (3.24.1).

Sixth, believers should draw comfort from the fact that due to God's sovereign predestining work on their behalf, they will persevere in the faith. Christians should focus their attention on Christ, since the Bible speaks of his ongoing future care for his children. "All whom [Christ] receives, the Father is said to have entrusted and committed to him to keep unto eternal life" (3.24.6).

---

10. Ibid., 242.
11. See Questions 10–12.

Summary

Calvin said little that had not been taught before him. Yet, his consistent Augustinianism combined with his intense biblicism flowed into an expression of theology that gripped the minds and hearts of his followers. People typically know him for his unflinching espousal of God's absolute sovereignty in all of life and in salvation. We have also seen, though, that Calvin taught true human responsibility—the responsibility of believers and unbelievers alike.

REFLECTION QUESTIONS

1. Before reading this, what were your impressions of John Calvin?

2. After reading this, how has your evaluation of Calvin changed?

3. Do you think Calvin was correct in teaching God's absolute providence over all things and events?

4. How much do you think people's sin affects their willingness and ability to come to Christ? Do you think Calvin was correct in his evaluation of the effects of human sin on our ability to come to Christ?

5. Do you agree with Calvin's teaching on predestination?

QUESTION 14

Were There "Calvinists" before Calvin?

John Calvin was not the first "Calvinist." Beginning with Augustine (354–430), the church wrestled with how God's sovereignty interacted with human responsibility in the arena of salvation. These discussions persisted throughout the medieval era and continued in the Protestant Reformation of the sixteenth century. Calvin would have been fine being called an "Augustinian" regarding the doctrine of salvation. Many Christians who lived before Calvin agreed with him in the main.

Augustine's "Calvinism"

The early church did not discuss the doctrine of predestination in much detail. These Christians wanted to distance themselves from any appearance of fatalism, so they typically eschewed predestination. Jaroslav Pelikan notes that both Roman Stoicism and a heretical movement called Gnosticism were fatalistic, and the church desired to avoid any appearance of condoning these errors. So "the defenders of the faith were obliged to define man's responsibility for his condition [in sin] much more carefully than they did the inevitability of the condition itself."[1] In other words, they stressed human free will to the exclusion of God's sovereignty in salvation.[2]

Augustine sharply disagreed with this. In a sense, the heretic Pelagius forced him to do it. Pelagius taught that people are born without the taint of sin and that, if they desire, they can serve God perfectly. This was the theology of salvation by works, and it was eventually condemned as heretical. In the process of refuting Pelagius, Augustine looked closely at the epistles of Paul.

---

1. Jaroslav Pelikan, *The Christian Tradition: A History of the Development of Doctrine (The Emergence of the Catholic Tradition [100–600])* (Chicago: University of Chicago Press, 1971), 1:280.
2. Pelikan refers specifically to Justin Martyr, Origen, Tertullian, and Irenaeus who touted humanity's free will (*The Christian Tradition* 1:282–83). See also Gregg Allison, *Historical Theology: An Introduction to Christian Doctrine* (Grand Rapids: Zondervan, 2011), 454–55.

The theology that came out of this controversy—a developed view of original sin along with its accompanying doctrine of divine predestination—put an end to Pelagianism in the Catholic church. On the nature of salvation, then, we can say that Augustine was a "Calvinist."[3]

Augustine believed in God's absolute sovereignty. Indeed, he did not shy away from espousing both eternal election and eternal reprobation:

> [God] has appointed them [people condemned in Adam] to be regenerated . . . whom he predestined to eternal life, as the most merciful giver of grace. To those whom he has predestined to eternal death, however, he is also the most righteous awarder of punishment, not only on account of the sins which they add in the indulgence of their own will, but also because of their original sin, even if, as in the case of infants, they add nothing to it.[4]

Commenting on Augustine's words, Gregg Allison explains, "So it all depends on God's sovereign will to choose some and pass over others."[5] To be fair, Augustine did not believe he could understand the doctrine of predestination perfectly, as Allison affirms: "To the charge that selective election seems totally unfair, Augustine appealed to the mystery of God's plan (Rom. 11:33; Ps. 25:10) and affirmed with Scripture that there is no unrighteousness with God (Rom. 9:14). . . . Augustine ultimately admitted that predestination is largely mysterious and a cause for wonderment."[6]

Consider Augustine's defense of sovereign predestination:

> What were we but sinful and lost? We did not lead Him to choose us by believing in Him; for if Christ chose people who already believed, then we chose Him before He chose us. . . . Here is the faulty reasoning of those who defend the foreknowledge of God in opposition to His grace. For they say that God chose us before the creation of the world, not in order to make us good, but because He foreknew we would be good. . . . Grace is no longer grace, if human goodness comes first. . . .

---

3. Augustine was only partially correct on his doctrine of justification, but that is not at the heart of what I am defining as "Calvinism."
4. Augustine, *On the Soul and Its Origin*, 16, in *Nicene- and Post-Nicene Fathers*, eds. Alexander Roberts, James Donaldson, Philip Schaff, and Henry Wace, 1st ser., 14 vols. (Peabody, MA: Hendrickson, 1994); quoted in Allison, *Historical Theology*, 456.
5. Allison, *Historical Theology*, 456–57.
6. Ibid., 457.

Listen, you ungrateful person, listen! "You did not choose Me, but I chose you" [John 15:16]. . . . We were evil, and we were chosen that we might become good by the grace of Him Who chose us. For salvation is not by grace if our goodness came first; but it is by grace—and therefore God's grace did not *find* us good but *makes* us good.[7]

Calvinism in the Middle Ages

In Augustine's later years, and in the years following his death in 430, the opponent of Augustianism became "semi-Pelagianism," a position which represented a synthesis of Augustine's view and that of the Pelagians. Even though two councils—Carthage (418) and Orange (529)—approved of Augustine's views, Alister McGrath comments that "Augustine's views on predestination were diluted somewhat, even though the remainder of his system was enthusiastically endorsed."[8]

Nevertheless, Augustine's powerful and trenchant apology for sovereign predestination cast a shadow for centuries to come. Bengt Häggland remarks that "Augustine's doctrine of grace and predestination prompted widespread controversy even before he died, and it continued to occupy the center of theological discussion throughout the Middle Ages."[9] Various factors—including the Council of Orange's watered-down Augustinianism and Pope Gregory I's (r. 590–604) adjustment of Augustine's thought and transportation of it into the medieval period—meant that most theologians did not adhere to Augustine's views.[10] Nonetheless, some were drawn to Augustine's theology.

A Saxon monk, Gottschalk of Orbais (c. 804–c. 869), taught double predestination and suffered imprisonment and harsh treatment for his views.[11] More significant thinkers were also Augustinian in many of their doctrines. Both Anselm of Canterbury (1033–1109) and Thomas Aquinas (1225–1274) also taught God's predestination of individuals to salvation.[12] Another significant medieval theologian, Bernard of Clairvaux (1090–1153), was an ardent Augustinian soteriologically. Anthony Lane summarizes Bernard's teaching

---

7. Augustine, *Sermons on John*, 86:2–3; quoted in N. R. Needham, *The Triumph of Grace: Augustine's Writings on Salvation* (London: Grace, 2000), 218–19 (italics original).
8. Alister E. McGrath, *Reformation Thought: An Introduction*, 2nd ed. (Oxford and Cambridge, MA: Blackwell, 1993), 75.
9. Bengt Häggland, *History of Theology*, 3rd ed., trans. Gene J. Lund (St. Louis: Concordia, 1968), 143.
10. For a discussion of semi-Pelagianism up to the Council of Orange, see Allison, *Historical Theology*, 457–59. On Gregory's adjustments of Augustine's thought, see Justo L. González, *A History of Christian Thought, Vol. 2: From Augustine to the Eve of the Reformation* (Nashville: Abingdon, 1970), 69–72.
11. John Hannah, *Our Legacy: The History of Christian Doctrine* (Colorado Springs: Navpress, 2001), 217.
12. Allison, *Historical Theology*, 459–61.

in *Grace and Free Will*, in which "he follows a strongly Augustinian line," in this way:

> He maintains that our good works are at the same time entirely the work of God's grace (leaving no room for boasting) and entirely the work of our own free will in that it is *we* who perform them (thus making them worthy of reward). The human will is always free in the sense that we will voluntarily and spontaneously. But left to themselves, fallen human beings will only to sin. We are free in the sense that we sin willingly, without anyone forcing us to sin—but not in the sense that we can do otherwise. Grace so moves the will that it freely and willingly chooses the good. Grace changes the will from evil to good—not by destroying its freedom but by transferring its allegiance.[13]

Significantly, a late medieval stream of thought that goes by the name *schola Augustiniana moderna* ("the modern Augustinian school") also arose. This revival of Augustine's thought developed largely in reaction to a Pelagian-like theology termed the *via moderna* ("modern way") or "nominalism." Thomas Bradwardine (1290–1349) and Gregory of Rimini (1300–1358), two fervent Augustinians, sought to transmit Augustine's soteriology to their own day.[14] Many of Augustine's themes—"an emphasis on the need for grace, on the fallenness and sinfulness of humanity, on the divine initiative in justification and on divine predestination"—were revived and transmitted by thinkers in this tradition. Thus, unlike those who argue that there were few historical precursors to Calvinism's soteriology, Alister McGrath remarks that "a school of thought which was strongly Augustinian in cast was in existence in the late Middle Ages on the eve of the Reformation."[15]

---

13. Tony Lane, *A Concise History of Christian Thought*, rev. ed. (Grand Rapids: Baker, 2006), 111.

14. Bradwardine's 1344 treatise, *The Cause of God Against the Pelagians*, is in Heiko A. Oberman, ed., *Forerunners of the Reformation: The Shape of Late Medieval Thought Illustrated by Key Documents*, trans. Paul L. Nyhus (New York: Holt, Rinehart and Winston, 1966), 151–64.

15. McGrath, *Reformation Thought*, 78–79. Also see Alister McGrath, *The Intellectual Origins of the European Reformation* (1987; Grand Rapids: Baker, 1994), 86–93. This historical data is opposed to Roger Olson's unfounded contention that "Calvinism stands in tension with the ancient faith of the Christian church and much of the heritage of evangelical faith. Some of its crucial tenets cannot be found before the church father Augustine in the fifth century, and others cannot be found before a heretic named Gottschalk (d. circa 867) or from him until Calvin's successor, Theodore Beza" (Roger E. Olson, *Against Calvinism* [Grand Rapids: Zondervan, 2011], 24).

Calvin's Historical Apology

During his lifetime John Calvin was accused by Catholic apologists of inventing new doctrines never held by the church. Jacob Sadoleto, a Catholic bishop who was later made a cardinal, for example, accused Calvin of novelty. He warned the Genevan church that they were in danger of losing their salvation because they were adhering to a novel teaching by following Protestantism.

Calvin's "Reply to Sadoleto" is one of the Protestant Reformation's masterpieces. In part, Calvin pointed out to Sadoleto that "you teach that all which has been approved for fifteen hundred years or more, by the uniform consent of the faithful, is, by our headstrong rashness, torn up and destroyed. . . . [but] our agreement with antiquity is far closer than yours." Calvin defended the Protestants, claiming "all we have attempted has been to renew that ancient form of the Church, which, at first sullied and distorted by illiterate men of indifferent character, was afterwards . . . almost destroyed by the Roman Pontiff and his faction." He appealed to "Chrysostom and Basil, among the Greeks, and [to] Cyprian, Ambrose, and Augustine, among the Latins" as holding to the same doctrine he taught.[16] Church history was on Calvin's side, not the Catholics'.

Defending his doctrine of predestination in the *Institutes of the Christian Religion*, Calvin especially appealed to Augustine.[17] Calvin argues that "if I wanted to weave a whole volume from Augustine, I could readily show my readers that I need no other language than his. But I do not want to burden them with wordiness." Instead, Calvin simply concurs with Augustine's reflection on Romans 9: "God's grace does not find but makes those fit to be chosen."[18]

Calvin taught that reprobation does not make God a tyrant. "With Augustine I say," Calvin writes, "the Lord has created those whom he unquestionably foreknew would go to destruction. This has happened because he has so willed it. But why he so willed, it is not for our reason to inquire, for we cannot comprehend it."[19] God had the right to ordain that humanity would fall into sin; he remained holy in doing it. Defending this view, Calvin references Augustine, who taught "the God and Lord of all things, who created all things exceedingly good, and foreknew that evil things would rise out of good . . . so ordained the life of angels and men that in it he might first of all show what their free will could do, and then what the blessing of his grace and the verdict of his justice could do."[20] God did not merely "permit" sin in the sense that he was not

---

16. John Calvin, "Reply to Sadoleto," in *A Reformation Debate: John Calvin and Jacopo Sadoleto*, ed. John C. Olin (1966; Grand Rapids: Baker, 1976), 62.
17. Instances of Calvin's references to Augustine in support of his doctrine of predestination include the following: John Calvin, *Institutes of the Christian Religion*, ed. John T. McNeill, trans. Ford Lewis Battles (Philadelphia: Westminster, 1960), 3.22.1, 8; 3.23.5, 7, 13, 14; 3.24.1, 13.
18. Calvin, *Institutes* 3.22.8, quoting Augustine, *Letters* 186.5.15.
19. Calvin, *Institutes* 3.23.5, referring to Augustine, *Letters* 186.7.23.
20. Calvin, *Institutes* 3.23.7, quoting Augustine, *On Rebuke and Grace* 10.27.

sovereignly in control of it and its effects. Instead, Calvin believed , along with Augustine, "the will of God is the necessity of things."[21]

Calvin also believed preaching was consistent with God's eternal predestination. He uses Augustine as support: "God could turn the will of evil men to good because he is almighty. Obviously he could. Why, then, does he not? Because he wills otherwise. Why he wills otherwise rests with him."[22] Our responsibility is to preach, not to ask questions.[23] In the most "Calvinistic" of doctrines—predestination—then, Calvin claimed Augustine to be his major historical support. Calvin was not novel in his teaching.[24]

Summary

History is not authoritative. The Bible is. However, this chapter has demonstrated that John Calvin's views were not unique when he expounded them in the sixteenth century. "Calvinism"—we should probably call it "Augustinianism" when it predates Calvin—had a long heritage before Calvin taught it.

REFLECTION QUESTIONS

1. What most surprised you in this historical overview?

2. Do you agree with Augustine that "God's grace does not find but makes those fit to be chosen"? Why?

3. Why do you think Calvin appealed to Augustine's predestinarian teaching so much?

4. Is it important to you that Calvin could reference other Christian thinkers who agreed with him regarding the sovereignty of God? Why?

5. How authoritative do you think the church's history is?

---

21. Calvin, *Institutes* 3.23.8, quoting Augustine, *On Genesis in the Literal Sense* 6.15.26.
22. Calvin, *Institutes* 3.24.13, quoting Augustine, *On Genesis in the Literal Sense* 11.10.13.
23. Augustine is central to Calvin's argument about this in *Institutes* 3.23.13–14. Augustine was newly accessible in the sixteenth century. Although his works had been unpublished for centuries, they were edited between 1490 and 1506 and published for a new audience in eleven volumes (McGrath, *Reformation Thought*, 13–14).
24. A helpful overview of predestinarian teaching from Augustine to Calvin is found in Herman Bavinck, *Reformed Dogmatics*, vol. 2, *God and Creation*, ed. John Bolt, trans. John Vriend (Grand Rapids: Baker, 2004), 347–66.

Who Was Jacob Arminius and What Did He Believe?

Jacob (or James) Arminius (1559–1609) gave his name to a system of doctrine that deviates from much of Calvinistic theology. Although his views are not heretical, they substantially changed the sovereign and particularistic emphases in Calvinism, even though some contemporary Arminians try to label their views as equally valid Protestant Reformation doctrines.

Arminius's Life and Doctrine

Arminius was born in the Netherlands in 1559. Though he suffered great family tragedy at a young age, he received a fine education, studying at Marburg, Leiden, Basel, and Geneva (1584–86). In Geneva, Theodore Beza (1519–1605) taught him and recommended him for a pastoral position, which Arminius took up at a Reformed church in Amsterdam in 1588. While in Amsterdam, though, Arminius's mind began to divert from the received Calvinistic teaching of his day. From Romans 7, he argued that the strife Paul speaks of in that chapter portrays an unregenerated person struggling to do good. Calvinists believed this gave too much power and desire to do good to those who were dead in sin and hated God. In Romans 9, Arminius believed Paul was not speaking of God's individual election but of a corporate dealing with groups; Pharaoh, Esau, and Jacob represented the groups of Egyptians, Edomites, and Israelites.

In 1608, Arminius finally published his views on central doctrinal issues such as providence, free choice, grace, assurance, and justification in his *Declaration of Sentiments* before the Estates General of Holland. Here he revealed his deviation from the Dutch Reformed church's doctrinal standards of the *Belgic Confession* and the *Heidelberg Catechism*. He abandoned both infralapsarianism and supralapsarianism, promoting a novel view.[1]

Arminus taught that there was not one eternal decree of God, as Calvinists supposed. Rather, there were four decrees. The first consisted of a general decree to appoint Christ as mediator of salvation in order to make salvation available to all persons because of God's desire that all would be saved. The second decree (hardly a "decree" to Calvinists) taught that God foreknew those who would receive Christ based on who would repent and trust Jesus. The third decree established the sufficient and efficient means—preaching and the sacraments—God would use for saving those whom he foreknew. Human choice, though, was all-determinative.[2] Finally, in the only decree that actually relates to particular individuals, God determines to save those he knows will repent and believe and to damn those he knows won't.[3]

Rather than being a slight intramural disagreement with Calvinism, Arminius's *Declaration* was an outright frontal assault on God's eternal and particular decree to save whom he chose of his own free will. Before he could develop his ideas at any length, Arminius died in 1609.[4]

Arminianism from 1609 to 1618

Arminius's disciples, though, were not silenced. They put forward their ideas in 1610 as a series of five ways in which they felt that the Calvinistic confessions of their church should be modified to allow for their views. Since their proposal was a legal appeal, it was titled the *Remonstrance* and those promoting these five theological views were labeled "Remonstrants." Because these "five points of Arminianism" are the antecedent of the "five points of Calvinism," we shall note them, along with brief explanations.

---

1. On infra- and supralapsarianism, see Question 33. The standard biography of Arminius is Carl Bangs, *Arminius: A Study in the Dutch Reformation* (Nashville: Abingdon, 1971). Also helpful are Richard A. Muller, *God, Creation, and Providence in the Thought of Jacob Arminius: Sources and Directions of Scholastic Protestantism in the Era of Early Orthodoxy* (Grand Rapids: Baker, 1991), 3–51; and Keith D. Stanglin and Thomas H. McCall, *Jacob Arminius: Theologian of Grace* (Oxford: Oxford University Press, 2012), 25–46.
2. Arminius's dependence upon Molinist middle knowledge theory has been suggested appropriately at this point by Eef Dekker, "Was Arminius a Molinist?" *Sixteenth Century Journal* 27, no. 2 (1996): 337–52.
3. James Arminius, "A Declaration of the Sentiments of Arminius, on Predestination, Divine Providence, the Freedom of the Will, the Grace of God, the Divinity of the Son of God, and the Justification of Man before God," in *The Works of Arminius*, trans. James Nichols (1825; Grand Rapids: Baker, 1996), 1:580–732. See A. Skevington Wood, "The Declaration of Sentiments: The Theological Testament of Arminius," *Evangelical Quarterly* 65, no. 2 (1993): 111–29.
4. For a helpful discussion of Arminius's theology in the *Declaration of Sentiments*, see Richard A. Muller, "Grace, Election, and Contingent Choice: Arminius's Gambit and the Reformed Response," in *The Grace of God: The Bondage of the Will*, eds. Thomas R. Schreiner and Bruce A. Ware (Grand Rapids: Baker, 1995), 2:251–78.

The first article deals with predestination, making God's decision to predestine conditional upon a human decision. God predestines those he knows will believe in Christ and persevere in the faith and determines to damn those who reject the gospel and his grace. The human decision is fundamental and logically first; God's choice is contingent upon the person's:

> God, by an eternal, unchangeable purpose in Jesus Christ, his Son, before the foundation of the world, hath determined, out of the fallen, sinful race of men, to save in Christ, for Christ's sake, and through Christ, those who, through the grace of the Holy Ghost, shall believe on this his Son Jesus, and shall persevere in this faith and obedience of faith, through this grace, even to the end; and, on the other hand, to leave the incorrigible and unbelieving in sin and under wrath, and to condemn them as alienate from Christ.[5]

God's election is not unconditional, for he elects those whom he knows will believe, persevere, and obey. They believe and are elected. Faith is not, then, a gift of God.

The second article teaches that Christ died equally and in the same way for all people. The only limitation placed on the efficacy of Christ's atonement is whether or not people choose to receive the benefits of his death for them:

> Jesus Christ, the Savior of the world, died for all men and for every man, so that he has obtained for them all, by his death on the cross, redemption and the forgiveness of sins; yet that no one actually enjoys this forgiveness of sins except the believer, according to the word of the Gospel of John iii.16. . . . And in the First Epistle of John 2:2.[6]

The third article initially seems to highlight the importance of God's grace, which is necessary if a fallen person is to believe in Christ:

> That man has not saving grace himself, nor of the energy of his free will, inasmuch as he, in the state of apostasy and sin, can of and by himself, neither think, will, nor do any thing that is truly good (such as saving Faith eminently is); but that it is needful that he be born again of God in Christ through his Holy Spirit, and renewed in understanding, inclination, or will, and all his

---

5. *The Five Arminian Articles*, in *The Creeds of Christendom, with a History and Critical Notes*, 6th ed., ed. Philip Schaff, rev. David S. Schaff (1931; Grand Rapids: Baker, 1990), 3:545.
6. Ibid., 3:546.

powers, in order that he may rightly understand, think, will, and effect what is truly good, according to the Word of Christ, John 15:5: "Without me ye can do nothing."[7]

The fourth article, though, neutralizes any Calvinistic tendencies in the previous one, arguing that both the Lord's prevenient grace (which is prior to salvation) and his assisting grace (given to sustain Christians in the faith) may be resisted and ultimately rejected.

> That this grace of God is the beginning, continuance, and ac-
> complishment of all good, even to this extent, that the regen-
> erate man himself, without prevenient or assisting, awaking,
> following and co-operative grace, can neither think, will, nor
> do good, nor withstand any temptations to evil; so that all
> good deeds or movements, that can be conceived, must be
> ascribed to the grace of God in Christ. But as respects the
> mode of the operation of this grace it is not irresistible, inas-
> much as it is written concerning many, that they have resisted
> the Holy Ghost (Acts 7:51), and elsewhere in many places.[8]

The Calvinistic fifth article notes that the Lord must continue his gracious support of believers if they are to persevere in the faith over the course of their lives. It does not take a position on whether or not a believer may finally abandon the faith.

The authorities at the Synod of Dort asked the Arminians for a clarification of their views, which was finally produced in December of 1618. Titled the *Sententiae* (usually known as the *Opinions of the Remonstrants*), it did not retract any of the Arminian theology from the *Remonstrance*. Instead, it defended Arminian tenets more stridently and elaborately, and it taught that Christians could finally fall away from God's grace.[9]

Developments in Arminianism

Arminianism was not static but evolved dynamically. Its development is a complex story, but historians have largely traced changes in the system in two different directions: Arminianism of the head and Arminianism of the heart.[10]

---

7. Ibid., 3:546–47.
8. Ibid., 3:547.
9. See "Appendix 6: The Opinions of the Remonstrants (1618)," in Matthew Barrett, *The Grace of Godliness: An Introduction to Doctrine and Piety in the Canons of Dort* (Kitchener, Canada: Joshua, 2013), 151–58.
10. Roger E. Olson, *Arminian Theology: Myths and Realities* (Downers Grove: InterVarsity Press, 2006), 16–17; J. I. Packer, "Arminianisms," in James I. Packer, *Honouring the People of God: Collected Shorter Writings of J. I. Packer*, vol. 4 (Carlisle, UK: Paternoster, 1999), 279–307.

The former was "an elastic, progressive, changing liberalism,"[11] leading J. I. Packer to the conclusion that the "continental Arminian school drifted into undogmatic moralism and pietism" and eventually denied the deity of Christ.[12] To Roger Olson, this stream of Arminianism encompasses "an optimistic anthropology that denies total depravity and the absolute necessity of supernatural grace for salvation," thus making it "heretical."[13] Olson highlights Arminians like Philip Limborch (1633–1712) and Charles Grandison Finney (1792–1875) who

> vulgarized Arminian theology by denying something Arminius, Wesley and all the faithful Arminians before him had affirmed and protected as precious to the gospel itself— human moral inability in spiritual matters, and the absolute necessity of supernatural prevenient grace for any right re- sponse to God, including the first stirrings of a good will to- ward God.[14]

Some contemporary Arminians are calling for a renewal of the purer, evangelical stream, Arminianism of the heart. This Arminianism—which began with Arminius and was revived by John Wesley (1703–91)—is of an evangelical sort, stressing original sin, human inability, and the necessity of prevenient grace for the salvation of any sinners.[15] It should be called, they maintain, "classical," "Reformed," or "Reformation" Arminianism.[16]

J. Matthew Pinson, an adherent of "Reformed Arminianism," summa- rizes this approach, while also distancing it from much of contemporary Arminian thought:

> Reformed Arminianism, unlike most Arminianism, posits a traditional Reformed notion of original sin and radical depravity that only the grace of God via the convicting and

---

11. Schaff, *Creeds of Christendom*, 1:509, cited in Packer, "Arminianisms," 287.
12. Packer, "Arminianisms," 288.
13. Olson, *Arminian Theology*, 17.
14. Ibid., 23, 27.
15. Ibid., 17–30.
16. F. Leroy Forlines, *Classical Arminianism: A Theology of Salvation*, ed. J. Matthew Pinson (Nashville: Randall House, 2011). J. Matthew Pinson, "Introduction," in Forlines, *Classical Arminianism*, v; see J. Matthew Pinson, "Jacobus Arminius: Reformed and Always Reforming," in *Grace for All: The Arminian Dynamics of Salvation*, eds. Clark H. Pinnock and John D. Wagner (Eugene, OR: Resource, 2015), 146–76. "A thorough analysis of Arminius's theology itself reveals that it was more a nuanced development of Reformed thought than a radical departure from it" (Pinson, "Jacobus Arminius," in *Grace for All*, 176). For further exemplars of both the "Reformed Arminian" and "Classical Arminian" label, see Jack W. Cottrell, "The Classical Arminian View of Election," in Chad Owen Brand, ed., *Perspectives on Election: Five Views* (Nashville: B&H, 2006), 71.

drawing power of the Holy Spirit can counteract. It puts forward a thoroughgoing Reformed, penal substitution view of atonement, with the belief that Christ's full righteousness is imputed to the believer in justification. Thus, it diverges from the perfectionism, entire sanctification, and crisis-experience orientation of much Arminianism, believing that one perseveres in salvation through faith alone. While believers can apostatize from salvation and be irremediably lost, this apostasy comes about through defection from faith rather than through sin.[17]

Adherents of this "classical" Arminian approach have two goals. First, they desire to show that not all "Arminian" approaches are equally good. Some classical Arminians, such as Pinson and F. Leroy Forlines, view Arminius as good, but they charge most subsequent Arminians with deviating from Arminius's thought. Another school of thought, represented by such thinkers as Olson and Thomas Oden, sees a continuing valid stream of Arminian theology from the seventeenth to the twenty-first centuries that's in line with Arminius himself.

A second observation of "Reformation Arminians" is that Arminius was a Reformed thinker. They argue that in the early seventeenth century there was no set view that constituted Calvinism; rather, it was "multi-faceted, dynamic, and ever-developing."[18] Since Calvinism was not codified, its scope should be broadened to include Arminianism.

Summary

Even given the common ground between Arminianism and Calvinism on some important doctrines, a chasm still remains regarding significant aspects of sinners' salvation. One says that man and God have to cooperate in salvation (Arminianism), while the other says salvation is a gift of God (Calvinism). They cannot both be correct. William Ames (1576–1633) who served as a theological advisor at the Synod of Dort rightly summarized what should be our attitude towards Arminianism:

> The view of the Remonstrants [i.e., the Arminians], as it is taken by the mass of their supporters, is not strictly a heresy, that is, a major lapse from the gospel, but a dangerous error tending toward heresy. As maintained by some of them,

---

17. J. Matthew Pinson, *Arminian and Baptist: Explorations in a Theological Tradition* (Nashville: Randall House, 2015), ix.

18. William den Boer, *God's Twofold Love: The Theology of Jacob Arminius (1559–1609)* (Gottingen: Vandenhoeck and Ruprecht, 2010), 43–44; quoted in Pinson, *Arminian and Baptist*, 3.

however, it is the Pelagian heresy, because they deny that the effective operation of inward grace is necessary for conversion.[19]

REFLECTION QUESTIONS

1. What most surprised you about Arminius's life and theology?

2. How would you summarize what Arminius taught regarding God's decrees?

3. Do you think John 3:16 and 1 John 2:2 teach that Christ died in the same way for all persons as Arminius maintained?

4. Do you think Romans 9 teaches corporate election in the Arminian sense (as opposed to individual election, as Calvinists maintain)?

5. Do you think that Arminianism is a valid stream of Calvinistic thought? Why?

---

19. William Ames, *De Conscientia* IV: iv, q. 4, in Packer, "Arminianisms," 303. We would do well to follow the advice of J. I. Packer who notes that "Arminianisms vary, so that blanket judgments are not in order: each version of post-Reformation semi-Pelagianism must be judged on its own merits" ("Arminianisms," 303).

What Did the Synod of Dort Teach? (Part 1)

Responding to the Arminian threat, representatives at the Synod of Dort produced an extensive pastoral and theological statement of Calvinism. Since it followed the arrangement of the five Arminian assertions in the *Remonstrance*, the *Canons of Dort* teaches the "five points of Calvinism."[1] The *Canons*, though, are not defensive. They are a positive biblical account of the doctrines refuted by the Arminians, demonstrating that Calvinism guards the integrity of the biblical gospel. In this chapter we will note Dort's formulation of the doctrines of predestination and Christ's atonement.

The Synod of Dort

The Synod of Dort (or Dortrecht) was a gathering of international Calvinists from November 1618 to May 1619.[2] Delegates came to Dort from Britain, Switzerland, Germany, and all the Dutch provinces and universities, convening in 154 formal sessions. At first, "thirteen Remonstrant leaders were summoned. After five weeks of clashes, they were dismissed and the synod defined its positions in opposition to the Remonstrants."[3]

Dort's representatives were not monolithic in their doctrine. A minority held to universal atonement.[4] Another minority group adhered to suprala-

---

1. Dort also answered the Arminian "Opinions." Each main point of doctrine is followed by a list of "rejection of [Arminian] errors."
2. Louis Praamsma, "The Background of the Arminian Controversy (1586–1618)," in *Crisis in the Reformed Churches: Essays in Commemoration of the Great Synod of Dort, 1618–1619*, ed. Peter Y. De Jong (Grand Rapids: Reformed Fellowship, 1968), 22–38.
3. Rudolph W. Heinze, *Reform and Conflict: From the Medieval World to the Wars of Religion, A.D. 1350–1648*, The Baker History of the Church, vol. 4 (Grand Rapids: Baker, 2005), 348.
4. William Robert Godfrey, "Tensions within International Calvinism: The Debate on the Atonement at the Synod of Dort, 1618–1619," Ph.D. dissertation, Stanford University, 1974.

psarianism.[5] But both these minority groups thought opposing the grave errors of Arminianism was more significant than holding out for a statement they could agree with perfectly, so they all signed the *Canons of Dort*.

The *Canons of Dort* are pastoral, evangelistic, God-honoring, and biblical. Although they occasionally employ the technical theological language of their day, they argue that Arminianism must be opposed, for "nothing less than the heart of the gospel was at stake" in the Calvinists' debates with Arminianism.[6] A wrong understanding of the manner in which the grace of God saves sinners (or whether it accomplishes God's desire of salvation) has huge ramifications. Only when we understand the gospel correctly will we give God the glory he deserves for saving us. Only when we understand the gospel correctly will we have assurance of salvation.[7]

The First Main Point of Doctrine: Divine Election and Reprobation

The Arminians had asserted that God predestined persons according to his foreknowledge of who would believe in Jesus, obey him, and persevere in the faith. Predestination was conditional upon the decisions of persons. To this the Calvinists responded with eighteen clarifying points asserting that God predestined individuals to life based on his eternal choice alone.

God's Love Is Displayed in the Gospel

God's glorious character is the main point of this first point of doctrine. The first two articles set forth both the justice and the love of God in the context of human sin. Because of all persons' sin, God would have been just to punish them all. "Since all people have sinned in Adam and have come under the sentence of the curse and eternal death, God would have done no one an injustice if it had been his will to leave the entire human race under the curse, and to condemn them on account of their sin" (article 1).[8] But, out of his love, God sent "his only begotten Son into the world, so that whoever believes in him should not perish but have eternal life" (article 2). The reality of sin and God's antidote in the gospel are the starting point to all discussions of predestination.

5. Matthew Barrett, *The Grace of Godliness: An Introduction to Doctrine and Piety in the Canons of Dort* (Kitchener, Canada: Joshua, 2013), 131–36.

6. Cornelis P. Venema, *But for the Grace of God: An Exposition of the Canons of Dort*, 2nd ed. (Grandville, MI: Reformed Fellowship, 2011), 17.

7. Ibid., 17–18.

8. I am using the text of the *Canons of Dort* in *Creeds and Confessions of Faith in the Christian Tradition*, Vol. 2, *Creeds and Confessions of the Reformation Era*, eds. Jaroslav Pelikan and Valerie Hotchkiss (New Haven, CT: Yale University Press, 2003), 569–600, reprinted in Barrett, *The Grace of Godliness,* 159–93.

The Gospel

All persons must trust in Jesus and are guilty for not doing so. In mercy, God sends gospel messengers, calling sinners to faith and repentance (article 3). God's wrath remains upon those who do not believe; but those who believe, who "embrace Jesus the Saviour with a true and living faith" are delivered from wrath and "receive the gift of eternal life" (article 4). All are responsible for their belief or unbelief. What differentiates people is their decision to trust Jesus.

Election Is Gracious, Whereas Reprobation Is Just

Seen from another angle, when we look behind people's actions, God's eternal choice to grant faith to some and not to others is what differentiates persons. Unbelief's cause is in sinners themselves; it "is not at all in God." Faith in Christ, however, "is the free gift of God" (article 5). This presupposes the first article's teaching on universal human sin. Finally, then, we arrive at eternal election. God's eternal decree is the cause of election and reprobation—"The fact that some receive from God the gift of faith within time, and that others do not, stems from his eternal decision." He softens the hearts of the elect and brings them to faith but "by his just judgment" leaves the non-elect in their sin. Both the elect and the non-elect were "equally lost" and deserving of condemnation. But God discriminates between humanity—in an "unfathomable," "merciful," and "just" manner. Though many resist God's right to distinguish between the elect and non-elect, "holy and godly souls" find consolation in it (article 6).

God Graciously Elects for His Own Purposes

The next five articles unpack the doctrine of election. Article 7 defines election as "God's unchangeable purpose by which . . . Before the foundation of the world, by sheer grace, according to the free good pleasure of his will, he chose in Christ to salvation a definite number of particular people out of the entire human race, which had fallen by its own fault from its original innocence into sin and ruin." Nothing in the elect commends them to God, but God effectually chose them and all the fruits of their salvation flow from his choice (article 7). God's choice is not based on foreseen faith or works. Rather, the elect are chosen "for the purpose of faith, of the obedience of faith, of holiness," and other gifts that accompany salvation. "Election is the source of each of the benefits of salvation" in them (article 9). The cause of election is "the good pleasure of God," not anything in persons since all are part of "the common mass of sinners" (article 10). Since election is done by the "most wise, unchangeable, all-knowing, and almighty" God, the elect will certainly be saved (article 11).

Election Leads to Assurance, Not Ungodliness

Election should result in assurance and holiness. The elect will have assurance, not by questioning God's eternal choice, but by seeing fruits of grace—"a true faith in Christ, a childlike fear of God, a godly sorrow for their sins, a hunger and thirst for righteousness"—in their lives (article 12). Certainty of election should result in humility and praise to and love for God not licentiousness (article 13).

Election Should Be Taught with Sensitivity

Pastors must wisely teach about divine election. The doctrine of election is biblical so it must be taught. But it must be proclaimed carefully ("with a spirit of discretion, in a godly and holy manner, at the appropriate time and place") and "for the glory of God's most holy name, and for the lively comfort of his people." We must eschew "inquisitive searching into the ways of the Most High" in election (article 14).

Unbelievers Should Come to Christ, Not Fear Reprobation

The final four articles consider the doctrine of reprobation, which had been briefly addressed in article six. The decree of reprobation does not make God the author of sin but shows him to be a just judge. He is "most just," exercising his "just judgment" in order to declare his "justice." This justice is manifest because those who are "passed by in God's eternal election" are guilty for "the common misery into which, by their own fault, they have plunged themselves" and are condemned for "their unbelief" as well as "for all their other sins." God is just to condemn them, both according to his eternal decree and according to their sin. Reprobation magnifies the "eternal and undeserved grace of our election" because the only thing differentiating Christians from the reprobate is God's gracious choice (article 15).

Unbelievers, though, should not assume they are damned. Reprobation should not terrify unbelievers seeking Christ or Christians lacking assurance, but it should horrify those who have rejected Christ (article 16). Finally, the section ends by warning against murmuring against God's right to exercise "this grace of an undeserved election" as well as "a just reprobation." For these things, God should be worshiped (article 18).

The Second Main Point of Doctrine: Christ's Death and Human Redemption through It

Whereas the Arminians had asserted that Christ's death on the cross was equally effective for all persons and that the only thing that differentiated persons was their response to Christ's atonement, Dort responded in nine articles, noting that Christ's death was effective only for those whom the Father had elected. They did not, however, "limit" Christ's work merely to those who were predestined; rather, they taught that his death had implications for all of humanity.

God's Mercy in Sending Jesus

God is both patient and the punisher of those who do wrong. On the one hand, God's justice requires the eternal punishment of our sins, since all have sinned "against his infinite majesty" (article 1). Therefore, in his infinite mercy God sent his Son as a sacrifice for us since we could not make satisfaction for our own sins. By being "made to be sin" and becoming "a curse for us, in our place," Jesus made "satisfaction for us" (article 2). God's love met the demands of his justice in Christ's death for the elect.

Christ's Death Is Infinitely Worthy and Sufficient to Atone for All Sin
Nothing was lacking in Christ's cross for the salvation of any sinner. Since he is the Son of God, Christ's death is "the only and entirely complete sacrifice" for sin and has infinite worth. Therefore, it is "more than sufficient to atone the sins of the whole world" (article 3). Its sufficiency derives from the nature of who Jesus is as well as from his role as the bearer of God's wrath. He "was not only a true and perfectly holy man, but also the only begotten Son of God" who was "of the same eternal and infinite essence" with the Father and the Spirit. He bore "God's anger and curse, which we by our sins fully deserved" (article 4). Nothing is lacking in Christ's death to pay for any person's sin.

The Gospel Must Be Preached to Everyone
The next two articles stress that the only limit to the cross's effectiveness is the unwillingness of sinners to trust Christ's work. "Whoever believes in Christ crucified shall not perish but have eternal life" (John 3:16). This glorious promise "ought to be announced and declared without differentiation or discrimination to all nations and people" (article 5). Some fail to believe, not because Christ's sacrifice "is deficient or insufficient," but because of their sin (article 6).

Christ Death for the Elect Gives Them Everything Necessary for Salvation
The particularity of the atonement is also taught in Scripture. Those who believe do so solely because of God's grace, "given to them in Christ from eternity," not because of their merit (article 7). Because of God's "entirely free plan" and his "very gracious will and intention," he determined that "the saving effectiveness of his Son's costly death should work itself out in all his chosen ones." Christ's death was only effective for those whom the Father had chosen because Christ "effectively redeem[ed] from every people, tribe, nation and language all those and those only who were chosen from eternity to salvation and given to him by the Father." Christ purchased the gift of faith for them, paid for all their sins, and committed to preserve them in the faith until heaven (article 8).

Christians Should Exult in Christ's Atonement
Since the purpose to effectively redeem a people proceeds from God's eternal love, his people will eternally praise him for the accomplishment of his love for them. Since Christ "laid down his life for her [the church] upon the cross, as a bridegroom for his bride," the church "steadfastly loves, persistently worships" God (article 9).

REFLECTION QUESTIONS

1. Do you think it was appropriate for a group of Calvinists to gather together to respond to Arminianism? Why? Could, or should, anything like this theological gathering ever happen in our day?

2. What most surprised you in this discussion of the *Canons of Dort*? Why?

3. Do you think it was significant that Dort asserted that the reality of human sin was necessary to consider before discussing either election or reprobation? Why?

4. Do you believe that predestination should lead to Christian assurance of salvation? Why?

5. Do you think it is helpful to conceive of Christ's death on the cross as both of infinite worth and also only effective for the elect? Why?

What Did the Synod of Dort Teach? (Part 2)

The third and fourth main points of doctrine in the *Canons of Dort* (written as one point) discuss the reality and extensiveness of human sin and the sovereign grace that is thus required to raise people from spiritual death to life. The fifth and final main point encourages believers that God will preserve his people through the vicissitudes of life and instructs them in how they can gain assurance of salvation.

The Third and Fourth Main Points of Doctrine: Human Corruption, Conversion to God, and the Way It Occurs

The Remonstrants' *Opinions* of 1618 combined their thoughts about human sin and Christian conversion under one head. So Dort treated these topics in one heading as well. Due to their guilt and inability, the elect can only be saved by the irresistible, sovereign grace of God, Dort asserted in seventeen articles.

All Humans Have Rebelled and Can Do Nothing to Save Themselves

Even though man was originally created holy and had many excellent gifts, he rebelled "against God at the devil's instigation and by his own free will." The result was horrific: he "brought upon himself blindness, terrible darkness, futility and distortion of judgment in his mind; perversity, defiance and hardness in his heart and will; and finally impurity in all his emotions" (article 1). Humanity is now bound to sin in mind, affections, and will. And this sinful disposition is passed to everyone through Adam, who, since he was corrupt, "brought forth corrupt children" (article 2).

All Unbelievers Deserve God's Eternal Wrath

Sin condemns every person before the holy God:

> Therefore, all people are conceived in sin and are born chil-
> dren of wrath, unfit for any saving good, inclined to evil,
> dead in their sins and slaves to sin; without the grace of the
> regenerating Holy Spirit they are neither willing nor able to
> return to God, to reform their distorted nature, or even to
> dispose themselves to such reform (article 3).

Even the knowledge of God that all have through creation is not able to save anyone (article 4). Given the reality and extent of human sin, God must sovereignly save sinners.

Only When the Spirit Applies the Gospel to Us Will We Be Eternally Saved
God typically follows a normal course to save people. God's law shows them their sin, but it is unable to save (article 5). God chooses, rather, to save those who believe the gospel by the power of the Holy Spirit (article 6). Those whom God chooses—who "receive so much grace"—should be a humble people for they contributed nothing to their salvation. They should gratefully adore God, and "certainly not inquisitively search into" the "severity and justice of God's judgments on the others, who do not receive this grace" (article 7).

God Sincerely Invites Sinners to Salvation in the Gospel
The gospel call, though, with all God's kind disposition, goes out to all who hear it. It is a sincere summons, for those who hear the gospel are "called seriously" to come to God. It's God's earnest declaration and invitation, promising "rest for their souls and eternal life to all who come to him and believe" (article 8). Not all believe, but as Jesus taught in the parable of the soils (Matt. 13), the cause of unbelief is in the sinner's heart alone. Unbelief is not due to any sin in God or any defect in the gospel. Unbelievers' lack of faith "must not be blamed on the gospel, nor on Christ, who is offered through the gospel, nor on God, who calls them through the gospel" (article 9). Sinners are completely responsible for not coming to Christ.

God Mysteriously and Effectually Grants Life to the Elect through the Gospel
Faith "must not be credited to man, as though one distinguishes himself by free choice from others." Rather, that some believe is due solely to God's grace who "grants them faith and repentance, and, having rescued them from the dominion of darkness, brings them into the kingdom of his Son" (article 10). This grace of God is effective in saving the elect because God's regenerating work is all-encompassing:

> By the effective operation of the same regenerating Spirit,
> [God] also penetrates into the inmost being of man, opens
> the closed heart, softens the hard heart and circumcises the

heart that is uncircumcised. He infuses new qualities into the will, making the dead will alive, the evil one good, the unwilling one willing and the stubborn one compliant; he activates and strengthens the will so that, like a good tree, it may be enabled to produce the fruits of good deeds (article 11).

Regeneration is "an entirely supernatural work," and a "most pleasing, a marvelous, hidden and inexpressible work." Those in whom the Lord works "are certainly, unfailingly and effectively reborn and do actually believe." As soon as God gives them life, their will "is also itself active," and the person believes and repents by virtue of divine grace received (article 12). Christians should revel in their regeneration, even though "in this life believers cannot fully understand the way this work occurs" (article 13).

Since God Grants Grace to Believe, Christians Should Be Thankful and Humble
Believers should take great hope because God did not leave them to themselves. No, God granted the elect the faith necessary to be saved. He "produces in man both the will to believe and the belief itself" (article 14). Those who have received this grace should overflow with thanks to God who gave them grace even though they deserved condemnation. Christians should pray for those not yet converted, asking God to grant them faith. All the while they should be marked by humility, since they contributed nothing to their salvation (article 15).

God's Grace Treats Us as His Image-Bearers in Regeneration
In regeneration, God "does not act in people as if they were blocks and stones," for he does not "abolish the will and its properties or coerce a reluctant will by force." Arminians charge that "irresistible grace" was akin to God bringing sinners into salvation kicking and screaming. Instead, God "spiritually revives, heals, reforms, and—in a manner at once pleasing and powerful—bends [the will] back" (article 16). In regeneration, God treats us as those created in his image.

God Uses Means to Bring Persons to Salvation
Just as God uses means to provide for our "natural life" (like eating and sleeping), he similarly uses means—supremely the means of preaching ("the holy admonitions of the gospel")—to bring about spiritual life. The gospel is thus "the seed of regeneration and the food of the soul." So we must preach the gospel to sinners if we hope to see them regenerated. In this way, the Lord will receive all the glory for the salvation of his people.

The Fifth Main Point of Doctrine: The Perseverance of the Saints
In their *Opinions*, the Arminians argued that a Christian could fall away from the faith and lose his or her salvation. Dort responded in the final section of

the *Canons,* opposing this non-Calvinistic doctrine. The *Canons* affirm that God will preserve his people in the faith through all the vicissitudes of life, and it also instructs them in the means they should use to arrive at assurance of salvation.

The Already-Not Yet Nature of Christians' Relationship to Sin
Christians have been freed from sin, yet they still struggle with sin. On the one hand, the whole Trinity has worked to accomplish our salvation: "Those people whom God according to his purpose calls into fellowship with his Son Jesus Christ our Lord and regenerates by the Holy Spirit, he also sets free from the reign and slavery of sin." Yet, "in this life" believers are not free "entirely from the flesh and the body of sin" (article 1). Christians will struggle with sin "until they are freed from this body of death and reign with the Lamb of God in heaven" (article 2).

Christians Can Only Persevere Because God Preserves Them in the Faith
Due to their indwelling sin Christians cannot persevere in the faith by their own power; they "could not remain standing in this grace if left to their own resources." But they do persevere because God is faithful to his promises. He demonstrates that by "powerfully preserving them in [grace] to the end" (article 3).

Believers' Struggle with Sin and Its Relationship to Assurance of Salvation
Christians will struggle with sin and its consequences in this life. They must be on guard against temptation, for God may yet permit them to fall into sin as he did David and Peter. Believers need to be careful lest they be "carried away by the flesh, the world, and Satan into sins, even serious and outrageous ones" (article 4). Sin has grievous effects—it offends God, grieves the Spirit, and leads one to be ineffective in the faith. It may even make one "sometimes lose the awareness of grace for a time." Yet, when in this situation, the promise remains that if believers repent, "God's fatherly face again shines upon them" (article 5).

God's Sovereign Election Leads Believers to Trust Him with the Difficulties of Life
God, whose purposes in election will not fail, will never let his children fall completely away so that they "plunge themselves, entirely forsaken by him, into eternal ruin." This is because he is "rich in mercy," and "his unchangeable purpose of election" means he has set his eternal love on his elect (article 6). When his people sin, God calls them back to himself in repentance—"by his Word and Spirit he certainly and effectively renews them to repentance so that they have a heartfelt and godly sorrow for the sins they have committed." Then they will have great joy and "experience again the grace of a reconciled God" (article 7).
Sin is of such great power that, left to themselves, Christians would certainly abandon their heavenly Father. Yet, the united effort of the Trinity works to keep them in the faith. Their falling away "cannot possibly happen, since

[God's] plan cannot be changed, his promise cannot fail, the calling according to his purpose cannot be revoked, the merit of Christ as well as his interceding and preserving cannot be nullified and the sealing of the Holy Spirit can neither be invalidated nor wiped out" (article 8). Christ's disciples have every reason to hope in the Lord's care for them, now and through all the turmoil of life.

Biblical and Pastoral Ways to Arrive at Assurance of Salvation

Believers can have assurance of their salvation, but it will be relative to the amount of faith they have in God's promises, especially the certainty of "the forgiveness of sins and eternal life" (article 9). However, judging our faith can be hard, if not impossible. So Christians should look to God's promises, the Spirit's testimony, as well as our lives in order to gain assurance:

> assurance does not derive from some private revelation beyond or outside the Word, but from faith in the promise of God which he has very plentifully revealed in his Word for our comfort, from the testimony of the Holy Spirit testifying with our spirit that we are God's children and heirs (Romans 8:16–17), and finally from a serious and holy pursuit of a clear conscience and of good works.

This is the way for one to obtain "well-founded comfort" (article 10).

Assurance Brings One Close to God and Leads One Far from Pride and Ungodliness

Temptations to sin may deprive believers of assurance, but believers should have hope, for "God, the Father of all comfort . . . by the Holy Spirit revives in them the assurance of their perseverance" (article 11). Against Catholic and Arminian arguments that having assurance of salvation will lead a person to be lax in his spiritual duties, Dort articulates the effects that assurance of salvation should have in a Christian's life. Certainty that one will persevere should lead to humility, love, prayer, perseverance in suffering, and joy, not to pride. In fact, assurance is "the true root" of these godly traits (article 12). Similarly, assurance that one will persevere will lead to godliness, not to licentiousness, for a believer dreads losing his or her sense of God's fatherly love "for the godly, looking upon [God's] face is sweeter than life, but its withdrawal is more bitter than death." Christians should do everything they can do to remain far away from sin and close to the Lord (article 13).

Out of His Great Love for Us, God Uses Means to Allow His People to Arrive at Assurance of Salvation

Assurance is not automatic. God employs means such as preaching and the private reading of the Bible—with its exhortations, threats, and promises—along with the sacraments to preserve his people (article 14). Misunderstandings abound regarding assurance. Unbelievers rail at it. Satan hates it. But God's people love it and find deep spiritual comfort from it: "The bride of Christ . . . has always loved this teaching very tenderly and defended it steadfastly as a priceless treasure; and God, against whom no plan can avail and no strength can prevail, will ensure that she will continue to do this. To this God alone, Father, Son, and Holy Spirit, be honour and glory forever. Amen" (article 15).

REFLECTION QUESTIONS

1. What surprised you the most in this chapter? Why?

2. Were there things you disagreed with in this chapter? What were they?

3. Why do you think the *Canons of Dort* spent so much time helping Christians find assurance of salvation?

4. Do you think Dort effectively balanced God's preservation of the elect with their duty to persevere in faith? Why?

5. What most challenged you in your walk with Christ in reading this chapter?

PART 2

Questions about Salvation

Humanity's Sin and the
Necessity of Divine Intervention

How Sinful Are People?

Without understanding the dire straits humanity is in, we will never comprehend the sovereign work of grace necessary to save any of us. If we're really okay, we can save ourselves. If we're pretty sick but God has given all of us a significant measure of grace, we can cooperate with it and be saved. But if we're dead spiritually, he must raise us to life. The Bible teaches the last of these views, as we'll see. Only the sovereign, particular, raising-from-death-to-life grace of God can rescue anyone out of the mire of sin.

Sin according to the Bible

The Bible says a great deal about sin. Here we will notice both what sin is and also how extensive sin's grip is on us. In the first place, the Bible carefully and fully defines sin. The Old Testament authors used many different words to convey the notion that sin is dreadful. It means "missing the mark" or "erring" (e.g., Exod. 32:30; Ps. 51:9). It is active rebellion against God's will (Prov. 28:13). Sin is going astray from the right path (Lev. 4:13) which leads to guilt before God (1 Kings 17:18). In the New Testament, the most common word for sin is *hamartia*, "missing the mark," which implies failure and wrongdoing (e.g., Matt. 1:21). Sin is also "unrighteousness," meaning that the deeds proceeding from it are opposed to God and goodness (1 Cor. 6:8). In addition, sin is "breaking the law" (Rom. 4:15; 1 John 3:4) and "godlessness" (Titus 2:12), among other things. Sin, then, is fundamentally something we do towards God, even though it has effects on other people (Ps. 51:4). Because of the Godward orientation of our sin, our transgressions deserve God's eternal wrath as a just punishment (Matt. 25:46; Rom. 6:23).

In the second place, sin affects everything we are as human beings—our bodies, our wills, our minds, our affections. Because of sin, every human gets sick and will die bodily. Additionally, sin affects that part of us (we usually call it the will) by which we make choices. This means that our choices are not oriented in a Godward direction, nor are they neutral. Jesus said that "everyone who commits sin is a slave to sin" (John 8:34). Paul noted that being "dead in the trespasses and sins in which you once walked," includes not just "walking," but also "following" the world's course, "living" in the flesh's passions, and "carrying out" the flesh's and the mind's desires (Eph. 2:1–3). Choosing happens, but because of sinners' spiritual deadness all their choices are opposed to God. Peter concurs, noting that the unrighteous false teachers whom he warns the church about "themselves are slaves of corruption. For whatever overcomes a person, to that he is enslaved" (2 Peter 2:19). Sin enslaves an unbeliever's will and orients it in an anti-God direction.

Sin also distorts our rationality. Our thinking about the issues that matter most in the universe (who God is, who we are, what is the path to salvation) are skewed in the wrong direction. Paul's dreadful summary of the consequences of sin shows humanity suppressing the truth of God in creation and in ourselves (Rom. 1:18–32). He tells the "wise" Corinthians that "in the wisdom of God, the world did not know God through wisdom" (1 Cor. 1:21). Even more starkly, he charges that "the natural person does not accept the things of the Spirit of God, for they are folly to him, and he is not able to understand them because they are spiritually discerned" (1 Cor. 2:14). The problem with unbelievers is that they are marked by "the futility of their minds" (Eph. 4:17).

Our affections and emotions—that part of us which determines what we love and hate and desire—are also grossly affected by sin. We see this in Romans 1 where Paul includes a description of the effects of sin on our sexual desires (Rom. 1:24–27). He cites one kind of love—that of money—as a root of all kinds of evils (1 Tim. 6:10). The apostle also laments the manner in which sin makes people "lovers of pleasure rather than lovers of God" (2 Tim. 3:4), demonstrating sin's effects on our affections.

So every part of who we are is affected by sin. This is what is meant by the (not very helpful) phrase "total depravity," which has been misunderstood to mean that every person is as bad as he possibly could be. That's not the case. By God's common grace, he restrains evil in all of us to some degree; all of us could be more evil than we are. "Total depravity" reminds us—as we've seen through our quick survey of the New Testament—that every part of us is affected by sin. We might better label our state "pervasive depravity" because sin has pervaded every part of us. Nothing in us is neutral. Lorraine Boettner comments that human depravity,

> which declares that men are dead in sin, does not mean that all men are equally bad, nor that any man is as bad as he could be, nor that any one is entirely destitute of virtue, nor that human nature is evil in itself, nor that man's spirit is inactive, and much less does it mean that the body is dead. What it does mean is that since the fall man rests under the curse of sin, that he is actuated by wrong principles, and that he is wholly

unable to love God or to do anything meriting salvation. His corruption is extensive but not necessarily intensive.[1]

Sin's Effect on Our Relationship to God

The Bible also teaches us God's evaluation of humanity due to our sin. Before the holy Judge, because of our sin, we are all condemned, defiled, unable to obey, deserving of wrath, and dead. First, we are condemned before the judgment seat of God both for Adam's sin imputed to us and also for our "own personal delinquencies" (Rom. 1:32; 2:8–9; 5:12–21), as J. I. Packer notes.[2] Second, we stand before the holy God defiled by the sin that is at the core of who we are. Jesus says that evil is located not in external actions, but "from within, out of the heart of man" all sorts of evil come forth that defile a person (Mark 7:21). Third, in relation to God the Lawgiver, we are unable to obey. Paul stresses this inability: "the mind that is set on the flesh is hostile to God, for it does not submit to God's law; indeed, it cannot. Those who are in the flesh cannot please God" (Rom. 8:7–8). We must not quickly skirt over Paul's "cannots" here.[3] It is not just that most people don't obey and please the Lord. It's not merely that many haven't found the means of doing the right thing apart from God's intervention. They don't do the right thing because they cannot. Packer concludes correctly that "when God commands those who are in the flesh to repent (Acts 17:31) and believe on his Son (Jn. 6:28f.), they cannot do it till their hearts are made new (cf. Jn. 3:5; 6:44; 1 Cor. 2:14)."[4] Fourth, we are under God's wrath, his enemies (Rom. 5:10). All of us deserve his eternal judgment, his awful wrath, according to Romans 1:18, 2:5, and 3:5. Fifth, due to our sin, we are dead spiritually, bound for an eternity apart from fellowship with God (Eph. 2:1; Rom. 6:23). We conclude, then, that sin is fundamentally the anti-God orientation that defines all humans outside of Christ. It is not just what people do; it's who they are. As Thomas Schreiner insists, "Those who are born in Adam do not merely sin; they are also slaves to sin. Sin, as an alien power, dominates them. They are under its rule and authority."[5]

Calvinism and Arminianism on Sin

Unlike Arminianism, Calvinism takes sin and its devastating effects on humanity to their correct biblical conclusion. Calvinism asserts that sin's gravity and its effects on all of us warrant nothing but our eternal condemnation. We are not able to cooperate with God toward our salvation since we're dead spiritually.

---

1. Loraine Boettner, *The Reformed Doctrine of Predestination* (1932; Grand Rapids: Eerdmans, 1957), 61.
2. J. I. Packer, *God's Words: Studies in Key Bible Themes* (1981; Grand Rapids: Baker, 1988), 75.
3. See Question 9.
4. Ibid., 77.
5. Thomas R. Schreiner, *Paul, Apostle of God's Glory in Christ: A Pauline Theology* (Downers Grove, IL: InterVarsity Press, 2001), 127.

The Westminster divines highlighted that our first parents' rebellion meant that they "became dead in sin, and wholly defiled in all the parts and faculties of soul and body" (Westminster Confession of Faith, 6.2). This sin is imputed to all their posterity who inherit "the same death in sin and corrupted nature" (6.3). Therefore all persons are "utterly indisposed, disabled, and made opposite to all good, and wholly inclined to all evil." Their "actual transgressions" flow from this corrupted nature (6.4), and so all persons are "bound over to the wrath of God" and "made subject to death, with all miseries spiritual, temporal, and eternal" (6.6). Because of humankind's corruption and spiritual inability, God graciously elects and calls certain ones to be his own (10.1–2).

Arminianism disagrees with Calvinism's assessment of the devastating effects of sin on humanity. In its popular form in much of evangelicalism, Arminianism affirms "a universal healing of total depravity by the grace of God through the atoning work of Christ on the cross," leading (in Arminians' conception of things) to original guilt not being imputed to persons. Therefore, as Roger Olson maintains, this branch of Arminianism "mitigated the corruption of inherited depravity. From the cross flowed into humanity a power of spiritual renewal 'removing so much of their spiritual death . . . and enabling them to seek the face of God, to turn at his rebuke, and, by improving that grace to repent and believe the gospel.'"[6]

Classical Arminians are significantly closer to Calvinism, declaring that Adam's sin is imputed to all humanity so that we are all guilty of original sin; because of this, humanity is depraved and our wills are bound in sin.[7] William Witt concludes, "Whatever may be true of successors to Arminius's theology, he himself held to a doctrine of the bondage of the will which is every bit as trenchant as anything in Luther or Calvin."[8] However, this view of sin is not the same as Calvinism's because in the Arminian scheme, God's sufficient, or prevenient, grace overcomes sin's debilitations so that all persons can receive Christ if they will just cooperate with this grace. As Olson notes:

> The moral ability to respond to the gospel freely—by the graciously freed will—is a free gift of God through Christ to all people in some measure. It does not mean that anyone can now seek and find God using natural ability alone! It is a supernatural endowment that can and usually is rejected

---

6. Olson, *Arminian Theology: Myths and Realities* (Downers Grove: InterVarsity Press, 2006), 153–54, quoting Richard Watson, *Theological Institutes* (New York: Lane & Scott, 1851), 2:57.
7. On "Classical Arminianism," see Question 15.
8. William Gene Witt, "Creation, Redemption and Grace in the Theology of Jacob Arminius" (Ph.D. diss., University of Notre Dame, 1993), 479, quoted in Olson, *Arminian Theology*, 142. See Keith D. Stanglin and Thomas H. McCall, *Jacob Arminius: Theologian of Grace* (Oxford: Oxford University Press, 2012), 150.

> or neglected. According to Arminian theology, because of
> Christ and by the power of the Holy Spirit all people are being
> influenced toward the good; the deadly wound of Adam is
> being healed. . . . no person is left by God entirely in that state
> of nature without some measure of grace to rise above it if he
> or she cooperates with grace by not resisting it.[9]

Whatever doctrine of depravity Arminianism has is destroyed by its under-standing of God's general grace to all people ("to all people in some measure," "all people are being influenced toward the good").[10] In essence, human in-ability is a null set since "no person is left by God entirely in that state of nature without some measure of grace" to cooperate with God and be saved. Arminian "total depravity" may exist in theory but it is not a reality. For that reason, Arminianism redefines what God's grace is in both its particularity and its sovereign power.

Summary

Sin is moral evil that makes us repugnant to God and spiritually impo-tent. The solution to the devastating reality of sin in our lives must come from outside of us, as Paul delights to remind us: "But now the righteousness of God has been manifested apart from the law" (Rom. 3:21); "But God" (Eph. 2:4); "For the grace of God has appeared" (Titus 2:11); "But when the good-ness and loving kindness of God our Savior appeared" (Titus 3:4). The biblical doctrine of sin leads us to the conclusion that God in his grace must sover-eignly and independently save dead and corrupt sinners. Praise him for his merciful kindness in Christ!

REFLECTION QUESTIONS

1. How would you define sin in your own words?

2. Do you think "total depravity" is a helpful way to describe humanity's status in sin? Why?

---

9. Olson, *Arminian Theology*, 155.
10. I pass over the obvious biblical inconsistency at this point in Arminianism's insistence that all persons everywhere are being reached in some measure by God so that they can cooperate with him towards salvation. This counters the clear biblical evidence that people, apart from hearing the gospel and responding to it in faith and repentance, have no hope and will spend eternity in hell (see, e.g., Acts 4:12; Rom. 10:10–17; Eph. 2:12). It is this conviction that has driven Calvinists historically to zealously evangelize the lost.

3. How do you think an Arminian would interpret Ephesians 2:1–10? Do you think it is a valid understanding of the salvation process taught here?

4. Thomas Schreiner has written: "Human beings apart from Christ are in a bleak state. They dishonor God, fail to keep his law and boast in their works anyway. Even if they tried to observe God's commands, they could not because they are slaves to sin. They are under the dominion of the world, the flesh and the devil. As children of Adam, they are born into the world separated from God and as sinners. The plight of human beings is such that a solution is needed."[11] Do you agree with his evaluation of humanity's plight? Why?

5. Can you think of any biblical evidence against the Calvinistic understanding of sin asserted in this chapter?

---

11. Schreiner, *Paul*, 150.

What Is Predestination according to Calvinism?

In this question we will notice how the Calvinistic tradition has conceptualized the doctrine of predestination. Our guide will be the Westminster Confession of Faith as well as several commentators on the Confession. The Calvinistic tradition has cogently defined predestination, trumpeted the doctrine's usefulness, and answered objections to it.

God's Sovereign Decree

God's predestinating activity flows from his sovereign decree, of which the Confession says:

> God, from all eternity, did, by the most wise and holy counsel of his own will, freely, and unchangeably ordain whatsoever comes to pass: yet so, as thereby neither is God the author of sin, nor is violence offered to the will of the creatures; nor is the liberty or contingency of second causes taken away, but rather established.
>
> Although God knows whatsoever may or can come to pass upon all supposed conditions, yet hath he not decreed anything because he foresaw it as future, or as that which would come to pass upon such condition. (WCF 3.1–2)

Roger Nicole delineates six affirmations the Confession makes here. First, "the decrees are eternal, as God is." In other words, "from all eternity he has made a plan and purpose," as Ephesians 1:4 shows: "he chose us in him before the foundation of the world."[1] Second, God's "decrees participate in God's wisdom," which is why the Confession says they are "most wise."[2] Third, God is not the "author of sin" since the decrees of God are an aspect of the "holy counsel of his own will."[3] Fourth, "the decrees of God are free," not constrained by anything outside of himself:

> There is no external power over God which compels him to decide or ordain anything. God is not moved by external powers which somehow make the decree inevitable. It is in his own sovereign freedom that God ordains and purposes whatever he has planned. . . . [T]he freedom of God is qualified by the beautiful things we read in Scripture about his nature. The character of God articulates what he will determine in his freedom—in the same way our character determines what we decide when it is given to us to make decisions.[4]

Fifth, God's decree is immutable since God "unchangeably" decreed all things. Sixth, the decree is "all-encompassing," meaning that "there is nothing in the whole world which is not included in God's purpose."[5] Eternal, wise, holy, free, immutable, all-encompassing—this is how we should positively understand God's decree.

The Confession also guards against four possible errors. First, "God is not the author of sin." "We recognize that sinful acts are encompassed in his total plan, but God is not himself the first cause of evil in them. The evil has to be adjudged in terms of another source or causation. This baffles us tremendously, as anything connected with evil ultimately does." Recognizing the significance of this, Dort averred, "By no means is God the author of evil, the very thought of which is blasphemy."[6] Second, humans are really responsible since "violence is not offered to the will of the creature."[7] People really do freely make their own choices.[8] Third, "the liberty or contingency of second causes is not taken away, but rather established" by God's decree. That is to say, God's decree encompasses

---

1. Roger Nicole, *Our Sovereign Saviour: The Essence of the Reformed Faith* (Fearn, UK: Christian Focus, 2002), 34. I have removed Nicole's italics throughout.
2. Ibid.
3. Ibid., 35.
4. Ibid., 36.
5. Ibid., 37.
6. Ibid., 37–38.
7. Van Dixhoorn summarizes the point here: "To invert Proverbs 16:33, 'every decision is from the Lord,' but 'the lot' is still cast into our own laps. God is sovereign, but in a very real way we are free, and in every way we are responsible for our actions" (Chad Van Dixhoorn, *Confessing the Faith: A Reader's Guide to the Westminster Confession of Faith* [Edinburgh: Banner of Truth, 2014], 45).
8. See Questions 9–12.

all the means by which he will accomplish that determination, including the agents who self-willingly do what God has ordained:

> God does not ordain things simply "out of the blue," so that history is only a conglomeration of unrelated events having no connection with one another. Rather, God has ordained things in a texture, so to speak, so that everything that happens is related to everything else. . . . God does not ordain things without the means whereby they take place. Specifically, he does not ordain the salvation of people without the preaching of the Word.[9]

Fourth, God's decree is not grounded in his foreknowledge of future human choices. "If the decree of predestination was grounded in foreknowledge, it would be disastrous for us. For how could God foreknow anything good about us apart from the grace he gives?" The usual Arminian prooftext for predestination according to foreknowledge, Romans 8:29, actually establishes the Calvinistic position:

> Here the word "foreknew" is used in the biblical sense of "love in advance," "choosing in advance," not simply to have advance information. It is perfectly obvious that if God simply has advance information about what we might do, then the information would be that all of us would be lost. None of us would respond to the invitation of his grace. In order that the purpose of predestination should be fulfilled, it is necessary that the Holy Spirit be active within our hearts to move us to respond, to change our wills and the dominant disposition of our natures, and thus enable us to repent and believe.[10]

Sovereign Predestination

The Confession next teaches individual election of particular sinners who are chosen for salvation only on the basis of God's grace.

> By the decree of God, for the manifestation of his glory, some men and angels are predestinated unto everlasting life; and others foreordained to everlasting death.

> These angels and men, thus predestinated, and foreordained, are particularly and unchangeably designed, and their

---

9. Nicole, *Our Sovereign Saviour*, 38–39.
10. Ibid., 39–40.

number so certain and definite, that it cannot be either in-
creased or diminished.

> Those of mankind that are predestinated unto life, God, be-
> fore the foundation of the world was laid, according to his
> eternal and immutable purpose, and the secret counsel and
> good pleasure of his will, hath chosen, in Christ, unto ever-
> lasting glory, out of his mere free grace and love, without any
> foresight of faith, or good works, or perseverance in either
> of them, or any other thing in the creature, as conditions,
> or causes moving him thereunto; and all to the praise of his
> glorious grace. (WCF 3.3–5)

A. A. Hodge notices here "that God has elected certain individuals to
eternal life, and all the means and conditions thereof, on the ground of his
sovereign good pleasure. He chooses them to faith and repentance, and not
because of their faith and repentance. That God does choose individuals
to eternal life is certain."[11] Additionally, the Confession denies election-
according-to-foreknowledge, for predestination "is not conditioned upon
foreseen faith or repentance, but in each case upon sovereign grace and personal love, according to the secret counsel of [God's] will."[12] Finally, "the ultimate end or motive of God in election is the praise of his glorious grace."[13]

The Confession also details that, in order to accomplish his decreed goals,
God uses "means":

> As God hath appointed the elect unto glory, so hath he, by
> the eternal and most free purpose of his will, foreordained all
> the means thereunto. Wherefore, they who are elected, being
> fallen in Adam, are redeemed by Christ, are effectually called
> unto faith in Christ by his Spirit working in due season, are
> justified, adopted, sanctified, and kept by his power, through
> faith, unto salvation. Neither are any other redeemed by
> Christ, effectually called, justified, adopted, sanctified, and
> saved, but the elect only. (WCF 3.6)

Although God's decree is one and integral, to accomplish his goal he uses various "means" or "parts" to work together to accomplish this one decree. Hodge
notes that "although the decree of God is one eternal, all-comprehensive
intention, the several elements embraced within it necessarily sustain the

---

11. A. A. Hodge, *The Confession of Faith* (1869; Edinburgh: Banner of Truth, 1958), 70.
12. Ibid.
13. Ibid., 71.

relation to one another of means to ends." Not only does he determine the end, but "God at the same time determines the means by which he intends to accomplish them."[14] The Confession next carefully explains God's interactions with the non-elect:

> The rest of mankind God was pleased, according to the unsearchable counsel of his own will, whereby he extendeth or withholdeth mercy, as he pleaseth, for the glory of his sovereign power over his creatures, to pass by; and to ordain them to dishonor and wrath for their sin, to the praise of his glorious justice. (WCF 3.7)

In its discussion of the doctrine of reprobation here, the Confession makes two related points. In the first place, as God has decreed the salvation of the elect, so "he has sovereignly decreed to withhold his grace from the rest" of mankind. We are not privy to his motivations, but we trust that this "rests upon the unsearchable counsel of his own will, and is for the glory of his sovereign power."[15] Second, there is no unrighteousness in this, for God treats the non-elect as they deserve, punishing them for their rebelliousness. He treats "all those left in their sins with exact justice according to their own deserts, to the praise of his justice, which demands the punishment of all unexpiated sin."[16]

Reprobation—God's eternal choice to condemn the non-elect—is an extremely difficult doctrine. Two theologians assist us in understanding that God's righteous character is not impugned by this teaching. No one can charge God with injustice for his treatment of the non-elect, as J. V. Fesko argues:

> The point the [Westminster] divines implicitly make with such a distinction, namely, the predestination of the elect and the preterition of the non-elect, is that God does not treat both groups in the same way. God positively and actively brings about the salvation of the elect, but he does not positively and actively bring about the reprobation of the non-elect. To do this would make God the author of sin, something the Confession 3.1 explicitly denies.[17]

---

14. Ibid., 72.
15. Ibid., 74.
16. Ibid.
17. J. V. Fesko, *The Theology of the Westminster Standards: Historical Context and Theological Insights* (Wheaton, IL: Crossway, 2014), 120.

All mankind justly deserves condemnation for their sin. God intervenes and rescues the elect while he allows the non-elect to continue in their initial direction.

Robert Letham notes two aspects of reprobation: "Negatively, God has determined to withhold grace from the nonelect. Positively, he has ordained them to wrath and dishonor." But those who are "passed by are ordained to wrath *for their sin*." The Westminster divines taught "a marked disparity between election and preterition (passing by). The latter is directly connected with the sin of the nonelect and is in perfect accord with God's justice. Election, on the other hand, is entirely a matter of free grace and love."[18] We must remember that God never does evil. The non-elect get what they deserve, and so God is just. The elect receive the benefits of Christ's work on their behalf, and so God is gracious. The Judge of all the earth always does what is just (Gen. 18:25).

The final section of this chapter of the Confession insists that predestination must be taught with care, since it may be misunderstood and can be applied wrongly by Christians to their harm:

> The doctrine of this high mystery of predestination is to be
> handled with special prudence and care, that men, attending
> the will of God revealed in his Word, and yielding obedience
> thereunto, may, from the certainty of their effectual vocation,
> be assured of their eternal election. So shall this doctrine af-
> ford matter of praise, reverence, and admiration of God; and
> of humility, diligence, and abundant consolation to all that
> sincerely obey the gospel. (WCF 3.8)

Calvinists have regularly asserted that pastors and teachers should be cautious in their teaching of predestination, especially placing the stress—as Scripture does—on God's unconditional election of Christians as opposed to his punishment of the reprobate, which is not dealt with often in the Bible.[19]

Summary

Calvinists have labored to understand and explain the contours of predestination because they believe it is taught in Scripture. They have sought to follow the Bible's lead in emphasizing God's majestic glory in predestination, his gracious choosing of undeserving sinners to be his children, his passing over some sinners, and his use of means in bringing the elect to faith. It may seem like Calvinists are fixated on this doctrine. They are not. Few, if

---

18. Robert Letham, *The Westminster Assembly: Reading Its Theology in Historical Context* (Phillipsburg, NJ: P&R, 2009), 186–87 (italics original).

19. For example, Francis Turretin, *Institutes of Elenctic Theology*, trans. George Musgrave Giger, ed. James T. Dennison, Jr. (Phillipsburg, NJ: P&R, 1992), 1.331.

any, Calvinists have made predestination the center of their theology. When Calvin wrote his comprehensive account of Christian theology, for example, he did not discuss predestination until the end of the third book of four.[20] Calvinists have been compelled, though, to defend predestination because it so frequently has been attacked by opponents of the doctrine. And they have observed that predestination is not an isolated doctrine. It affects our view of God in his sovereign glory, our prayers, our trust in him, our evangelism and missions, our confidence when we feel spiritually depressed. Predestination is a worship-inspiring, hope-giving, joy-producing, evangelism-prompting doctrine. That is why Calvinists emphasize it.

REFLECTION QUESTIONS

1. What surprised you the most in the Westminster Confession of Faith's teaching on predestination?

2. Are there places where you think that the Confession is wrong on predestination? Where? Why?

3. Evaluate this comment from Chad Van Dixhoorn on the difference between Calvinism and Arminianism on predestination: "Consider too how God did not merely make salvation a possibility for all people (as our Arminian brethren teach), but a reality for his chosen people (as our Reformed fathers taught). That is to say, God did not build a wide bridge part-way to heaven. No, in Jesus Christ he built a secure bridge all the way to heaven."[21] Do you think he is right? Why?

4. Do you think the Confession and the theologians in this chapter were helpful in the way they discussed reprobation? Why?

5. Does the fact that God uses means to save the elect motivate you to share the gospel? Why?

---

20. John Calvin, *Institutes of the Christian Religion*, ed. John T. McNeill, trans. Ford Lewis Battles (Philadelphia: Westminster, 1960), 3.21–24.
21. Van Dixhoorn, *Confessing the Faith*, 58.

What Does the Bible Teach about Election and Predestination?

The Scripture unapologetically teaches that our God is a choosing Sovereign. His choosing, or election, of his people is asserted in both the Old Testament and the New Testament. It is a matter of praise and consolation that should produce humility among his children. Christians should not argue with God about his right to predestine his people, for were it not for the Lord's predestination no one would go to heaven.

Predestination and Election

Though the terms "predestination" and "election" are closely related in the Bible, they have slightly different meanings. Predestination refers to God's eternal determination for all human beings, elect and non-elect, as well as for angels. Robert L. Dabney calls it God's "purpose concerning the everlasting destiny of His rational creatures."[1] This includes those God will save as well as those whom he will condemn. Election is a subset of predestination, referring specifically to those whom God has chosen for salvation. Election, writes J. I. Packer, is "a gracious, sovereign, eternal choice of individual sinners to be saved and glorified in and through Christ."[2] The two words have slightly different meanings—this is why we speak of "unconditional election" (referring only to the elect) but "double predestination" (referring both to the elect and

---

1. Robert L. Dabney, *Systematic Theology*, 2nd ed. (1878; Edinburgh: Banner of Truth, 1985), 223.
2. J. I. Packer, "Election," in *New Bible Dictionary*, 2nd ed., ed. J. D. Douglas (Leicester: InterVarsity Press, 1982), 316. D. A. Carson offers a broader definition, calling predestination "the fore-ordination of events by God" while election "refers to soteriological predestination" (*Divine Sovereignty and Human Responsibility: Biblical Perspectives in Tension* [Grand Rapids: Baker, 1994], 2).

non-elect)—and are worth examining individually to see the Bible's teaching.[3] After our examination of the two words in the next section, I will generally employ them synonymously since their meanings overlap a great deal.

Predestination and Election in Scripture

God is always the subject of the verb *prohorizō* ("predestine") in the New Testament. Louis Berkhof notes, "The decree of predestination is undoubtedly in all its parts the concurrent act of the three persons in the Trinity, who are one in their counsel and will. But in the economy of salvation, as it is revealed in Scripture, the sovereign act of predestination is more particularly attributed to the Father, John 17:6, 9; Rom. 8:29; Eph. 1:4; I Pet. 1:2."[4] Three biblical texts are instructive.

In Romans 8:28, Paul encourages his Christian readers by noting that they can have confidence that all things will work together for their good. But that verse doesn't stand on its own. Paul gives them a reason—a "for" or "because"—they can be certain that this will happen. "*For* those whom he foreknew he also predestined to be conformed to the image of his Son, in order that he might be the firstborn among many brothers. And those whom he predestined he also called, and those whom he called he also justified, and those whom he justified he also glorified" (8:29–30). In this "golden chain of salvation," Paul says the bedrock of Christian assurance goes all the way back to eternity where God chose to place his love on his people (that's the meaning of "foreknowledge"). Because of his love, God decided to ordain them for salvation (predestining them to the image of Christ). The rest of the "chain" follows since it's grounded in the eternal decision of the omnipotent God. God loved his own from eternity; destined them for salvation; in time efficaciously called them to himself by his Spirit through the gospel; they believed and so were justified; and their eternal standing with him is so secure that he speaks of their future eternal status with him ("glorification") in the past tense. All good things come to God's people because of his gracious predestination.

We notice two additional instances of predestination language in Paul's great benediction in the opening chapter of Ephesians. In this hymn of praise ("Blessed be the God and Father our Lord Jesus Christ," 1:3), twice the apostle speaks of God's predestining his people for salvation. In love, he declares, God "predestined us for adoption through Jesus Christ, according to the purpose of his will" (1:5). In Christ, believers "have obtained an inheritance, having been predestined according to the purpose of him who works all things according to the counsel of his will" (1:11). We notice that God's predestination is purposeful (note the "purpose" and "counsel" of his will that guides his

---

3. As we noticed in the previous question, the Westminster divines preferred to speak of God's "predestination" of the elect and his "foreordination" of the non-elect.
4. Louis Berkhof, *Systematic Theology*, 4th ed. (Grand Rapids: Eerdmans, 1941), 112–13.

decision); it is also closely related to Jesus Christ; and it is guided by God's affection (it is done in love and it results in adoption).[5]

Election (*eklegomai* is the Greek verb) means that God chooses some for salvation. Berkhof calls it "that eternal act of God whereby He, in His sovereign good pleasure, and on account of no foreseen merit in them, chooses a certain number of men to be recipients of special grace and of eternal salvation."[6] The God of the Bible is a choosing God. He regularly—for his own good purpose and not owing to anything in the chosen one—selects one person or group of people over another. Israel's history proves this. God chose Abraham and his descendants. He made an everlasting covenant with him and his descendants, and promised that Abraham's seed should be a blessing to all the earth. God chose this particular group of people; he did not choose all the other families of the earth at that time.

Why did God choose them? "It was not because you were more in number than any other people that the LORD set his love on you and chose you, for you were the fewest of all peoples, but it is because the LORD loves you and is keeping the oath that he swore to your fathers" (Deut. 7:7–8). The Lord chose Israel simply because he loved them. Of course, this means there were numerous other peoples God did not choose, whom he did not love savingly.

Throughout the Old Testament, God discriminates, electing some and not others. For example, he chose Moses (Ps. 106:23), Aaron (Ps. 105:26), the priests (Deut. 18:5), the prophets (Jer. 1:5), the kings (1 Sam. 10:24; 2 Sam. 6:21), and the Messiah of Isaiah's prophecy ("Here is my servant, whom I uphold, my chosen one, in whom I delight" [Isa. 42:1]). God's choice brought blessing to the people of Israel. But his not choosing the rest of mankind meant that they were outside of salvation. The Gentiles who were not part of God's chosen people were "separated from Christ, alienated from the commonwealth of Israel and strangers to the covenants of promise, having no hope and without God in the world" (Eph. 2:12). The non-chosen had no hope. God's choosing a person or group has eternal consequences.

The New Testament also teaches election. Paul reminded the Corinthians that "God chose what is foolish in the world to the shame the wise; God chose what is weak in the world to shame the strong; God chose what is low and despised in the world, even things that are not, to bring to nothing things that are, so that no human being might boast in the presence of God" (1 Cor. 1:27–29). Peter urged his Christian readers to "make your calling and election sure" (2 Peter 1:10).

Jesus said, "many are called, but few are chosen" (Matt. 22:14). He did not pray for everyone's salvation but for those who belonged to the Father, or

---

5. Many of these same ideas are conveyed in the Old Testament as well. Consider, for example, Psalm 139:16 and Isaiah 46:9–11.

6. Berkhof, *Systematic Theology*, 114.

(which is the same thing) for those whom the Father had given to him: "I am not praying for the world but for those whom you have given me, for they are yours" (John 17:9). Similarly, Jesus clarified that unbelievers did not believe in him because the Father had not given them to the Son: "You do not believe because you are not among my sheep. My sheep hear my voice, and I know them, and they follow me. I give them eternal life, and they will never perish, and no one will snatch them out of my hand. My Father, who has given them to me, is greater than all, and no one is able to snatch them out of the Father's hand" (John 10:26–29). Jesus reiterates this point when he says, "All that the Father gives me will come to me, and whoever comes to me I will never cast out" (John 6:37). Who comes to Christ for salvation? Only the ones whom the Father has given to him, the ones he has chosen.

The Biblical Doctrine of Election

The Bible asserts that God's election is gracious, sovereign, individually-oriented, and for God's glory.[7] First, election is a gracious choice. Paul teaches in Romans 11:5 that "there is a remnant, chosen by grace." He tells Timothy that God "saved us and called us to a holy calling, not because of our works but because of his own purpose and grace, when he gave us in Christ Jesus before the ages began" (2 Tim. 1:9). Predestination is gracious because the objects of God's predestining love deserve nothing except his eternal condemnation. And it gives them every blessing—now and forever—that they can have in Christ. God's people have received awe-inspiring blessings from his predestination (Eph. 1:3–5), which is "to the praise of his glorious grace" (v. 6). Instead of the judgment we deserved, we received adoption—all because of God's grace.

Second, election is God's sovereign, purposeful choice. Nothing outside of him determines his choice. His choice flows out of "the purpose of his will" and is made "according to his purpose" (Eph. 1:5, 9). God's purpose alone leads to his choice. Francis Turretin reminds us that "purpose" (*prothesis*) "is often used by Paul in the matter of election to denote that this counsel of God is not an empty and inefficacious act of willing, but the constant, determined and immutable purpose of God (Rom. 8:28; 9:11; Eph. 1:11)."[8]

God's sovereign choice explains why some respond to the gospel summons. The non-elect sinner cannot believe in Christ on his or her own, as Paul notes: "The man without the Spirit does not accept the things that come from the Spirit of God, for they are foolishness to him, and he cannot understand them, because they are spiritually discerned" (1 Cor. 2:14). God, though, sovereignly gives his chosen ones faith (Eph. 2:8). "And as many as

---

7. I am here following Packer, "Election," 316–17.

8. Francis Turretin, *Institutes of Elenctic Theology*, trans. George Musgrave Giger, ed. James T. Dennison, Jr. (Phillipsburg, NJ: P&R, 1992), 1:334.

were appointed to eternal life believed" (Acts 13:48). "We know, brothers loved by God, that he has chosen you, because the gospel came to you not only in word, but also in power and in the Holy Spirit and with full conviction" (1 Thess. 1:4–5).

Third, election is God's choice of individuals through union with Christ. As Ephesians 1:3–14 proclaims, God has blessed them (v. 3), chosen them (vv. 4, 11), predestined them (v. 5), redeemed and forgiven them (v. 7), made known to them the mystery of his will (v. 9), and sealed them (v. 13). And in so doing, he has united them with Christ, who is the means by which he has done these things. Jesus, in fact, is the central character in this extended hymn of praise. Christians are blessed "in Christ" (v. 3), are chosen "in him" (v. 4), are given glorious grace "in the Beloved" (v. 6), have redemption "in him" (v. 7), have received the mystery which God purposed "in Christ" (v. 9), the mystery which unites all things together "in him" (v. 10), have an inheritance "in him" (v. 11), have put their hope "in Christ" (v. 12), have been sealed "in him" (v. 13), and have believed "in him" (v. 13). God's eternal choice, Christians' present belief, and their eternal hope—all these glorious realities find their focal point in Jesus.[9]

Fourth, election is praiseworthy, as Paul stresses in Ephesians. He calls believers to praise God (1:3), urging us to do so "to the praise of his glorious grace" (v. 6) and "to the praise of his glory" (vv. 12, 14). God's ultimate purpose in graciously resurrecting dead-in-sin persons through his grace, Paul teaches us, is "so that in the coming ages he might show the immeasurable riches of his grace in kindness toward us in Christ Jesus" (Eph. 2:7). Far from being a matter of speculation or debate—or even an issue to cause us to doubt God's justice or fairness in dealing with us—God's predestinating choice should lead his people to worship him.

Summary

The doctrine of election has attracted much unwarranted criticism over the centuries. Undoubtedly, there are many reasons for this censure. We cannot, though, escape the fact that the Bible teaches God's eternal election and predestination of individuals to salvation for his praise. And who would want to escape it really? For apart from our Father's eternal choice of us to

---

9. Van Dixhoorn points out the significance that God predestined the elect "in Christ." This matters since Jesus "is the chosen one of God, the foreordained one, and we are saved as we are united to him." Paul taught this in several places: "We are 'predestined . . . through Jesus Christ' (Eph. 1:5), his purpose for us is 'set forth in Christ' (Eph. 1:9), his grace is given us 'in Christ Jesus before the ages began' (2 Tim. 1:9). In short, 'God has not destined us for wrath, but to obtain salvation through our Lord Jesus Christ' (1 Thess. 5:9)" (Chad Van Dixhoorn, *Confessing the Faith: A Reader's Guide to the Westminster Confession of Faith* [Edinburgh: Banner of Truth, 2014], 51).

salvation no one would be saved. And apart from his choice, no one we share the gospel with would ever respond in faith.

REFLECTION QUESTIONS

1. In your own words define "predestination" and "election." Do you think it's worth keeping the two concepts separate? Why?

2. Can you think of biblical texts that contradict the doctrine defended in this chapter? How do they do that?

3. Can you think of additional biblical texts that support the doctrine defended in this chapter? How do they do that?

4. If you agree with the doctrine defended here, why do you think other born again Christians disagree with it?

5. Does the doctrine of election spur you on to do evangelism? Why? Do you think it encouraged the apostles? Why?

Is Election Unconditional?

God eternally chose his people for salvation apart from anything they would do. Indeed, they were unable to do anything good—even having the smallest amount of faith in Christ—because they were dead in sin (Eph. 2:3) and could not obey God (Rom. 8:7–8). To buttress human autonomy and because they misunderstand the meaning of "foreknowledge," Arminians propound conditional election. That is the belief that God elects some people on the condition of his prior knowledge of their faith in Christ. Yet, the Bible teaches the opposite. God's choice of his people is not conditioned upon anything they do. Divine election is unconditional.

Unconditional Election in the Bible

Bruce Ware defines unconditional election as

> God's gracious choice, made in eternity past, of those whom he would save by faith through the atoning death of his Son, a choice based not upon anything that those so chosen would do, or any choice that they would make, or on how good or bad they might be, or on anything else specifically true about them (i.e., their qualities, characters, decisions, or actions) in contrast to others, but rather based only upon God's own good pleasure and will.[1]

There is no place for any human effort—whether faith, obedience, or perseverance, or any combination of them—as the reason for God's predestination

---

1. Bruce A. Ware, "Divine Election to Salvation: Unconditional, Individual, and Infralapsarian," in *Perspectives on Election: Five Views*, ed. Chad Owen Brand (Nashville: B&H, 2006), 4.

of the elect. He chooses to love them because that was his choice, not because he foreknew what they would do.

Ephesians 1:3–11 proves the unconditionality of election in three ways. First, God's election is eternal: "he chose us in him before the foundation of the world" (v. 4). Greg Welty observes that "God's action of election does not await our fulfillment of certain conditions."[2] Second, election is personal. God chose and predestined "us" (vv. 4, 5). "We" were predestined (v. 11). The Lord did not choose an abstract group that would be populated by those who met his condition for salvation. Rather, he chose particular individuals to be Christians. Welty's critique of Arminianism in this regard is cogent:

> God did not choose abstract categories or hypothetical con-
> ditionals and say, 'I thus choose you, O abstract category or
> hypothetical conditional! Whoever ends up having faith in
> Christ will end up being saved.' . . . Interesting theory, but far
> from the thought of the apostle Paul. God elects people, not
> categories or conditions.[3]

Third, election is grounded in God's will, not a human choice. "Paul repeatedly and emphatically draws our attention to *God's* will as the foundation of our salvation."[4] The apostle's exclamations that we were chosen "according to the purpose of his will" (v. 5), on the basis of "the mystery of his will . . . according to his purpose" (v. 9), and especially that we were predestined "according to the purpose of him who works all things according to the counsel of his will" (v. 11) establishes that God's choice, not ours, is the foundation of election.

Unconditional election is taught throughout the New Testament. In John 17:2, Jesus says of himself to the Father, "You have given him authority over all flesh, to give eternal life to all whom you have given him." Verses 6, 9, and 24 repeat the same idea. Ware comments,

> Just as the disciples become the disciples because the Father
> gives these ones to Jesus, so also all future believers come
> to believe in Christ through the message of the disciples be-
> cause God has given these to his Son. Belief is necessary, to
> be sure. But those who believe are those given to Christ by
> the Father. The unconditional election of the Father, then,

2. Greg Welty, "Election and Calling: A Biblical Theological Study," in *Calvinism: A Southern Baptist Dialogue*, eds. E. Ray Clendenen and Brad J. Waggoner (Nashville: B&H, 2008), 218.
3. Ibid.
4. Ibid., 219 (italics original).

accounts for the subsequent faith and salvation of those to whom the Son grants eternal life.[5]

Acts 13:48 also teaches unconditional election, for Luke reports that "as many as were appointed to eternal life believed." There is no way around the order of thought to arrive at Arminian conclusions.[6] Rather, "God's appointment of those who would receive eternal life preceded the belief of these very people."[7] Andrew Davis notes of this verse: "God is the agent, and He ordained or appointed these people for eternal life before the foundation of the world, and as a result of that, they believed the gospel that Paul and Barnabas preached that day. Election is the cause of faith, not the other way around."[8] Second Timothy 1:9 likewise asserts that God appointed his own to salvation "before the ages began." Ware observes that since "no one existed when God's election took place, God's election of those whom he would save simply could not have to do with something about them."[9] The elect were chosen by their sovereign Father unconditionally.

Biblical texts that teach that "election is the ground of faith" also communicate unconditional election since faith is the condition of salvation. If God chooses to give faith unconditionally, his choice of some for salvation is likewise unconditional. Davis highlights two texts. On James 2:5 ("Listen, my beloved brothers, has not God chosen those who are poor in the world to be rich in faith and heirs of the kingdom, which he has promised"), he comments, "The order of this verse is election first, faith next." Second Thessalonians 2:13 ("But we ought always to give thanks to God for you, brothers beloved by the Lord, because God chose you as the firstfruits to be saved, through sanctification by the Spirit and belief in the truth") garners this comment: "Election precedes faith and is the ground if it. God elected them for final salvation, and therefore He elects that they will have faith. Election is the cause of faith, not the other way around."[10] John Murray similarly observes that "the faith which God foresees is the faith he himself creates (cf. John 3:3–8; 6:44, 45, 65; Eph. 2:8; Phil. 1:29; II Pet. 1:2). Hence his eternal foresight of faith is preconditioned by his decree to generate this faith."[11] The Bible unswervingly teaches unconditional election.

---

5. Ware, "Divine Election," 7.
6. One Arminian reverses the logical order of Luke's words here, maintaining that "the Gentiles believed and entered the category of the appointed ones" (William W. Klein, *The New Chosen People: A Corporate View of Election* [Grand Rapids: Zondervan, 1990], 121). See Ware, "Divine Election to Salvation," 8 n. 7.
7. Ware, "Divine Election," 8.
8. Andrew M. Davis, "Unconditional Election: A Biblical and God-Glorifying Doctrine," in *Whomever He Wills: A Surprising Display of Sovereign Mercy*, eds. Matthew M. Barrett and Thomas J. Nettles (Cape Coral: Founders, 2012), 67.
9. Ware, "Divine Election," 15.
10. Davis, "Unconditional Election," 66–68.
11. John Murray, *The Epistle to the Romans* (Grand Rapids: Eerdmans, 1968), 316.

Answering Arminian "Foreknowledge" Objections

However, that's not the stance of Arminians. For example, Jack Cottrell estimates that God's predestining work is based upon his prior knowledge of free human choices, saying the Lord

> does not predestine certain unbelievers to become believers and the rest to remain in their unbelief. Those who accept Christ through faith do so of their own free choice. Their choice of Jesus Christ is not predestined. That choice, however, is foreknown; and as a result the choosing ones become the chosen ones, who are then predestined to receive the full blessings of salvation.[12]

Roger Olson concurs, reporting that Arminians "believe that God foreknows every person's ultimate and final decision regarding Jesus Christ, and on that basis God predestines people to salvation or damnation. But Arminians do not believe God predetermines or preselects people for either heaven or hell apart from their free acts of accepting or resisting the grace of God."[13] Arminians thus assert conditional election, the view that God's eternal choice is conditioned upon something he sees in the individual.

Arminians teach that God elects according to his foreknowledge of those who will receive the gospel. This seems reasonable based on the English word: the suffix "fore" (i.e., prior) plus "knowledge" (i.e., awareness of a fact). The problem with this interpretation, though, is at least threefold. First, "know" in the Bible often has connotations not of intellectual awareness but of loving the chosen one. Older translations alluded to this when they said a husband went into his home and "knew" his wife, meaning not that he had an intellectual conversation with her but that he had intimate sexual relations with her. He loved her. So "Adam knew Eve his wife, and she conceived, and bare Cain" (Gen. 4:1 KJV). Amos 3:2, where the Lord says of Israel, "you only have I known of all the families of the earth," is also instructive. Clearly Yahweh had cognizance of other peoples, but he knew Israel in the sense that he had set his affection upon her. This is why the NIV translates this as "you only have I chosen of all the families of the earth." John Murray observes, "Many times in Scripture 'know' has a pregnant meaning which goes beyond that of mere cognition. It is used in a sense practically synonymous with 'love', to set regard upon, to know with peculiar interest, delight, affection, and action."[14] After a

---

12. Jack W. Cottrell, "The Classical Arminian View of Election," in *Perspectives on Election: Five Views*, ed. Chad Owen Brand (Nashville: B&H, 2006), 81.
13. Roger E. Olson, *Arminian Theology: Myths and Realities* (Downers Grove, IL: InterVarsity Press, 2006), 180.
14. Murray, *Romans*, 317 (referencing Gen. 18:19; Exod. 2:25; Ps. 1:6; 144:3; Jer. 1:5; Amos 3:2; Hos. 13:5; Matt. 7:23; 1 Cor. 8:3; Gal. 4:9; 2 Tim. 2:19; and 1 John 3:1).

careful consideration of "know" in the Old Testament and "foreknow" in the New Testament, S. M. Baugh concludes that the meaning is one of personal commitment: "It would be best to say that phrase *God knows us* expresses a relationship of commitment."[15]

Second, the grammar of Romans 8:28–30 refutes the Arminian notion of predestination according to foreknowledge. Christians can be certain that God works everything for their good (v. 28) because of God's foreknowledge-predestination-calling-justification-glorification (vv. 29–30). Foreknowledge, then, begins this irrevocable series of events from eternity past to eternity future. The apostle doesn't tell us that God knew that the elect would receive Jesus and so he predestined them. Instead, he penned, "*whom* he foreknew he predestined" (v. 29). "Whom" is a relative pronoun, telling us that persons—not something they were to do—were the object of God's loving choice.[16] Paul teaches that God knew the elect from eternity in the sense that he loved them. Welty comments, "God foreknows individuals, which is to say He *foreloves* them; and in virtue of that special, distinguishing love, He marks them out for a peculiar destiny."[17]

Third, if God elects us according to his prior knowledge of our choice, our salvation is dependent to some degree on us. In this sense, we can't say that it ultimately is "to the praise of his glorious grace" (Eph. 1:6). D. A. Carson illustrates this by noting that five prisoners accepting a pardon of forgiveness "are distinguishable from [five others] who reject the offer solely on the basis of their own decision to accept the pardon. The only thing that separates them from those who are carted off to prison is the wisdom of their own choice. That becomes a legitimate boast. By contrast, in the Calvinistic scheme, the sole determining factor is God's elective grace."[18] According to Arminianism, believers can boast in their salvation in comparison to others' damnation. This overturns God's sovereign grace that effectively accomplishes the salvation of his beloved ones. "What do you have that you did not receive? If then you received it, why do you boast as if you did not receive it?" (1 Cor. 4:7).

Even though Arminians sometimes charge that holding to unconditional election will hamper our evangelism and missions, it actually empowers us to share the gospel indiscriminately. Consider Paul, the same apostle who said "whom he foreknew he also predestined." This Paul taught that persons needed to be confronted with the gospel and call on Jesus to be saved (Rom. 10:8–17).

---

15. S. M. Baugh, "The Meaning of Foreknowledge," in *Still Sovereign: Contemporary Perspectives on Election, Foreknowledge, and Grace*, eds. Thomas R. Schreiner and Bruce A. Ware (Grand Rapids: Baker, 2000), 193 (italics original).

16. Murray, *Romans*, 316–17.

17. Welty, "Election and Calling," 224 (italics original). The Old Testament background in which the Lord tells his people he chose them simply because he loved them (e.g., Deut. 7:6–8; 10:15–16) and Jesus's warning to those whom he never knew (Matt. 7:23) confirms this understanding (ibid., 224–25).

18. D. A. Carson, *Exegetical Fallacies*, 2nd ed. (Grand Rapids: Baker, 1996), 121–22.

He lived that way too (Rom. 15:17–24). In Acts, for instance, we see him constantly reasoning with his listeners, urging them to listen to what he is saying (e.g., Acts 13:38–41), and holding them accountable for whether they obey the gospel or not (13:46) while at the same time being confident that among all his listeners "as many as were appointed to eternal life believed" (13:48). He reasoned with his listeners (17:17) and commanded them to repent (17:30–31). He took his role as ambassador so seriously that he was once stoned for preaching and left for dead (14:19); within a matter of days he was preaching again (14:20–21)! This same apostle who took people's responsibility to respond to the gospel seriously (20:20–21; 26:24–29) also believed that God's unconditional election was an incentive to evangelism (18:6–11). Rather than seeing this biblical doctrine as a hindrance to evangelism, then, we should follow Paul's example, taking to heart that God has chosen a people and calls us to preach the gospel indiscriminately to everyone so that the elect will hear, believe, and be saved.

Summary
The biblical doctrine of unconditional election highlights that salvation is from the Lord (Jonah 2:9) who in love chose us when we were dead in sin (Eph. 1:4–5; 2:3). It is a glorious act of his sovereign, loving, good pleasure that should give us comfort (Rom. 8:28), produce humility (1 Cor. 4:7), lead us to praise God (Eph. 1:6), and empower us to take the gospel to the ends of the earth (Acts 13:48).

REFLECTION QUESTIONS

1. How would you define "unconditional election" in your own words?

2. Do you think there are significant arguments against unconditional election? If so, what are they?

3. How would you respond to Arminian objections that unconditional election violates true human freedom?

4. How does Ephesians 1:3–11 help to establish the doctrine of unconditional election?

5. Do you agree with D. A. Carson's illustration that apart from unconditional election, Christians have reason to boast of their salvation? Why?

Is Predestination Fair?

In the Bible, predestination serves several purposes. It should lead us to worship the God who saves (Eph. 1:3–14). It should cause us to thank God for his electing love (1 Thess. 1:2–5). It explains people's rejection of the gospel (Matt. 11:25–30), while giving us hope that some we share with will come to faith (Acts 13:48). It should humble us (Rom. 9:19–21). But the Bible never presents predestination as a doctrine that should make us question God's fairness. It is fair for God to predestine the eternal destinies of all people.

Arminian Critiques

No Calvinistic teaching has been criticized as much as the doctrine of predestination. Arminians attack what they see as the arbitrariness of the doctrine, as well as its double nature—for in choosing one person for eternal life, God did not choose another who was equally unworthy of salvation. This was John Wesley's critique in his mis-named *Predestination Calmly Considered*.[1] To him, Calvinism's understanding of predestination logically had to include God eternally decreeing to damn the non-elect: "You know if God hath fixed a decree that *these men only* shall be saved, in such a decree it is manifestly implied that *all other men* shall be damned."[2] Since double predestination calls the character of God into question, it is wrong. We can summarize Wesley's argument in the form of a syllogism:

---

1. Packer shrewdly observes, "Many of its words are in capital letters and it is filled with exclamation marks! For some reason [Wesley] found it hard to be calm when he discussed this subject. Others, too, have had this problem" (J. I. Packer, "Predestination in Christian History," in *Honouring the People of God: Collected Shorter Writings of J. I. Packer, Vol. 4* [Carlisle, UK: Paternoster, 1999], 215).
2. John Wesley, *Predestination Calmly Considered*, in *John Wesley*, ed. Albert C. Outler (New York: Oxford University Press, 1964), 432 (italics original).

Major premise: unconditional predestination logically requires unconditional reprobation.

Minor premise: reprobation is contrary to what the Bible reveals of the character of God.

Conclusion: therefore, unconditional predestination is an unbiblical doctrine.

Wesley exclaimed, "Unconditional election I cannot believe, not only because I cannot find it in Scripture, but also (to waive all other considerations) because it necessarily implies unconditional reprobation. *Find out any election which does not imply reprobation and I will gladly agree to it.*"[3] Roger Olson concurs with Wesley since, to him, double predestination "cannot be reconciled with the character of God revealed in Jesus Christ, who wept over Jerusalem when its inhabitants did not accept him as their Messiah."[4] Calvinistic double predestination is nonsensical, "a sacrifice of the intellect."[5] Calvinism's appeal to mystery regarding God's dealings with the non-elect, he characterizes as a "blatant contradiction."[6]

Calvinists and Double Predestination

Calvinists have never emphasized double predestination nor have they explained it as crassly as the Arminians noted above. The Synod of Dort, for example, explains,

> The fact that some receive from God the gift of faith within time, and that others do not, stems from his eternal decision. For all his works are known to God from eternity (Acts 15:18; Ephesians 1:11). In accordance with this decision he graciously softens the heart, however hard, of his chosen ones and inclines them to believe, but by his just judgment he leaves in their wickedness and hardness of heart those who have not been chosen. And in this especially is disclosed to us his act—unfathomable, and as merciful as it is just—of distinguishing between people equally lost. This is the well-known decision of election and reprobation revealed in God's Word.[7]

---

3. Ibid., 434 (italics original).
4. Roger Olson, *Against Calvinism* (Grand Rapids: Zondervan, 2011), 103.
5. Ibid., 107.
6. Ibid., 105.
7. *The Canons of Dort* 1.6, in Matthew Barrett, *The Grace of Godliness: An Introduction to Doctrine and Piety in the Canons of Dort* (Kitchener, Canada: Joshua, 2013), 160–61. Also see, e.g., R. C. Sproul, *Chosen by God*, rev. ed. (Carol Stream, IL: Tyndale House, 1986), 119.

We see, first, that the in-time decisions of persons (elect and reprobate alike) are rooted in God's eternal decree. He is not determined by them; they are determined by him. Second, God acts consistently with his holiness—graciously towards the elect, and justly towards the non-elect. Third, he acts differently towards the two groups—he changes the elects' hearts, while he chooses not to act upon the non-elect. All this shows that God is a God who distinguishes "between people equally lost."

Double predestination means that God has eternally determined the final destiny of both Christians and non-Christians (often called the "reprobate"). Calvinists, though, disagree about exactly how to formulate the doctrine. Robert Dabney, for example, thought that "preterition" (i.e., God's leaving the non-elect to bear the consequences of their sin) was true. But he denied God's "pre-damnation" of the reprobate since it seemed to make God at least partly responsible for their sin.[8] Louis Berkhof, on the other hand, argued for both preterition and God's eternal decree of the "precondemnation" of the non-elect. He comments, "We are not warranted in excluding" precondemnation "from the decree of reprobation, nor to regard it as a different decree. The positive side of reprobation is so clearly taught in Scripture as the opposite of election that we cannot regard it as something purely negative."[9] He explains, "Since the Bible is primarily a revelation of redemption, it naturally does not have as much to say about reprobation as about election. But what it says is quite sufficient."[10]

Calvinists, like the Bible, stress God's mercy in saving any in election. Nonetheless, they see in Scripture several instances which speak of God's active relation to the non-elect. Herman Bavinck notes many biblical texts that inform this doctrine:

> [God] makes weal and creates woe; he forms the light and creates the darkness (Isa. 45:7; Amos 3:6); he creates the wicked for the day of evil (Prov. 16:4), does whatever he pleases (Ps. 115:3), does according to his will among the inhabitants of the earth (Dan. 4:35), inclines the heart of all humans as he wills (Prov. 16:9; 21:1), and orders their steps (Prov. 20:24; Jer. 10:23). Out of the same lump of clay he makes one vessel for beauty and another for menial use (Jer. 18; Rom. 9:20–24), has compassion upon whomever he wills and hardens the heart of whomever he wills (Rom. 9:18). He destines some people to disobedience (1 Pet. 2:8), designates some

---

8. Robert L. Dabney, *Systematic Theology* (1871; Edinburgh: Banner of Truth, 1985), 239.
9. Louis Berkhof, *Systematic Theology*, 4th ed. (Grand Rapids: Eerdmans, 1941), 116.
10. Ibid., 118.

for condemnation (Jude 4), and refrains from recording the names of some in the Book of Life (Rev. 13:8; 17:8).[11]

Romans 9:6–29 is certainly the "central passage on reprobation," and therefore on double predestination.[12] The context is significant because, after Paul's exclamation that God will always keep his people (8:31–39), the apostle anticipates a question. How can these gospel truths be true if God has deserted his people, Israel? Can he be trusted to keep his promises (9:1–6)? Yes, Paul urges, because ethnicity is not what determines whom God will save. Being a descendent of Abraham never led to heaven (9:6–9). Rather, God has always had a chosen people, even among ethnic Jews—Isaac, not Ishmael; Jacob, not Esau. God's sovereign choice alone determines who experiences salvation (9:9–11). Election is not based on any works of the individual—either works done in the past or foreseen to be done. This is why Paul stresses in the case of the twins that God's choice occurred before they were born or had done anything either good or bad (9:11). Douglas Moo stresses that "God's purpose in election is established not simply by virtue of God's prediction of Jacob's prominence over Esau, but by the fact that this prediction was made apart from any basis in the personal circumstances of Jacob and Esau."[13]

Election is not based on any efforts on man's part to secure God's favor (9:15–18). In his freedom, God treats some sinners as they deserve. He raises up Pharaoh and hardens him and others as he desires: "So then he has mercy on whomever he wills, and he hardens whomever he wills" (9:18). Moo is right that the hardening "is a sovereign act of God that is not *caused* by anything in those individuals who are hardened."[14] Thomas Schreiner aptly comments that

> Pharaoh was raised up for judgment. A careful analysis of the OT text also reveals that God's hardening of Pharaoh precedes and undergirds Pharaoh's self-hardening. . . . One cannot elude the conclusion that Paul teaches double predestination here, and this is not contrary to the gospel, but it secures the theme that faith is wholly a gift of God.[15]

---

11. Herman Bavinck, *Reformed Dogmatics*, vol. 2, *God and Creation*, ed. John Bolt, trans. John Vriend (Grand Rapids: Baker, 2004), 341. He actually lists many other biblical references to this effect.

12. John M. Frame, *Systematic Theology: An Introduction to Christian Belief* (Phillipsburg, NJ: P&R, 2013), 222.

13. Douglas J. Moo, *The Epistle to the Romans*, New International Commentary on the New Testament (Grand Rapids: Eerdmans, 1996), 580.

14. Ibid., 598 (italics original).

15. Thomas R. Schreiner, *Romans*, Baker Exegetical Commentary on the New Testament (Grand Rapids: Baker, 1998), 510.

The Lord ultimately destroys Pharaoh and others for their sin (9:21–22). Yet, in his sovereign freedom, the Lord selects some out of the mass of sinful humanity for salvation:

> Has not the potter no right over the clay, to make out of the same lump one vessel for honored use and another for dishonorable use? What if God, desiring to show his wrath and to make known his power, has endured with much patience vessels of wrath prepared for destruction, in order to make known the riches of his glory for vessels of mercy, which he has prepared beforehand for glory? (Rom. 9:21–23)

Schreiner is perceptive: "By definition the Creator has absolute freedom to do what he wants with his creatures, just as a potter exercises sovereignty over the clay he forms."[16] There is no injustice in this, since Paul argues throughout this chapter that the Creator owes mercy to no one. In other words, "God's hardening does not, then, *cause* spiritual insensitivity to the things of God; it maintains people in the state of sin that already characterizes them."[17] God's sovereign plan is what determines whom he will save. At the same time Paul holds humans responsible for their choices (see Rom. 10:8–17).

Romans 9 teaches a double predestination that both highlights God's rights over his creatures and reminds us that we're all responsible individuals. Paul's purpose in highlighting it is to buttress his assertion in Romans 8 that God will always protect his children. He also intended it as support for indiscriminate gospel preaching, as Romans 10 shows.

So, Is It Fair?

We are now ready to answer the question before us. Our fundamental presupposition is that God never does anything wrong. Predestination, then, is just since it's revealed in Scripture and since it's an action of the holy God. God's grace in salvation is "right," "just," and "good." Grace and predestination to life are not "fair," though, because the elect receive what they do not deserve. With these preliminary observations in mind, we can respond to the question in at least five different ways.

First, *the* question is what does the Bible say, not what do I think the Bible should say. He's the Creator; we're his creatures. He's the potter; we're the clay. He determines what is right; we don't. We must seek to understand the Bible on this topic, not import our ideas of what God can and can't do.

Second, we must fight against any tendencies to consider God as a blind force, perhaps even an out-of-control power. That is not who he is. As we

---

16. Ibid., 516.
17. Moo, *Romans*, 599 (italics original).

strive to submit to his revelation of himself to us in Scripture, we need to hold on to the fact that he is personal, loving, feeling, and compassionate as well as sovereign, all-knowing, and eternal.[18] God is love (1 John 4:8). He is "the LORD, a God merciful and gracious, slow to anger, and abounding in steadfast love and faithfulness" (Exod. 34:6).

Third, we must always remember the fundamental asymmetry between election and reprobation. The non-elect receive exactly what they deserve. Their sin does not flow from the Lord; it flows from themselves and they are responsible for it. They will be condemned not for what God did to them but for their own rebellion. They will receive justice. The elect, on the other hand, are saved purely as a result of God's gracious intervention in their lives. They receive what they don't deserve. In neither case is God unjust. He chooses to save some of those who deserve condemnation but not all. Why he loves some savingly but not others, we don't know. "The secret things belong to the LORD our God" (Deut. 29:29). "Who has known the mind of the Lord, or who has been his counselor?" (Rom. 11:34).

Fourth, Arminians have problems with predestination. In their scheme, God knows the future perfectly—including who will and will not freely choose Christ and who will be punished eternally for their sins. Yet, knowing all this, God still chooses to create the world, give people free will, and punish those who don't receive Jesus. But he didn't have to. He could have chosen not to create the world in order not to condemn anyone eternally. At the end of the day, Arminians struggle with salvation's "fairness" as much as they think Calvinists do.

Fifth, the Bible is fundamentally a message of redemption. Berkhof was right that there are relatively few biblical texts that speak of God's eternal relationship to the non-elect. Rather than letting predestination, then, become a doctrine that makes us question God's goodness or that leads us to stop sharing the gospel, we should be spurred on like Paul with the truth that the Lord has his people and we have the privilege of speaking the gospel to everyone, telling them to repent and trust in Jesus and warning them of judgement to come.[19] God's sovereignty in salvation guards our proclamation of the gospel and reminds us that our heavenly Father has shown "his love for us in that while we were sinners, Christ died for us" (Rom. 5:8).

REFLECTION QUESTIONS

1. Do you agree with Wesley's evaluation of Calvinism's doctrine of predestination? Why?

---

18. See Question 5.
19. See Questions 36 and 37.

2. Do you think Dort's explanation of the doubleness of predestination is biblical? Why?

3. Do you prefer Dabney's or Berkhof's understanding of God's eternal relationship with the non-elect noted above? Why?

4. What other aspects of Romans 9–11 influence the fairness of God's predestination? Does Ezekiel 18:25–29 affect your thinking about God's fairness? How?

5. In your own words, can you explain why Arminians also struggle with the fairness of salvation?

The Extent of Christ's Atonement

Did Jesus Die for the Sins of the Whole World?

The extent of the atonement has been the most debated of the five points of Calvinism because of the Bible's assertion, for instance, that Jesus died "for the sins of the whole world" (1 John 2:2). Many Christians thus reject the "L" (limited atonement) of Calvinism. After noticing the New Testament texts usually assembled to argue for unlimited atonement, we will see how two different groups—Arminians and "multiple-intention" Calvinists—dispute limited atonement. Our desire is largely to explain these views, but we will also point out their deficiencies as we go along. The next three chapters will positively develop the biblical doctrine of definite atonement.

"Universal" Texts

Numerous New Testament texts seem to teach a universal atonement.[1]

- Behold, the Lamb of God, who takes away the sin of *the world*! (John 1:29)
- For in [Christ] all the fullness of God was pleased to dwell, and through him to reconcile to himself *all things*, whether on earth or in heaven, making peace by the blood of his cross. (Col. 1:19–20)
- This is good, and it is pleasing in the sight of God our Savior, who desires *all people* to be saved and to come to the knowledge of the truth. (1 Tim. 2:4)
- For to this end we toil and strive, because we have our hope set on the living God, who is the Savior of *all people*, especially of those who believe. (1 Tim. 4:10)

---

1. Italics have been added to the following Bible quotations.

- But we see him who for a little while was made lower than the angels, namely Jesus, crowned with glory and honor because of the suffering of death, so that by the grace of God he might taste death for *everyone*. (Heb. 2:9)
- But false prophets also arose among the people, just as there will be false teachers among you, who will secretly bring in destructive heresies, even denying the Master who *bought them*, bringing upon themselves swift *destruction*. (2 Peter 2:1)
- [Jesus Christ] is the propitiation for our sins, and not for ours only but also for the sins of *the whole world*. (1 John 2:2)

Others, like John 3:16 and 2 Peter 3:9, will be addressed later.[2] Still others, such as Romans 5:18 and 2 Corinthians 5:14–15, are not powerful arguments for the unlimited view because, read in an unlimited light, they argue not for evangelical universal atonement but for universalism, the belief that all persons are going to heaven. These texts demonstrate that the Bible often refers to "fewer than every single individual" when it says, "all."

Arminianism's Universal Atonement

Arminians take the "universal" texts literally. They truly mean that Jesus died in the same way for every human being. To protect themselves from becoming universalists, Arminians then assert that the atonement of Jesus was universal but not efficacious in itself. Something else had to happen in order to make it effective to bring salvation to people. That something else is the individual's belief which then brings the atoning work of Christ into the person's life. Thus, according to Roger Olsen, "Arminians believe that Christ's death on the cross provided *possible* salvation for everyone, but it is actualized only when humans accept it through repentance and faith."[3] Arminians, he explains, "do believe that Christ died for everyone, but the benefit of his death (setting aside condemnation for actual sins, in contrast to Adamic sin) is applied by God only to those who repent and believe."[4]

Arminius himself held to universal atonement, the belief "that, according to the Scriptures, Christ died for all people without prejudice to anyone and that his death satisfied the demands of justice for those who believe."[5] Referencing John 1:29; 3:16; 4:42; 6:51; 2 Corinthians 5:19, and 1 John 2:2; 4:14, Arminius argued,

---

2. See Question 34.
3. Roger E. Olson, *Arminian Theology: Myths and Realities* (Downers Grove, IL: InterVarsity Press, 2006), 222 (italics original).
4. Ibid., 223.
5. Ibid., 226.

It is manifest, as well from these passages as from the usage of Scripture, that by the word "world" in those places is meant simply the whole body of mankind. But, in my opinion, there is no place in all Scripture in which it can be shown beyond all controversy that the word "world" signifies *the elect*. Christ is said to have died *for all*. (Heb. ii. 9, and elsewhere.) He is called "the Saviour of *all men*, specially of those that believe;" (1 Tim. iv. 10) which expression cannot, without twisting and injury, be explained respecting conservation in this life.[6]

The New Testament, however, knows nothing of *possible* salvation flowing from Christ's death. "Christ also suffered once for sins, the righteous for the unrighteous, that he might bring us to God" (1 Peter 3:18). Jesus did not make salvation possible for everyone; he actually saves. As the following three chapters will prove, on the cross Jesus truly substituted himself for those for whom he intended to die. And he truly bore the penalty for their sin so that there was nothing left for them to do to obtain the salvation procured for them. This leads to the fundamental dilemma for the Arminian view of the atonement, as John Owen maintained:

God imposed his wrath due unto, and Christ underwent the pains of hell for, either all the sins of all men, or all the sins of some men, or some sins of all men. . . . If the first [the Arminian position], why, then, are not all freed from the punishment of all their sins? You will say, "Because of their unbelief; they will not believe." But this unbelief, is it a sin, or not? If not, why should they be punished for it? If it be, then Christ underwent the punishment due to it, or not. If so, then why must that hinder them more than their other sins for which he died from partaking of the fruit of his death? If he did not, then did he not die for all their sins.[7]

Owen is correct. Arminians cannot have it both ways. If Jesus died for all the sins of everyone, then everyone must go to heaven. Yet, this is unbiblical universalism. If they maintain that he died for all sins but unbelief, then he did not atone for that sin and the sinner must do something to merit his or

6. James Arminius, "Examination of Dr. Perkins's Pamphlet on Predestination," in *The Works of James Arminius*, eds. James Nichols and William Nichols (1875; Grand Rapids: Baker, 1986), 3:329 (italics original); quoted in ibid., 226.

7. John Owen, *Salus Electorum, Sanguis Jesu; or, The Death of Death in the Death of Christ*, in *The Works of John Owen* (1647; Carlisle, PA: Banner of Truth, 1967), 10:173–74.

her salvation. This seems to be both works righteousness and a slighting of the fullness of Christ's atonement.

"Multiple-Intention" Atonement

The "multiple-intentions" view is a modified Calvinistic position for it holds that Christ died for the elect. More than that, though, Jesus died for the sins of all the world and in order to make cosmic redemption. John Hammett argues that the typical question, "For whom did Christ die?," needs to be expanded to answer the more biblical query, "What did God intend to accomplish by Christ's death?"[8] He answers his question in this way: "there are three intentions in the atonement: universal, particular, and cosmic. . . . the atonement is in some sense universal and in some sense particular, but *multiple-intentions* best comprehends all of the biblical teaching on the atonement, particularly biblical teaching on the extent of the atonement."[9] His key argument for holding both to limited and unlimited atonement is that "salvation involves both a divine provision and a human appropriation. Even if the human appropriation is a divine gift or divinely enabled, it is still separate from the provision. Thus, the divine provision can be universal without resulting in universal salvation."[10]

This view has the advantage of seeming to take both the "particular" and the "universalistic" texts seriously. Hammett notes that "by far the most important advantage is that it allows for the most natural exegesis both to universal and to particular texts. It also allows for a clear and unmistakable basis for calling all to repentance and faith and for affirming that Christ has secured the salvation of the elect in his atonement." In other words, his view has "all the virtues of both traditional positions with few of the problems of either."[11] We will notice how he understands some central texts.

Second Peter 2:1 speaks of "false prophets" and "false teachers" "who will secretly bring in destructive heresies, even denying the Master who bought them, bringing upon them swift destruction." Hammett claims that Christ

> "bought" the false teachers in a soteriological sense; that is, they were included in the universal provision Christ made on the cross. But they never personally appropriated that provision, so they were never saved. . . . Are there some for whom Christ died who will in the end be lost? This is certainly what 2 Pet 2:1 seems to affirm.[12]

---

8. John S. Hammett, "Multiple-Intentions View of the Atonement," in *Perspectives on the Atonement: Three Views*, eds. Andrew David Naselli and Mark A. Snoeberger (Nashville: B&H, 2015), 148.

9. Ibid., 149 (italics original).

10. Ibid., 153.

11. Ibid., 183.

12. Ibid., 155.

He rejects the interpretation that these false teachers merely seemed to be Christians to the church members, because that interpretation

> seems to appeal mainly to those who approach the verse with a commitment to definite atonement. But when a commitment to a theological position requires one to deny what a verse straightforwardly appears to affirm, it would seem that the theological position needs reexamination. When one places the earlier verses affirming that Christ died for the world, or all people, alongside this verse from 2 Peter, the biblical case for a divine intention to provide atonement universally is strong.[13]

Hammett apparently believes that multiple-intentions advocates approach the biblical text without biases—or at least with fewer prior theological commitments than their five-point brethren.

First John 2:2 ("He is the propitiation for our sins, and not for ours only but also for the sins of the whole world") is central to the multiple-intentions position. In this regard, Hammett quotes Gary Shultz approvingly: "There is no clearer statement in Scripture indicating that Christ died to pay the penalty of all people."[14] Unfortunately, Hammett's exegesis does not prove multiple intentions. He fails to interact with the meaning of "propitiation" and how it functions as the logical limiting factor in the verse since "world" can mean a variety of things. Biblically, a propitiation is an accomplished fact, not a hypothetical possibility. Jesus propitiated God's wrath for a certain number of people, either the elect or all humanity. If the former, we have definite atonement. If the latter, universalism. That seems to be all that 1 John 2:2 can mean.

A troubling aspect of the "multiple-intentional" view is its view of cosmic redemption based on Colossians 1:20—God was pleased through Christ "to reconcile to himself all things, whether on earth or in heaven, making peace by the blood of his cross." Avoiding universalism, Hammett argues that it is "possible to understand how cosmic reconciliation need not imply that all of humanity, or fallen angels, have been restored to fellowship with God and will enjoy the blessings of salvation."[15] "Reconciliation" here, he maintains, means "all things being put in right relation to Christ."[16] This interpretation of reconciliation allows Hammett to suggest,

---

13. Ibid., 157.
14. Ibid., 151, quoting Gary Lee Shultz Jr., "A Biblical and Theological Defense of a Multi-Intentioned View of the Atonement" (Ph.D. dissertation, The Southern Baptist Theological Seminary, 2008), 120.
15. Hammett, "Multiple-Intentions View of the Atonement," 185.
16. Ibid., 186, quoting Richard Melick Jr., *Philippians, Colossians, Philemon* (Nashville: Broadman, 1991), 227.

For those who come in faith and repentance, right relationship is salvation. For those who have rejected Christ and
rebelled against him, right relationship involves judgment
and punishment. For the material creation, reconciliation
will mean restoration to the original condition of peace, harmony, and order that sin disturbed. Even those who might
desire to continue their rebellious ways will be subdued.[17]

The problem with this view is simply that this is not what "reconciliation"
means, especially in the context of Jesus's having made "peace by the blood
of the cross" (Col. 1:20). John Piper is right: "To say that blood-bought peace
describes the relationship between God and those in hell surely must eventually make a heaven of hell or rob heaven of peace."[18] Piper's interpretation that
"the blood of Christ has secured the victory of God over the universe in such
a way that the day is coming when 'all things' that are in the *new* heavens and
the *new* earth will be reconciled to God with no rebel remnants" makes more
sense of the immediate context, understands "reconciliation" in its biblical
sense, and avoids the problems inherent in the multiple-intentions view.[19]

Summary

Arminians cast the cross of Christ as having made salvation possible,
if only people will do something to make it effective. Multiple-intention
Calvinists attempt to interpret texts of the death of Christ in a literal way.
Unfortunately, this ties them in unnecessary biblical and theological knots.
As the next three chapters will demonstrate, Christ died for his people and
won their salvation on the cross.

REFLECTION QUESTIONS

1. Can you think of other problems with the Arminian view of the atonement? What are they?

2. Can you think of other biblical problems with the multiple-intentions
   view? What are they?

---

17. Ibid.
18. John Piper, "'My Glory I Will Not Give to Another': Preaching the Fullness of Definite
    Atonement to the Glory of God," in *From Heaven He Came and Sought Her: Definite
    Atonement in Historical, Biblical, Theological, and Pastoral Perspective*, eds. David Gibson
    and Jonathan Gibson (Wheaton, IL: Crossway, 2013), 654. See ibid., 648–64, for Piper's
    extensive critique of the multiple-intentions position.
19. Ibid., 655 (italics original).

3. Do you think Jesus died on the cross for more reasons than to procure the salvation of the elect? What are those reasons?

4. Do you think only those holding to the views examined in this chapter can make a free offer of the gospel to non-Christians? Why?

5. Do you think that Jesus died for you just like he died for those damned eternally in hell? If that position is true, what differentiates you from that person who is going to pay for his or her sins forever? How does that inform your view of what Jesus accomplished on the cross?

Does the Bible Teach Definite Atonement? (Part 1)

By God's grace and according to his sovereign intention, Christ's death on the cross paid all the debt that God's people owed for their sin. The work of Christ on the cross actually accomplished the goal of bringing the two estranged parties together (the "at-one"-ment) by effecting the salvation of the elect. Calvinism thus believes in a "definite atonement" or a "particular redemption." Christ's death was directed towards, and actually saved, a definite, particular group of people, the elect of God.

Clarifying the Question

Louis Berkhof identifies what question we are asking here:

> The question with which we are concerned at this point is not (a) whether the satisfaction rendered by Christ was in itself sufficient for the salvation of all men, since this is admitted by all; (b) whether the saving benefits are actually applied to every man, for the great majority of those who teach a universal atonement do not believe that all are actually saved; (c) whether the *bona fide* offer of salvation is made to all that hear the gospel, on the condition of repentance and faith; . . . nor (d) whether any of the fruits of the death of Christ accrue to the benefit of the non-elect in virtue of their close association with the people of God. . . . On the other hand, the question does relate to the design of the atonement. Did the Father in sending Christ, and did Christ in coming into world, to make atonement for sin, *do this with the design or for the purpose of*

saving only the elect or all men? That is the question, and that only is the question.[1]

As Berkhof reminds us, there are several questions we are *not* asking at this point. We deal with several of them in other chapters.[2] The proper question is the one of God's intention. Did God intend his Son's death to redeem all men, at least potentially, or did he intend Christ's death to secure the forgiveness of a definite number of people? That is the only question we are asking here.

The New Testament gives us several reasons for holding to definite atonement. The next two chapters will examine the three most significant reasons for believing in a definite intent in Christ's atonement. First, though, we have to deal with some easily misunderstood terms.

Disputed Terms

In the previous chapter, we noted several texts employed by those who disagree with definite atonement. Since the New Testament uses the words "world," "all," "many," and other seemingly universalistic terms in conjunction with Christ's work, some Christians hold to a universal, general atonement. We must pay careful attention to this line of reasoning because we must let God's word determine our theology. In fact, though, the language of the Bible argues for a definite atonement, especially when we note that words like "world" and "all" which in English sound universalistic, are often given a different range of meaning in Scripture. For example, when Mark writes that "all the country of Judea and Jerusalem were going out to [John] and were being baptized by him in the river Jordan" (1:5), no one assumes that every single individual in Judea actually heard and was baptized by John. Clearly, here, "all" means "a lot." Context is king in our understanding even of what appear to be all-encompassing statements.

---

1. Louis Berkhof, *Systematic Theology*, 4th ed. (Grand Rapids: Eerdmans, 1941), 393–94 (italics original).
2. See Questions 5, 17, and 37. Importantly, we are not questioning the value of Jesus's death. Most Calvinists believe there are no limits to the value of the cross, as Roger Nicole avers, "It is freely granted that what Christ suffered is so immense, in fact so infinite, that it would be amply sufficient to atone for all the sins of all the people of all ages in the whole world and in a thousand worlds besides, if these existed . . . the work of Christ is strictly infinite in its value" (*Our Sovereign Saviour: The Essence of the Reformed Faith* [Fearn, UK: Christian Focus, 2002], 58). The Synod of Dort likewise propounded the view that Christ's death is perfect, of infinite worth and able to cover the sins of all the world: "This death of God's Son is the only and entirely complete sacrifice and satisfaction for sins; it is of infinite value and worth, more than sufficient to atone for the sins of the whole world" (2.3).

World

"World" (*kosmos*) is a common word, especially in John. Note these important instances:[3]

- Behold, the Lamb of God, who takes away the sin of *the world*! (John 1:29)
- we know that this is indeed the Savior of *the world*. (John 4:42)
- I did not come to judge the world but to save *the world*. (John 12:47)
- God . . . gave us the ministry of reconciliation; that is, in Christ God was reconciling *the world* to himself, not counting their trespasses against them. (2 Cor. 5:18–19)
- He is the propitiation for our sins, and not for ours only but also for the sins of *the whole world*. (1 John 2:2)

Like all words, "world" has a range of meanings. In John, "world" can have at least three different connotations. First, it can refer to the fallen arena, the part of the created order that's in opposition to the Lord, in which God acts to save sinners. In this sense, Jesus is the true light who came "into the world" (1:9), the one "the Father consecrated and sent into the world" (10:36).[4] Second, "world" can be used to make a sharp distinction between God's people and everyone else "out there." For instance, in John 17, Jesus prayed for his people but most definitely not for "the world" (17:9).[5]

The third meaning of "world" is the most important for our discussion. "World" in John often emphasizes "Christ's work as encompassing all people without distinction, not just the Jewish people." In other words, "Christ's redemption transcends ethnic boundaries to include not simply Jews but Gentiles as well."[6] This seems to be the case with Jesus's interaction with a non-Jewish woman in John 4. The shocking reality is that Jesus has come to redeem not just Jews but also Samaritans. Because of this woman's witness, many Samaritans trusted in Jesus (4:39) which led them to exclaim that Jesus is "the Savior of the world" (4:42). Matthew Harmon's conclusion is correct: "They believe that Jesus is not merely the Savior of the Jewish people, but rather of the whole world, even Samaritans. They recognize that his salvation transcends even the sharp divide between Jew and Samaritan to encompass

---

3. Italics have been added to the following Bible quotations.
4. See 1 John 4:1, 3, 9.
5. I get these two categories and the one to follow from Matthew S. Harmon, "For the Glory of the Father and the Salvation of His People: Definite Atonement in the Synoptics and Johannine Literature," in *From Heaven He Came and Sought Her: Definite Atonement in Historical, Biblical, Theological, and Pastoral Perspective*, eds. David Gibson and Jonathan Gibson (Wheaton, IL: Crossway, 2013), 281–87.
6. Ibid., 282.

all who believe without distinction."[7] "World" here does not refer to every individual on planet earth ("all without exception"), but rather to all sorts of people ("all without distinction").

This same distinction helps to explain 1 John 2:2, "He is the propitiation for our sins, and not for ours only but also for the sins of the whole world." We must note that the propitiatory (i.e., wrath-bearing and -averting) work of Christ is not spoken of as being potential. It accomplishes what he intended to do.[8] The question is, Who is the "whole world"? The parallel language in John 11:52 is enlightening. Jesus's death is "not for the nation only, but also to gather into one the children of God who are scattered abroad." The parallel uses of "not only . . . but also" add light to the meaning of John's epistle. In John 11, Christ's work is described as not being for Jews alone but also for all God's children "scattered abroad," certainly meaning Gentiles. The same applies in 1 John 2; Christ propitiated the sins not just of believing Jews but—remarkably!—of believing Gentiles as well. John intends us to understand that "Jesus is the propitiation for Jewish believers' sins, and not only for ours but also for the sins of Gentile believers too." Harmon is correct: "The death of Christ—portrayed here as an *actual* propitiation for the sins of the world, not a *potential* one—is for all without distinction, not all without exception."[9]

All

Besides the "world," other texts speak of Christ's work being directed towards "all." Paul speaks of "God our Savior, who desires all (*pantas*) people to be saved and to come to a knowledge of the truth" (1 Tim. 2:3–4). Even though "all" can mean "everyone without exception" at times, it can also connote "all sorts of" or "all kinds of." Only context determines its meaning. The context here suggests that Paul means God wants "all kinds of people" to come to salvation. The apostle urged Timothy to pray for "all people" (*pantōn*) (2:1), and he explains the limitations of "all people" in the next verse when he says the sorts of people he should intercede for: "kings and all who are in high positions" (2:2). So the "all people" is really "all *kinds* of people." According to George Knight, "The meaning would fit in the other occurrences of the phrase in 1 Timothy and Titus (especially Titus 3:2)," and "It is also the most natural understanding in a number of the Pauline passages where an absolute universalism is a virtual impossibility and a reference to all *kinds* of individuals is more likely."[10] The immediate context confirms that "all kinds of people" is the correct way to understand "all people," for Paul says that Christ

---

7. Ibid., 283.
8. See Question 23, specifically John Owen's lengthy quotation.
9. Harmon, "For the Glory of the Father," 285.
10. George W. Knight III, *The Pastoral Epistles: A Commentary on the Greek Text*, New International Greek Testament Commentary (Grand Rapids: Eerdmans, 1992), 115 (italics original).

"gave himself as a ransom for all" (2:6). Rather than teaching that Christ actually redeemed all persons (for "the verse and context say nothing about Christ being the *potential* ransom of everyone"), Paul here asserts that "Christ purchased salvation from all kinds of individuals from various people groups."[11] The next verse, where Paul speaks of his particular ministry to the Gentiles (2:7), confirms this understanding. Jesus ransomed all kinds of people, Jews and Gentiles.

Another significant text in this discussion is Romans 8:32, "He who did not spare his own Son but gave him up for us all (*pantōn*), how will he not also with him graciously give us all things?" Even though some interpret "all" here to refer to all persons without exception, a consideration of the context actually argues against such an interpretation. The preceding verses contain Paul's particular teaching that God's elect can have confidence that God works for them (8:28) because God foreknew-predestined-called-justified-glorified them (8:29–30). These verses teach that God's saving work is directed to the elect, and we have no reason to suppose that verse 32 expands the scope of God's work in Christ to "all without exception." In addition, the following context shows that God's work is here directed only to the elect. They are called "the elect," the ones who are justified (8:33). They are the ones not only for whom Christ died but also for whom he rose (8:34). They are the ones for whom he intercedes on the Father's behalf (8:34). They are the ones who have certainty that nothing will ever separate them from God's love in Christ (8:35–39). We have no contextual reason for assuming that the "us all" of verse 32 is any different from the ones discussed in verses 28–31 or 33–39. In other words, the context of Romans 8:32 leads to the conclusion that "us all" means "all the elect." John Murray is contextually correct: "The love implied in verse 32, the love of giving the Son, cannot be given a wider reference than the love which, according to verses 35–39, insures the eternal security of those who are its objects."[12]

Finally, 2 Corinthians 5:14–15 ("the love of Christ controls us, because we have concluded this: that one has died for all [*pantōn*], therefore all [*pantes*] have died; and he died for all [*pantōn*], that those who live might no longer live for themselves but for him who for their sake died and was raised") should also be considered. Verse 15 will not allow us to understand "died for all" in verse 14 as "all persons without exception." Indeed, the ones for whom Christ died are the ones who are "no longer [to] live for themselves" (v. 15), which is surely a description of Christians. Murray is right that "since 'those who live'

---

11. Thomas R. Schreiner, "'Problematic Texts' for Definite Atonement in the Pastoral and General Epistles," in *From Heaven He Came and Sought Her: Definite Atonement in Historical, Biblical, Theological, and Pastoral Perspective*, eds. David Gibson and Jonathan Gibson (Wheaton, IL: Crossway, 2013), 379.
12. John Murray, *Redemption Accomplished and Applied* (Grand Rapids: Eerdmans, 1955), 69. See pages 65–69 for his discussion of the context.

do not embrace the whole human race, neither can the 'all' referred to in the clause, 'he died for all' embrace the entire human family."[13] More than that, these "all" are united with Christ in his death and resurrection (v. 15). On the basis of Paul's teaching in Romans 6:3–4 and Colossians 2:11–14, regarding the union of Christians with Christ in his death and resurrection, we conclude that the "all" of 2 Corinthians 5:14 are the elect, the ones for whose "sake [Christ] died and was raised" (5:15).

This might not seem like such a big deal for us since most of us reading this book are probably Gentile Christians who for centuries have assumed that the unusual situation in the church is a converted Jew, not a converted Gentile. But in the time in which the New Testament was written, it was ground-breaking for the gospel to go to the Gentiles and for the church to accept Gentiles without attempting to make them conform to Jewish rites. For the apostles to proclaim that the finished work of Christ was for the sake of all kinds of people—Jews and Gentiles—was truly good news.

REFLECTION QUESTIONS

1. Do you agree with Berkhof's assertion that the proper question for us to answer is the one of God's intention in the atonement? Why?

2. Do you think the difference between "all without exception" and "all without distinction" is useful? How would explain the distinction in your own words?

3. Can you think of other uses of "world" or "all" in conjunction with the work of Christ that should be discussed in relationship to the design of the atonement? How would you explain them in light of this chapter?

4. Does the extent of Christ's atonement matter? Why?

5. How do you think John 3:16 contributes to discussions of the extent of the atonement? Do you think it disproves definite atonement?

---

13. Ibid., 72.

Does the Bible Teach Definite Atonement? (Part 2)

The New Testament always speaks of Christ's work on the cross as complete. It doesn't need any additions to it to make it effective. It redeems, reconciles, propitiates God's wrath. In a word, it saves. The New Testament also teaches us that the Father, Son, and Holy Spirit had the same intention in the death of Christ. All three persons of the Trinity desired that Christ's death would atone for the sins of the elect. Both the finished work of Christ and the unity of the Trinity lead us to the doctrine of definite atonement.

Christ's Complete Work of Redemption

The New Testament does not speak of a *potential* salvation procured by our Savior if we just add our part. Rather, Christ accomplished his work. Here we will look at three aspects of our Lord's atoning work, his reconciliation, redemption, and propitiation. Jesus's work in each of these three manners shows the definiteness of his accomplishment.

Reconciliation

Due to the Lord's holiness and our utter sinfulness, we needed someone outside of us to bring about a reconciliation between us and God. Jesus did that for his people. So Paul exults,

> All this is from God, who through Christ reconciled us to himself and gave us the ministry of reconciliation; that is, in Christ God was reconciling the world to himself, not counting their trespasses against them, and entrusting to us the message of reconciliation. Therefore, we are ambassadors for Christ, God making his appeal through us. We implore you on behalf of Christ, be reconciled to God. For our sake

he made him to be sin who knew no sin, so that in him we
might become the righteousness of God. (2 Cor. 5:18–21)

The question to ask about this is, Did God *really* reconcile sinners to himself
through Christ?

Similarly, the apostle proclaims, "If while we were enemies we were reconciled to God by the death of his Son, much more, now that we are reconciled,
shall we be saved by his life" (Rom. 5:10). This is complete reconciliation.
"God . . . through Christ reconciled us to himself." "We were reconciled to
God by the death of his Son." There is no hypothetical reconciliation that we
somehow have to activate. Those not reconciled are still at enmity with God.
God reconciled his people to himself through the cross.

Redemption

According to Wayne Grudem, "Because we as sinners are in bondage to
sin and to Satan, we need someone to provide redemption and thereby 'redeem' us out of that bondage. . . . a price was paid (the death of Christ) and
the result was that we were 'redeemed' from bondage."[1] A real price was completely paid. This is what Paul relishes in when he says that God "has delivered us from the dominion of darkness and transferred us to the kingdom of
his beloved Son, in whom we have redemption, the forgiveness of sins" (Col.
1:13–14). Jesus spoke of himself in similar terms: "For even the Son of Man
did not come to be served, but to serve, and to give his life as a ransom for
many" (Mark 10:45). He is the one who would pay the price to redeem his
people out of bondage. What type of redemption, however, is it when some
of those who are "redeemed" by Jesus are still in bondage to sin and Satan
and are far away from Christ? John Murray perceptively writes, "What does
redemption mean? It does not mean redeemability, that we are placed in a
redeemable position. It means that Christ purchased and procured redemption." Those arguing for a universal atonement err because

> It is to beggar the concept of redemption as an effective se-
> curement of release by price and by power to construe it as
> anything less than the effectual accomplishment which se-
> cures the salvation of those who are its objects. Christ did not
> come to put men in a redeemable position but to redeem to
> himself a people.[2]

Christ redeemed his people by his death on the cross.

---

1. Wayne Grudem, *Systematic Theology: An Introduction to Biblical Doctrine* (Grand Rapids:
   Zondervan, 1994), 580.
2. John Murray, *Redemption Accomplished and Applied* (Grand Rapids: Eerdmans, 1955), 63.

Propitiation

"Propitiation" means that by virtue of Christ's wrath-bearing work for his people on the cross, the wrath of God against his people is assuaged. Murray explains that

> Propitiation presupposes the wrath and displeasure of God, and the purpose of propitiation is the removal of this displeasure. Very simply stated the doctrine of propitiation means that Christ propitiated the wrath of God and rendered God propitious to his people.[3]

Christ's propitiatory work is done for God's people. This is what Paul means in Romans 3:25, what John intends in 1 John 2:2 and 4:10, and it is the point of Hebrews 2:17. What type of propitiation is it, though, if some of those for whom Jesus propitiated God's wrath are still subject to that wrath?

Consider Hebrews 2:17. Jesus was made like his brothers "so that he might become a merciful and faithful high priest in service to God, to make propitiation for the sins of the people." As the true High Priest, Jesus offers the sacrifice of himself which bears the wrath of God that certain ones ("the people") deserved. He substitutes himself in their place. It's not potential. It's complete. He has taken away the wrath of God that these represented people deserved. This helps us make sense of this passage as a whole. Earlier the writer had said that Jesus is "crowned with glory and honor because of the suffering of death, so that by the grace of God he might taste death for everyone" (2:9). In this instance we must let context determine who the "everyone" is. The writer gives us that context. In the next verse, he says that Jesus brought "many sons to salvation" (2:10). He has begun to narrow the range of the "everyone," now to "many sons." He narrows it further when he says those Jesus suffered for are his "brothers" (2:11). Further narrowing the possible meaning of "everyone," he calls them "the children God has given me" (2:13) and "the offspring of Abraham" (2:16), calling to mind God's promise that Abraham would be the father of many people, those who have the faith of Abraham (see Rom. 4:3, 16–18). It is these, then, for whom Christ died to make propitiation; these ones are "the people" (2:17).[4]

---

3. Ibid., 30.
4. A persuasive biblical-theological argument for definite atonement follows based on the priesthood of Christ. Just as the Old Testament priests offered sacrifices and prayed for a particular people (Israel, not all the nations), so does Christ the great High Priest. Since he specifically prayed only for his people (John 17:9, 20), he dies for the same ones. See Stephen J. Wellum, "The New Covenant Work of Christ: Priesthood, Atonement, and Intercession," in *From Heaven He Came and Sought Her: Definite Atonement in Historical, Biblical, Theological, and Pastoral Perspective*, eds. David Gibson and Jonathan Gibson (Wheaton, IL: Crossway, 2013), 519–39.

Propitiation is central to the gospel message since the gospel is supremely the message of God in his love and justice forgiving his elect who deserve only eternal wrath. To deny the doctrine of propitiation, according to Murray, "is to undermine the nature of the atonement as the vicarious endurance of the penalty of sin. In a word, it is to deny substitutionary atonement."[5] And, we might add, it is to deny definite atonement as well.

Jesus reconciled certain people. Jesus redeemed certain people. Jesus is the propitiation for certain people. This is what the New Testament teaches. It never speaks of potential reconciliation, of hypothetical redemption, of a propitiation waiting to be effected by us. General redemptionists who dispute these facts unwittingly tone down the power of the cross to save sinners because they assert that we have to add something to Jesus's work to make it effective. Murray correctly concludes that for Christians, "security inheres in Christ's redemptive accomplishment."[6]

Trinitarian Unity in Salvation

To Arminians, the Father, because of his infinite foreknowledge of human choices, chose a certain number of people to be Christians; not all are elect. The Son died in the same way for all persons. The Spirit convicts of sin and draws those who hear the gospel to Christ, but only seals those who repent and believe. The result is disunity in the Trinity. As J. I. Packer observes, whereas Calvinism "presents the three great acts of the Holy Trinity for the recovering of lost mankind—election by the Father, redemption by the Son, calling by the Spirit—as directed towards the same persons, and as securing their salvation infallibly," Arminianism "gives each act a different reference (the objects of redemption being all mankind, of calling, all who hear the gospel, and of election, those hearers who respond), and denies that any man's salvation is secured by any of them."[7]

What God has determined to do, each individual Person of the Godhead cooperates to accomplish. This is the case in redemption no less than in creation. For this reason, each Person of the Trinity is united in focusing God's saving grace on the elect, as this definition of definite atonement clarifies: "in the death of Jesus Christ, the triune God intended to achieve the redemption of every person given to the Son by the Father in eternity past, and to apply the accomplishments of his sacrifice to each of them by the Spirit."[8]

---

5. Murray, *Redemption Accomplished and Applied*, 32–33.
6. Ibid., 64.
7. J. I. Packer, "'Saved by His Precious Blood': An Introduction to John Owen's *The Death of Death in the Death of Christ*," in *A Quest for Godliness: The Puritan Vision of the Christian Life* (Wheaton, IL: Crossway, 1990), 128.
8. David Gibson and Jonathan Gibson, "Sacred Theology and the Reading of the Divine Word: Mapping the Doctrine of Definite Atonement," in *From Heaven He Came and*

Scripture is replete with the notion that the Persons of the Trinity are united in their intention on the cross. Consider, first of all, instances in the ministry of Jesus. John 6:37–40, 44 is worth quoting at length:

> All that the Father gives me will come to me, and whoever comes to me I will never cast out. For I have come down from heaven, not to do my own will but the will of him who sent me. And this is the will of him who sent me, that I should lose nothing of all that he has given me, but raise it up on the last day. For this is the will of my Father, that everyone who looks on the Son and believes in him should have eternal life, and I will raise him up on the last day. . . . No one can come to me unless the Father who sent me draws him. And I will raise him up on the last day.

The Father and the Son certainly have the same intention in the Son's work. The Father gives a particular group of people to the Son, and the Son then comes to earth to do the Father's will, which is to lose none of the ones the Father has given him. The Son gives them eternal life and only these ones believe in him because the Father draws them to the Son.[9] As Matthew Harmon comments, "the Father gives a specific group of people to the Son for whom he *then* comes to die in order to give them eternal life. Particularism attends the planning and the making of the atonement, not just its application."[10]

Paul is even more explicit in teaching the unity of the Trinity in Christians' salvation. In addition to texts that lead us to the doctrine of the Trinity (such as 1 Cor. 12:4–6; 2 Cor. 13:14; and Eph. 4:4–6), others show us the unity of the Godhead in redemption. Galatians 4:4–6 is one example. "God [the Father] sent forth his Son" in order "to redeem those who were under the law," and "God has sent the Spirit of his Son into our hearts, crying, 'Abba! Father!'" Jonathan Gibson comments, "God the Father sends his two Emissaries to accomplish and apply redemption: the Son to *redeem us* from under the law . . . and the Spirit to *be in our hearts.* . . . The obedience of Son and Spirit to the Father ensures harmony of purpose."[11]

Sought Her: Definite Atonement in Historical, Biblical, Theological, and Pastoral Perspective, eds. David Gibson and Jonathan Gibson (Wheaton, IL: Crossway, 2013), 33.

9. Matthew S. Harmon, "For the Glory of the Father and the Salvation of His People: Definite Atonement in the Synoptics and Johannine Literature," in *From Heaven He Came and Sought Her: Definite Atonement in Historical, Biblical, Theological, and Pastoral Perspective,* eds. David Gibson and Jonathan Gibson (Wheaton, IL: Crossway, 2013), 270.

10. Ibid., 271 (italics original). Also see John 12:49–50; 14:30–31; 17:1–26.

11. Jonathan Gibson, "The Glorious, Indivisible, Trinitarian Work of God in Christ: Definite Atonement in Paul's Theology of Salvation," in *From Heaven He Came and Sought Her:*

Paul's great hymn of praise in Ephesians 1:3–14 also shows the unity of the Trinity in our salvation. God the Father elected and predestined certain ones to salvation (1:4–5). Jesus redeemed them by his blood (1:7). The Spirit sealed these same people (1:13). The Father, Son, and Spirit all have the same persons and goal in mind—the salvation of the elect. As Daniel Montgomery and Timothy Paul Jones note, "The Son's death purchased—or redeemed—precisely the same people the Father chose and the Spirit seals. This work was *selective, effective,* and *definite.*"[12]

Michael Horton summarizes well how the unity of the Trinity leads to the doctrine of definite atonement:

> The Father chose many, but not all, to eternal life and entrusted their salvation to the Son (John 6:38–39; 15:16; 17:9; Rom. 8:29; Eph. 1:4–5, 7, 15). Scripture also teaches that the Spirit effectually calls the elect and unites them to Christ. Although they do indeed believe in Christ, it is because of God's sovereign grace rather than their own free will: the Spirit brings the elect to Christ, giving them faith (John 1:12–13; 6:44; 15:16; Rom. 8:30; 9:6–24; Eph. 2:8; 2 Thess. 2:13). . . . Our entire salvation is credited not to the cooperation of sinners with God, but to the cooperation of the persons of the Trinity. In unity with the Father and the Spirit, the Son's purpose was to save the elect.[13]

REFLECTION QUESTIONS

1. Do you think the completed work of Christ on the cross is a strong argument for definite atonement? Why?

2. Can you think of other biblical metaphors besides redemption, reconciliation, and propitiation that argue for a definite atonement?

Definite Atonement in Historical, Biblical, Theological, and Pastoral Perspective, eds. David Gibson and Jonathan Gibson (Wheaton, IL: Crossway, 2013), 361 (italics original). See also Romans 8:1–11; 2 Timothy 1:9–10; Titus 3:4–6; and 1 Peter 1:1–2.

12. Daniel Montgomery and Timothy Paul Jones, *Proof: Finding Freedom through the Intoxicating Joy of Irresistible Grace* (Grand Rapids: Zondervan, 2014), 39 (italics original).

13. Michael Horton, *For Calvinism* (Grand Rapids: Zondervan, 2011), 94. The classic treatment of this is found in John Owen, *Salus Electorum, Sanguis Jesu; or, The Death of Death in the Death of Christ,* in *The Works of John Owen* (1647; Carlisle, PA: Banner of Truth, 1967), 10:163–79.

3. Do you think it's possible for the Father to intend the salvation of only the elect while the Son dies for everyone's salvation?

4. Do you think Arminianism's belief in universal atonement leads to a disunited Trinity? Why?

5. Read John 17:1–26. Does Jesus's prayer only for the elect have any bearing on the extent of the atonement?

Does Substitutionary Atonement Imply Particular Redemption?

The doctrine of penal substitution—that our Lord Jesus Christ substituted himself in our place and bore the penalty for our sin—is at the heart of the gospel.[1] Without it, we have no hope of peace with God now or ever. Gloriously, though, this doctrine is revealed throughout the Bible. Its truth is one more reason we should hold to definite atonement, for the Bible teaches that Jesus substituted himself for particular persons and bore their penalty completely.

Substitution in the Bible

The notion that a substitute is needed to pay the penalty for sinners is a common idea throughout Scripture. God himself provided a ram as a sacrifice in place of Isaac (Gen. 22:13). The Mosaic law stipulated that the priest should sacrifice a goat or a bull as a sin offering "for the people" and that another goat, after the priest symbolically transferred the sins of the people onto its head, should be sent into the desert as a scapegoat (Lev. 16). The whole sacrificial system was built on the premise that animals were being slaughtered in the place of sinful Israelites.

Substitution is the central idea in the important "Servant Song" of Isaiah 53. The personal pronouns make this point explicitly. The servant bore "*our* griefs and carried *our* sorrows" (53:4). He was "wounded for *our* transgressions; he was crushed for *our* iniquities"; the chastisement that was placed on him "brought *us* peace" so that "with his stripes *we* are healed" (53:5). The punishment deserved by "*us* all" was placed on him by God (53:6). Indeed he was "stricken for the transgression of *my* people" and "he bore the sin of *many*" (53:8, 12). The suffering servant—whom New Testament authors identify as

---

1. See "The Heart of the Gospel," in J. I. Packer, *Knowing God* (Downers Grove, IL: InterVarsity Press, 1973), 161–80.

Jesus (see, e.g., Matt. 8:17; Mark 15:28; Acts 8:32; 1 Peter 2:22, 24)—stands in the place of a particular group of people. Alec Motyer is correct that the "many" of Isaiah 53:11–12 includes not only believing Israelites but also those he died for from among the nations (see Rev. 7:9).[2] This glorious song of hope highlights the "element of definiteness, of effected and effectual atonement."[3] The substitute died in the place of his people; because of his death for them, they receive salvation.

Substitution is also a central notion in the New Testament, as an examination of the prepositions used to speak of the work of Christ demonstrates.[4] The New Testament authors used four different prepositions to speak of the work of Christ: *anti*, *hyper*, *peri*, and *dia*. Here are some of their uses:

Anti

- the Son of Man came not to be served but to serve, and to give his life as a ransom for (*anti*) many. (Matt. 20:28)[5]

Murray J. Harris is correct: "The life of Jesus, surrendered in a sacrificial death, brought about the release of forfeited lives. He acted on behalf of the many by taking their place."[6] According to Matthew Harmon, the substitution presented here is a definite replacement: "His life is given in exchange for (αυτι) that of the many, not for all without exception."[7]

Hyper

- while we were still weak, at the right time Christ died for (*hyper*) the ungodly. . . . but God shows his love for us in that while we were still sinners, Christ died for (*hyper*) us. (Rom. 5:6, 8)

---

2. J. Alec Motyer, "'Stricken for the Transgression of My People': The Atoning Work of Isaiah's Suffering Servant," in *From Heaven He Came and Sought Her: Definite Atonement in Historical, Biblical, Theological, and Pastor Perspective*, eds. David Gibson and Jonathan Gibson (Wheaton, IL: Crossway, 2013), 265–66.
3. Ibid., 262.
4. R. E. Davies, "Christ in Our Place—The Contribution of the Prepositions," *Tyndale Bulletin* 21 (1970): 71–91.
5. Also see Mark 10:45.
6. Murray J. Harris, "Some Theologically Important Instances of the Major Prepositions," in *The New International Dictionary of New Testament Theology*, ed. Colin Brown (Grand Rapids: Zondervan, 1986), 3:1180.
7. Matthew S. Harmon, "For the Glory of the Father and the Salvation of His People: Definite Atonement in the Synoptics and Johannine Literature," in *From Heaven He Came and Sought Her: Definite Atonement in Historical, Biblical, Theological, and Pastoral Perspective*, eds. David Gibson and Jonathan Gibson (Wheaton, IL: Crossway, 2013), 276.

- He who did not spare his own Son but gave him up for (*hyper*) us all, how will he not also with him graciously give us all things? (Rom. 8:32)
- the life I now live in the flesh I live by faith in the Son of God, who loved me and gave himself for (*hyper*) me. (Gal. 2:20)
- Christ redeemed us from the curse of the law by becoming a curse for (*hyper*) us. (Gal. 3:13)
- Husbands, love your wives, as Christ loved the church and gave himself up for (*hyper*) her. (Eph. 5:25)
- Christ Jesus, who gave himself for (*hyper*) us to redeem us from all lawlessness and to purify for himself a people for his own possession. (Titus 2:13–14)
- we see . . . Jesus, crowned with glory and honor because of the suffering of death, so that by the grace of God he might taste death for (*hyper*) everyone. (Heb. 2:9)
- to this you have been called, because Christ also suffered for (*hyper*) you. (1 Peter 2:21)
- Christ also suffered once for (*peri*) sin, the righteous for (*hyper*) the unrighteous, that he might bring us to God. (1 Peter 3:18)
- By this we know love, that he laid down his life for (*hyper*) us. (1 John 3:16)[8]

Jesus says this of himself: "I am the good shepherd. The good shepherd lays down his life for (*hyper*) the sheep. . . . I lay down my life for (*hyper*) the sheep" (John 10:11, 15). D. A. Carson's exposition of this passage, and its use of *hyper*, reminds us of the substitutionary significance of this preposition:

> The words "for (*hyper*) the sheep" suggest sacrifice. The preposition, itself ambiguous, in John always occurs in a sacrificial context. . . . The shepherd does not die for his sheep to serve as an example, throwing himself off a cliff in a grotesque and futile display while bellowing, "See how much I love you!" No, the assumption is that the sheep are in mortal danger; that in their defence the shepherd loses his life; that by his death they are saved. That, and that alone, is what makes him *the good shepherd.*[9]

---

8. Also see Mark 14:24; John 6:51; 2 Corinthians 5:21; Galatians 1:4; Ephesians 5:2; 1 Timothy 2:5–6.
9. D. A. Carson, *The Gospel according to John* (Grands Rapids: Eerdmans, 1991), 386 (italics original).

Dia

- by your knowledge this weak person is destroyed, the brother for (*dia*) whom Christ died. (1 Cor. 8:11)
- you know the grace of our Lord Jesus Christ, that though he was rich, yet for (*dia*) your sake he became poor, so that you by his poverty might become rich. (2 Cor. 8:9)

Peri

- this is my blood of the covenant, which is poured out for (*peri*) many for the forgiveness of sins. (Matt. 26:28)
- God has done what the law, weakened by the flesh, could not do. By sending his own Son in the likeness of sinful flesh and for (*peri*) sin, he condemned sin in the flesh. (Rom. 8:3)
- He is the propitiation for (*peri*) our sins, and not for (*peri*) ours only but also for (*peri*) the sins of the whole world. (1 John 2:2)
- In this is love, not that we have loved God but that he loved us and sent his Son to be the propitiation for (*peri*) our sins. (1 John 4:10)

These prepositions remind us that the substitutionary death of Jesus is at the heart of what the gospel is. Christ died for our sins, in our place, as our substitute. Robert Letham correctly notes, "Christ himself willingly submitted to the just penalty which we deserved, receiving it on our behalf and in our place so that we will not have to bear it ourselves."[10]

Penal Substitution and Particular Redemption

What exactly did Jesus do when he substituted himself for us on the cross? He bore the penalty we deserved from God for our sin. This is the heart of the biblical doctrine of justification by faith alone. Thomas Schreiner explains penal substitution in this way:

> The penalty for sin is death (Rom 6:23). Sinners deserve eternal punishment in hell from God himself because of the sin and guilt. God's holy anger is directed (Rom 1:18) against all those who have sinned and fallen short of the glory of God (Rom 3:23). And yet because of God's great love, he sent Christ to bear the punishment for our sins. Christ died in our place, took to himself our sin (2 Cor

---

10. Robert Letham, *The Work of Christ* (Downers Grove, IL: InterVarsity Press, 1993), 133.

> 5:21) and guilt (Gal 3:10), and bore our penalty so that we
> might receive forgiveness of sins.[11]

God sacrifices himself in our place.[12] Fundamentally Jesus bears the wrath of
God which we deserve due to our sin. Hence, it is *penal* (meaning that it relates to the penalty due one in a legal system) and it is *substitution* (Jesus died
for us, in our place).

Everything we have seen about substitution, especially its penal character,
leads us to the conclusion that on the cross Jesus died particularly for his
people. Considering Jesus's real substitution, the only two consistent options
for one's view of the extent of the atonement are definite atonement or universal salvation. Universalism, though, is unbiblical. This means that evangelical Arminians have to redefine the nature of Christ's substitution, saying
that while it was meant for everyone it is limited in its effect. Something is
lacking in Christ's death (namely, our putting it into action via our faith) in
itself. Raymond Blacketer identifies this problem with Arminianism:

> For Arminius the work of Christ on the cross does not ef-
> fect salvation (understood as propitiation, satisfaction or re-
> demption) for any person or group; instead, it only makes
> salvation *possible*. The cross brings about a new legal situ-
> ation. . . . The condition that [God] prescribes is faith; and
> it is up to the individual sinner to use the universal grace
> provided by God to take that step of faith.[13]

Arminians limit the effectiveness of the atonement. Christ does what he can
for everybody, but a person must do something on his own to make Christ's
substitution effective. In this sense, then, we assert that it is Arminians who
"limit" the atonement, taking away the effectiveness of Jesus's death in the
place of sinners.

Because the Bible teaches penal substitution, however, Calvinism teaches
that the atonement's effectiveness is definite. It is intended for God's elect,
those whom he chose to be his own, as the doctrine of propitiation reminds
us. Four New Testament passages speak of Christ's work for his people in
terms of "propitiation" (Rom. 3:25; Heb. 2:17; 1 John 2:2; 4:10).[14]

---

11. Thomas R. Schreiner, "Penal Substitution View," in *The Nature of the Atonement*, eds. James
    Beilby and Paul R. Eddy (Downers Grove, IL: InterVarsity Press, 2006), 72–73.
12. See "The Self-Substitution of God" in John R. W. Stott, *The Cross of Christ* (Downers Grove, IL:
    InterVarsity Press, 1986), 133–63.
13. Raymond A. Blacketer, "Definite Atonement in Historical Perspective," in *The Glory of the
    Atonement: Biblical, Theological and Practical Perspectives*, eds. Charles E. Hill and Frank
    A. James III (Downers Grove, IL: InterVarsity Press, 2004), 319.
14. The only other use of this word in the New Testament is Luke 18:13.

Romans 3 is significant in this regard. God is outraged by human sin. So he gives us over more and more to our desires and their consequences (Rom. 1:18–32). He also expresses his righteous, awful wrath against those who rebel against his rule, as Paul says three times (Rom. 1:18; 2:5; 3:5). This, combined with the fact that all people seek their own desires and do not seek God, leaves all humanity in an awful predicament. No one seeks God; all hate him; and God's wrath is directed against them all (3:9–20).

No one can be saved, unless God in his love and kindness chooses to rescue guilty sinners. And he has! So Paul says, "but now" (3:21) God has acted to rescue people from their sin and rebellion. He has paid the penalty for their sin, by sending his own Son as the "propitiation" (3:25) for his people, the one who bears the punishment they deserve so that they are no longer liable for it. Jesus willingly takes their place, dying for them, so that they no longer need fear the wrath of God. All the penalty of their sin is erased; not a bit still needs to be paid by them. For this reason, Paul says that the gift of Christ's grace is to be received by faith, not by works (3:25–31). Packer is right: "By undergoing the cross, Jesus expiated our sins, propitiated our Maker, turned God's no to us into a yes, and so saved us."[15]

The doctrine of propitiation—both its particularity and its effectiveness—leads us to determine that penal substitution is a biblical doctrine. And it leads us to conclude, with Packer, whose words are worth quoting at length:

> Substitution is a definite and precise relationship whereby the specific obligations of one or more persons are taken over and discharged by someone else. . . . Should we not then think of Christ's substitution for us on the cross as a definite, one-to-one relationship between him and each individual sinner? This seems scriptural, for Paul says, "He loved *me* and gave himself for *me*" (Gal. 2:20). But if Christ specifically took and discharged my penal obligation as a sinner, does it not follow that the cross was decisive for my salvation not only as its sole meritorious ground, but also as guaranteeing that I should be brought to faith, and through faith to eternal life? . . . Once this is granted, however, we are shut up to a choice between universalism and some form of the view that Christ died to save only a part of the human race.[16]

---

15. J. I. Packer, "What Did the Cross Achieve? The Logic of Penal Substitution," in J. I. Packer and Mark Dever, *In My Place Condemned He Stood: Celebrating the Glory of the Atonement* (Wheaton, IL: Crossway, 2007), 73.

16. Ibid., 90 (italics original). Also see Garry J. Williams, "The Definite Intent of Penal Substitutionary Atonement," in *From Heaven He Came and Sought Her: Definite Atonement in Historical, Biblical, Theological, and Pastoral Perspective*, eds. David Gibson and Jonathan Gibson (Wheaton, IL: Crossway, 2013), 461–82.

REFLECTION QUESTIONS

1. How important do you think substitution is to the doctrine of the atonement?

2. How would you define penal substitution?

3. There are other biblical motifs used to speak of the atonement, such as Christ triumphing over evil on the cross and being an example to us. Do you think Protestants have been correct to believe that penal substitution is the most important of the biblical metaphors? Why?

4. How do you think Arminians would counter Packer's notion that penal substitution implies definite atonement?

5. Do you agree that definite atonement is the logical and biblical conclusion of penal substitution?

God's Powerful Grace and
His Preservation of His People

Is God's Grace Effective?

Calvinists affirm that God's saving grace is sovereign (accompanied by almighty power), particular (directed towards the elect), and effective (the older word used was "efficacious"). It will accomplish what God intends, the saving of the elect. To fit the TULIP mnemonic, this is often called "irresistible grace." "Irresistible," though, carries too many wrong connotations, so we will stick with "effective," or "efficacious." When God calls the elect to himself through the preaching of the gospel, that call is accompanied with divine authority and power. The elect will definitely come. God's call effectively accomplishes what he intends.

Efficacious Grace in Calvinism

Calvinists believe that God's eternal determination to save the elect works itself out in human history to accomplish his intention. From before the foundation of the world, God the Father chose certain ones to be his people. This "unconditional election" was done apart from anything he foresaw in them. Then, in human history, Jesus came and lived for and died for these elect ones— "when the fullness of time had come, God sent forth his Son . . . to redeem those who were under the law, so that we might receive adoption as sons" (Gal. 4:4–5). This is particular redemption. Finally, God the Holy Spirit brings life to the elect by sovereignly calling them through the preaching of the gospel and granting them new life so that they repent and believe. This is the effective grace we're considering in this question.[1] The three Persons of the divine Trinity work in concert to achieve God's will, the salvation of his chosen people.

---

1. Greg Welty reminds us that as we move "from unconditional election to effectual calling, we move from God's *planning* of salvation in eternity past to God's *bringing about* that salvation in the historical present" ("Election and Calling: A Biblical Theological Study," in *Calvinism: A Southern Baptist Dialogue*, eds. E. Ray Clendenen and Brad J. Waggoner [Nashville: B&H, 2008], 233).

Calvinistic confessions teach God's efficacious grace. A classic instance is the Westminster Confession of Faith, which asserts,

> All those whom God hath predestinated unto life, and those only, he is pleased, in his appointed and accepted time, effectually to call, by his Word and Spirit, out of that state of sin and death in which they are by nature, to grace and salvation by Jesus Christ: enlightening their minds, spiritually and savingly, to understand the things of God, taking away their heart of stone, and giving unto them an heart of flesh; renewing their wills, and by his almighty power determining them to that which is good; and effectually drawing them to Jesus Christ; yet so as they come most freely, being made willing by his grace. (WCF 10.1)

God's effective grace is particularly directed towards the elect. By the word and his Spirit, God in his grace creates new life in the elect, changing their minds, hearts, and wills. The elect person comes freely since God has graciously made him or her willing to come: "This effectual call is of God's free and special grace alone, not from anything at all foreseen in man, who is altogether passive therein, until, being quickened and renewed by the Holy Spirit, he is thereby enabled to answer this call, and to embrace the grace offered and conveyed in it" (WCF, 10.2). God the Father calls his own, and the Holy Spirit makes these passive agents (the elect) willing to embrace the grace offered in the gospel. This is God's effective grace.

John Murray reminds us that God's effective call comes with the full force of the Lord's sovereign authority:

> It is very striking that in the New Testament the terms for calling, when used specifically with reference to salvation, are almost uniformly applied, not to the universal call of the gospel, but to the call that ushers men into a state of salvation and is therefore effectual. . . . With scarcely an exception the New Testament means by the words "call," "called," "calling" nothing less than the call which is efficacious unto salvation.[2]

The Biblical Doctrine of God's Effective Grace

The following survey of the New Testament proves Murray's assertion correct. God's efficacious call sovereignly grants faith to his elect. The Bible asserts that God effectively calls the elect to salvation through the gospel, the preaching of his word. When Lydia heard the gospel message, "The Lord

---

2. John Murray, *Redemption Accomplished and Applied* (Grand Rapids: Eerdmans, 1955), 88.

opened her heart to pay attention to what was said by Paul" (Acts 16:14). God sovereignly opened her heart; then, paying attention to the gospel, she believed. The following texts assert the sovereign efficacy of God's calling. It accomplishes his goal of saving the elect:

- To all those in Rome who are loved by God and called to be saints. (Rom. 1:7)
- God is faithful, by whom you were called into the fellowship of his Son, Jesus Christ our Lord. (1 Cor. 1:9)
- But when he who had set me apart before I was born, and who called me by his grace. (Gal. 1:15)
- To this he called you through our gospel, so that you may obtain the glory of our Lord Jesus Christ. (2 Thess. 2:14)

Five New Testament passages, especially, demonstrate that effectual calling is a biblical doctrine. First, Romans 8:30—"And those whom he predestined he also called, and those whom he called he also justified, and those whom he justified he also glorified"—teaches it. Starting in verse 29, Paul moves from foreknowledge to predestination to calling to justification to glorification. They are all intricately united, they are effective to accomplish their goal, and they result in the salvation of the elect. God's calling is as sure as his predestining. Murray notes that

> the call is stated to be according to God's purpose and finds its place in the centre of that unbreakable chain of events which has its beginning in the divine fore-knowledge and its consummation in glorification. This is just saying that the effectual call insures perseverance because it is grounded in the security of God's purpose and grace.[3]

Christians can take comfort, Paul assures them (v. 28), because God's foreordained purpose for them in love is to make them like Jesus (v. 29). And they can take comfort, Matthew Barrett reminds us, due to the grammar of verse 30:

> There is an "exact correspondence" between those predestined and those called, made evident by the demonstrative pronoun "these" [*toutous*]. "This leaves little room for the suggestion that the links in this chain are not firmly attached to one another, as if some who were 'foreknown' and 'predestined' would not be 'called,' 'justified,' and 'glorified.'" The links in the chain are unbreakable. The link we want to pay

---

3. Ibid., 91.

special attention to is the verb "he called" which, "denotes
God's effectual summoning into relationship with him."[4]

If God's calling here can be resisted, believers have no assurance for the future
whatsoever. Why trust God (v. 28) if human obstinacy can thwart his desire to
bring his people forever into relationship with him (vv. 29–30)? This cannot
be the case. The "calling" mentioned here is effective.

Second, Peter exhorts his readers to "be all the more diligent to make your
calling and election sure" (2 Peter 1:10). This makes no sense if Peter were intending the general "call" of the gospel, since he is writing to Christians (1:1)
who have already experienced the inner renewal of the Spirit on their hearts.
Greg Welty remarks, "Clearly Peter was not asking his readers to make sure
they heard the gospel outwardly and verbally. Rather, he was using 'calling' in
its inward, effectual sense: make certain that *you are a believer*."[5]

Third, Jude 1 teaches this effective call—"to those who are the called, beloved in God the Father, and kept for Jesus Christ." The same three things are
true of these people: God loved them; they are being kept secure for the final
day when they go to be with Jesus; and they are "called" to belong to Christ.
Certainly not everyone who hears the gospel call outwardly but does not respond in repentance and faith is called in this sense. This verse teaches God's
efficacious call to create new hearts within the elect.

Fourth, the parallel between God's sovereign work in creation and his sovereign work in new creation is stunning. Paul reports to the Corinthian believers,

> the god of this world has blinded the minds of unbelievers,
> to keep them from seeing the light of the gospel of the glory
> of Christ, who is the image of God. For what we proclaim is
> not ourselves, but Jesus Christ as Lord, with ourselves as your
> servants for Jesus's sake. For God, who said, "Let light shine
> out of darkness," has shone in our hearts to give the light of
> the knowledge of the glory of God in the face of Jesus Christ.
> (2 Cor. 4:4–6)

The parallel is remarkable. Just as God spoke "let there be" in creation
and light came into being (Gen. 1:14–19), so he shines in the hearts of believers so that they see the beauty of Jesus. Light came into being by God's
sovereign call; spiritual life comes into being by God's sovereign call. God

---

4. Matthew M. Barrett, "The Scriptural Affirmation of Monergism," in *Whomever He Wills: A
   Surprising Display of Sovereign Mercy*, eds. Matthew M. Barrett and Thomas J. Nettles (Cape
   Coral, FL: Founders, 2012), 128–29; quoting Douglas J. Moo, *The Epistle to the Romans*, New
   International Commentary on the New Testament (Grand Rapids: Eerdmans, 1996), 535.
5. Welty, "Election and Calling," 236 (italics original).

works in the elect, and they definitely are saved. John Piper's conclusion is apropos: "A real light—spiritual light—shone in our hearts. . . . God causes the glory—the self-authenticating truth and beauty—of Christ to be seen and savored in our hearts."[6]

Finally, Jesus's words in John 6 teach God's effective grace. Notice Jesus's words:

- All that the Father gives me will come to me, and whoever comes to me I will never cast out. (v. 37)
- No one can come to me unless the Father who sent me draws him. And I will raise him up on the last day. It is written in the Prophets, "And they will all be taught by God." Everyone who has heard and learned from the Father comes to me. (vv. 44–45)
- This is why I told you that no one can come to me unless it is granted him by the Father. (v. 65)

We previously noted D. A. Carson's observation that these verses refute Arminian notions of "prevenient grace."[7] Instead, verse 65 teaches God's effective grace; God "grants" the ability to come to Christ to a person and then the individual willingly comes. Welty comments that "according to verse 65, no one can exercise saving faith unless 'it' (the faith, the coming to Christ) has been 'granted' by God." In other words, "it is precisely in terms of a distinction which the Father makes—in whom He grants to come to Jesus—that Jesus explains the unbelief of those who rejected him. But this explanation (which is the explanation Jesus gives) couldn't *be* the explanation if the Father drew everyone equally."[8] Carson further clarifies that a central note of verse 45 is that the Father lovingly draws the elect to himself by means of the Spirit's inward illumination: "When he compels belief, it is not by the savage constraint of a rapist, but by the wonderful wooing of a lover. Otherwise put, it is by an insight, a teaching, an illumination implanted within the individual" in fulfilment of Old Testament promises such as Isaiah 54:13, Jeremiah 31:31–34, and Ezekiel 36:24–26.[9] Like Paul, Jesus taught the Father's effective grace and calling.

Summary

God's effective grace and calling matter for a believer. His sovereign call should give us confidence that all things are working together for our good (Rom. 8:28–39). Whatever comes, we can trust the Lord. As Bruce Ware

---

6. John Piper, *Five Points: Towards a Deeper Experience of God's Grace* (Fearn, UK: Christian Focus, 2013), 34.
7. D. A. Carson, *The Gospel According to John* (Grand Rapids: Eerdmans, 1991), 293. See Question 7.
8. Welty, "Election and Calling," 238 (italics original).
9. Carson, *John*, 293.

reminds us, "Everything about this doctrine elicits our humble amazement at a gracious God who would call undeserving and blind sinners out of darkness into his marvelous light. To God alone belongs all glory and honor! Praise be to his great and gracious name!"[10]

REFLECTION QUESTIONS

1. How would you explain "effective" or "efficacious" grace to someone in your own words?

2. Does this doctrine matter? What do you think would be lost if someone did not believe in God's efficacious grace?

3. Do you see much difference between Arminian "prevenient grace" and Calvinistic "efficacious grace"? What is it?

4. Has understanding God's effective grace in your life better led you to worship God and to share the gospel more? Why?

5. Daniel Montgomery and Timothy Paul Jones write that through irresistible, or effective, grace, "God unshackles us from the enslaving contagion of sin so that we glimpse the overwhelming beauty of Jesus and his kingdom."[11] Have you had that experience of tasting or seeing the beauty of Jesus? If so, can you describe it? If not, what should you do?

---

10. Bruce A. Ware, "Effectual Calling and Grace," in *Still Sovereign: Contemporary Perspectives on Election, Foreknowledge, and Grace*, eds. Thomas R. Schreiner and Bruce A. Ware (1995; Grand Rapids: Baker, 2000), 227.

11. Daniel Montgomery and Timothy Paul Jones, *Proof: Finding Freedom through the Intoxicating Joy of Irresistible Grace* (Grand Rapids: Zondervan, 2014), 91.

Can People Resist the Holy Spirit?

The Bible teaches that sinners regularly resist God's overtures of grace in their lives. Calvinists, therefore, believe that God's grace is often "resistible." God's "outward call" goes out to all persons, many of whom resist it. But when the Lord's "inward call" comes to an individual with the life-giving power of the Holy Spirit, the person is changed and he responds in repentance and faith. This question is dealing with God's outward call, his grace that can be, and often is, resisted by sinners.

Arminian Misunderstandings of Irresistible Grace

Human beings have significant freedom of choice. Created in the image of God, we love and hate different things, and we choose from myriads of options all the time. Not only do we choose whether we will drink coffee or tea, but we also choose whether we will trust in Jesus or not. If we deny this truth, we treat one another as less than the image-bearers of God that we are.

One might conclude from this that Arminianism is correct in its charge that Calvinism denies real human responsibility by teaching that God's grace is "irresistible." For example, Roger Olson repeatedly charges Calvinists with believing in a being akin to Satan due to their belief in efficacious grace. Arminians, he writes, "have good reason to wonder how exactly to distinguish between the God [Calvinism] centers itself on and Satan—except that Satan wants all people to be damned to hell and God wants only a certain number damned to hell."[1] This is a truly unfortunate statement on Olson's part, but he insists that at this point Calvinism "injures God's reputation by necessarily undermining God's goodness and love."[2] Unfortunately, in addition to his acerbic tone, Olson's use of biblical evidence to show the error of efficacious grace proves his misunderstanding of Calvinism's compatibilism,

---

1. Roger E. Olson, *Against Calvinism* (Grand Rapids: Zondervan, 2011), 159.
2. Ibid., 163.

which asserts true divine sovereignty as well as real human responsibility.[3] One instance will suffice. Olson quotes Jesus's words in Matthew 19:24 ("Again I tell you, it is easier for a camel to go through the eye of a needle than for a rich person to enter the kingdom of God") and comments,

> What sense does this verse make in light of irresistible grace? Is Jesus saying it is harder *for God* to save a rich man than a poor one? How could that be? If everyone, without exception, only gets into the kingdom of God by God's work alone without any required cooperation on his or her part, then Jesus's saying makes no sense at all.[4]

Olson fails to see that the God of the Bible is absolutely sovereign in salvation (that's the reason Jesus responded to the disciples' incredulous reaction with the words, "With man this is impossible, but with God all things are possible" [v. 26]), while at the same time people are truly accountable for their decisions. Rich people are in danger of allowing their opulence to blind them to their real need of forgiveness for their sin. For this, they are responsible. Truly. But God can still save them.

People Are Responsible for Resisting the Gospel

The Bible teaches that people regularly resist the Holy Spirit's overtures to them. Even though God had called Israel to himself out of love for them (Gen. 12:1–3; Deut. 7:7–8), he continually called on the people to love him wholeheartedly, or, in the language of the Old Testament, to circumcise their hearts (Deut. 10:14–16; Jer. 4:4).[5] More often than not they failed to do this. The history of Israel—beginning with their grumblings after crossing through the Red Sea, serialized in Judges, and reaching its climactic fulfillment in Israel's and Judah's exile from the land—is largely the story of repeated rejection of Yahweh's injunctions to his people through the prophets. They were responsible for their rejection of the Lord.

Stephen takes up this issue in Acts 7. His audience was Jewish, made up of synagogue attendees (Acts 6:9) who stirred up the people and brought the deacon of the early church (6:5) before the elders, scribes, and council of the Jews (6:12). Stephen addressed them as "brothers and fathers" (7:2), throughout identifying with them as a Jew (e.g., calling Abraham "our father" [7:2]). Stephen's speech to them is a remarkable and selective history lesson,

---

3. See Questions 10–12.
4. Olson, *Against Calvinism*, 165 (italics original).
5. Although the Lord called on the people of Israel to circumcise their hearts in Deuteronomy 10, later he promised that he would circumcise their hearts for them (Deut. 30:6). They were responsible to do it; and he did it for them. This is an instance of compatibilism.

showing Israel's repeated rejection of God's appointed messengers, sent to call them back to faithfulness to him. The patriarchs were jealous of Joseph (7:9); they questioned Moses's right to interfere in their lives (7:27); they rejected Moses, refusing to obey him and returning to Egypt in their hearts (7:35, 39); they sought the fullness of God in temple worship, not realizing that this was as nothing to the Lord (7:47–50); for this reason, Yahweh would raise up for them in the future a truthful prophet (7:37). Stephen, then, was acting similarly to an Old Testament prophet when he cried out, "You stiff-necked people, uncircumcised in heart and ears, you always resist the Holy Spirit. As your fathers did, so do you. Which of the prophets did not your fathers persecute? And they killed those who announced beforehand the coming of the Righteous One, whom you have now betrayed and murdered, you who received the law as delivered by angels and did not keep it" (7:51–53). As Israel had largely rejected God's overtures through the Old Testament prophets, so they had now resisted his overtures through the prophet promised, the Messiah Jesus Christ. In this sense, they were culpable for their resistance.

We notice the same thing in Jesus's ministry. Jesus "was in the world, and the world was made through him, yet the world did not know him. He came to his own, and his own people did not receive him" (John 1:10–11). Later, after the declaration of God's great love and Jesus's call to all persons to come to him for forgiveness so that they will escape God's eternal punishment (3:16–18), John records this: "And this is the judgment: the light has come into the world, and people loved the darkness rather than the light because their deeds were evil. For everyone who does wicked things hates the light and does not come to the light, lest his deeds should be exposed" (3:19–20). People heard the gospel summons through Jesus. Yet, many of them resisted his appeal to them because they hated it and loved their life of sin instead.

Paul taught the same truth, insisting that non-Christians are constantly resisting the Lord's overtures to them. They do it as they reject God's testimony of himself to them in creation. They are responsible because in "their unrighteousness [they] suppress the truth" revealed to them (Rom. 1:18). God has revealed essential aspects of his character in creation (1:19–20), but unbelievers continually reject it because they idolize themselves instead of worshiping the true God (1:21–23). Therefore, "they are without excuse" (1:20). In a real sense, they resist God's revelation of himself to them in creation. Similarly, unbelievers resist what their consciences tell them. They do not know "that God's kindness is meant to lead [them] to repentance" (2:4). "Because of [their] hard and impenitent heart," Paul charges, they "are storing up wrath" for themselves "on the day of wrath when God's righteous judgment will be revealed" (2:5). They sin against the Lord when they reject his appeal to their consciences (2:15). Paul's conclusion is that "all have turned aside; together they have become worthless; no one does good; not even one" (3:12). "All have sinned and fall short of the glory of God" (3:23).

People are responsible for sinning. Unbelievers resist God's revelation of himself to them in creation and in conscience as well as in the call of the gospel. They resist the Lord's overtures to them every minute of every day.

The General, Resistible Call of the Gospel

The preceding biblical texts show us that we need to distinguish between two "calls" in the Bible. On the one hand, there is the general call (*vocatio externa*), which "refers to the call to all people to pay heed to the revelation of God."[6] Anthony Hoekema defines it this way: "The offering of salvation in Christ to people, together with an invitation to accept Christ in repentance and faith, in order that they may receive the forgiveness of sins and eternal life."[7] This general, outward call of God occurs through creation and conscience, summoning people to "acknowledge and honor their Creator (Ps. 19:1–4; Acts 17:24; Rom. 1:19–21; 2:14–15)."[8] But it also occurs through God's verbal summons to sinners to "repentance and faith in Christ so that they may receive eternal life and be forgiven of their trespasses (Matt. 28:18–20; Acts 1:6–8; 26:16–23; Rom. 10:8–15; 1 Cor. 15:1–8)."[9] This general, outward call goes to all persons. It's a real summons to submit to God. When the gospel is extended, it includes the offer of salvation. Yet people resist it all the time, because "the gospel call goes to all people but it is clearly not intended to be effectual for all of them, for we know that not all do in fact believe."[10]

But, on the other hand, God calls some sovereignly to faith in Christ. Unlike the external call, this internal, "invincible and irresistible," call (*vocatio interna*) of God always accomplishes its goal, which is the salvation of God's chosen ones. Bruce Ware says it is "God's inward and ultimately persuasive summons to repent of sin and to turn to Christ for salvation."[11] John Calvin agreed, noting that "only when God shines in us by the light of His Spirit is there any profit from the Word. Thus the inward calling, which alone is effectual and peculiar to the elect, is distinguished from the outward voice of men."[12] We will avoid many theological problems if we keep the general and outward call distinct from the special, inward, invincible call of God that is for the elect alone.

---

6. Matthew Barrett, *Salvation by Grace: The Case for Effectual Calling and Regeneration* (Phillipsburg, NJ: P&R, 2013), 70.

7. Anthony A. Hoekema, *Saved by Grace* (Grand Rapids: Eerdmans, 1989), 68.

8. Barrett, *Salvation by Grace*, 70.

9. Ibid., 71.

10. Ibid.

11. Bruce Ware, "Effectual Calling and Grace," 211.

12. John Calvin, *The Epistles of Paul the Apostle to the Romans and to the Thessalonians*, Calvin's New Testament Commentaries, vol. 8, trans. Ross MacKenzie, ed. David W. Torrance and Thomas F. Torrance (1960; Grand Rapids: Eerdmans, 1973), 232.

The general call is a staple of Calvinistic confessions as well as of the Bible. The Westminster Confession of Faith distinguishes God's inward call from a more general outward call that goes out to all who hear the summons of the gospel. "Others, not elected, although they may be called by the ministry of the Word, and may have some common operations of the Spirit, yet they never truly come to Christ, and therefore cannot be saved" (10.4). God's general summons for all who hear to listen, obey, and come, is not the same as his powerful, life-giving call that comes with all the regenerating power of the Spirit of God.

The New Testament is replete with examples of people hearing the gospel, but not heeding the summons of the Lord to repent and obey the gospel (e.g., Matt. 11:28; Luke 14:23; Acts 17:30; much of the ministry of Paul recorded for us in Acts). The classic text in this regard is Matthew 22:1–14, the parable of the wedding feast. Many were invited to come (vv. 3–4) but refused to come (vv. 5–6), so that the king invited others to come in their place (vv. 9–10) but nonetheless cast out one who did not belong among the invited guests (vv. 11–13). Jesus concludes by teaching this application: "For many are called, but few are chosen" (v. 14). Greg Welty notes of this text: "The first group received the outer call or invitation, which was resisted; but the second group responded to the summons: they were 'gathered together.' Thus, the word 'called' . . . envisioned in verse 14 is an outward call to all, a call that can and often is successfully resisted by those to whom it comes."[13]

Another significant text speaking of this "general call" is 1 Corinthians 1:23–24. Paul recounts, "We preach Christ crucified, a stumbling block to Jews and folly to Gentiles, but to those who are called, both Jews and Greeks, Christ the power of God and the wisdom of God." Clearly many listeners to Paul, according to John Piper, did not respond in faith; the only ones who did so were those "called," meaning that "they are called in such a way that they no longer regard the cross as foolishness. . . . Something happened in their hearts that changed the way they saw Christ. Let's describe this not as the general call but as the effectual call of God."[14] Just in the next chapter Paul tells the Corinthians that "the natural person does not accept the things of the Spirit of God, for they are folly to him, and he is not able to understand them because they are spiritually discerned" (1 Cor. 2:14). Paul does not write that unbelievers usually don't comprehend. Instead, they can't understand these things apart from God's intervention. But that doesn't keep Paul from preaching the gospel indiscriminately.

Summary

People continually resist God's overtures of grace to them in the gospel, in creation, and in their consciences. For this, they will be held accountable

---

13. Greg Welty, "Election and Calling," 235.
14. John Piper, *Five Points: Towards a Deeper Experience of God's Grace* (Fearn, UK: Christian Focus, 2013), 32.

by the Lord on the final day. Until then, we must be ever more zealous to call them to abandon the emptiness of their sin and turn to Jesus for forgiveness, where they will find rest for their souls (Matt. 11:29).

REFLECTION QUESTIONS

1. In your own words, how would you answer the question, "Can sinners resist God's offer of grace in the gospel?"

2. How would you respond to Olson's charge that the God of Calvinism is little different than Satan?

3. Can you think of other biblical texts where people are held accountable for resisting God's offer of grace to them?

4. Do you think it is helpful, and biblical, to distinguish between the outward (resistible) call of the gospel and the inward (irresistible) call of God the Holy Spirit? Why?

5. Has reading this chapter caused you to feel compassion towards those who have not come to faith in Christ? If not, consider Jesus's words in Matthew 23:37. How do you think you should feel about unbelievers?

What Is Regeneration?

The heart of being an evangelical Christian is believing that all people, as Jesus told Nicodemus, must be "born again" (John 3:3). We hold dear the truth that God "has caused us to be born again to a living hope" (1 Peter 1:3). People must be born again to inherit eternal life. Calvinists believe that in his sovereign grace, God gives new life to his elect who then repent of their sins and trust in Jesus. In other words, we believe that God sovereignly grants new life to us (we are regenerated) and then we ourselves believe (we convert). Regeneration precedes faith according to Calvinism.

The Divide

Calvinists' views are significantly different from Arminians'. Holding to prevenient grace, Arminians deny that God chooses to be gracious to a particular set of individuals. Rather, based on his foreknowledge of who will respond to the gospel, God chooses those future responders. When they repent and believe of their own free will, they are born again. In other words, in Arminianism faith precedes regeneration. Believing in Christ causes one to be born again. For this reason, Arminians are synergists. They maintain that sinners cooperate with God in the process of salvation.

Calvinists believe that because of the utter sinfulness, and resulting spiritual inability, of humanity, regeneration must precede faith. One is born from above, born by the power of the Holy Spirit (John 3:5–8) and then, as a result, the person believes in Jesus. For this reason, Calvinists are monergists, that is, those who hold that God is the sole cause of salvation since sinners are mired in sin. Monergism comports with the Bible's teaching on sin, God's efficacious grace, and the relationship between regeneration and faith.

The Biblical Warrant for Monergistic Regeneration

According to Anthony Hoekema, "Regeneration is a radical change from spiritual death to spiritual life, brought about in us by the Holy Spirit—a change in which we are completely passive. This change involves an inner renewal of our nature, is a fruit of God's sovereign grace, and takes place in union with Christ."[1] A sampling of biblical texts confirms the truthfulness of this definition.

First, regeneration is instantaneous, not a process. "The Lord opened [Lydia's] heart" (Acts 16:14); "even when we were dead in our trespasses, [God] made us alive together with Christ—by grace you have been saved" (Eph. 2:5); "And you, who were dead in your trespasses and the uncircumcision of your flesh, God made alive together with [Christ], having forgiven us all our trespasses" (Col. 2:13). God regenerates his elect suddenly, by his grace and power alone. Second, regeneration is a supernatural change, wrought by almighty God.

Believers "were born, not of blood nor of the will of the flesh nor of the will of man, but of God" (John 1:13). God is the agent in a Christian's spiritual birth.

Third, regeneration results in a complete, radical transformation of the changed person. The individual is, spiritually, a completely new person: "if anyone is in Christ, he is a new creation. The old has passed away; behold, the new has come" (2 Cor. 5:17). Since he or she is a born again person, his or her life must now bear appropriate spiritual fruit. "No one born of God makes a practice of sinning, for God's seed abides in him, and he cannot keep on sinning because he has been born of God" (1 John 3:9). These biblical texts highlight the radical, life-giving, monergistic nature of regeneration. We see why, therefore, John Murray avers that in regeneration

> God effects a change which is radical and all-pervasive, a change which cannot be explained in terms of any combination, permutation, or accumulation of human resources, a change which is nothing less than a new creation by him who calls the things that be not as though they were, who spake and it was done, who commanded and it stood fast. This, in a word, is regeneration.[2]

Think about this question: How does an unbelieving person meet the conditions required for salvation? What radical change must take place for a person to pass from death to life, from the kingdom of darkness to light? The answer is that an individual has to repent and believe the gospel. This is what Jesus taught: "the kingdom of God is at hand; repent and believe the gospel" (Mark 1:15); "repentance and forgiveness of sins should be proclaimed in his name to all nations" (Luke 24:47). Peter taught it as well: "repent and be baptized every one of you in the name of Jesus Christ for the forgiveness of your sins" (Acts 2:38); "God exalted him at his right hand as Leader and Savior, to give repentance to Israel and forgiveness of sins" (Acts 5:31). And Paul

---

1. Anthony A. Hoekema, *Saved by Grace* (Grand Rapids: Eerdmans, 1989), 101.
2. John Murray, *Redemption Accomplished and Applied* (Grand Rapids: Eerdmans, 1955), 96.

testified "both to Jews and to Greeks of repentance toward God and of faith in our Lord Jesus Christ" (Acts 20:21).

But due to humanity's enmity against God on account of our sin, apart from his intervention at the very core of our being (our "hearts" biblically), we will never change our course radically from pursuing our own interests to pursuing God's (this is what *metanoia* ["repentance"] means). Nor we will believe in Jesus on our own. Biblically defined, faith is more than intellectual cognizance of a thing. Rather, "faith is knowledge passing into conviction, and it is conviction passing into confidence. . . . The specific character of faith is that it looks away from itself and finds its whole interest and object in Christ. He is the absorbing preoccupation of faith."[3] Repentance and faith, then, indicate that a radical change has already transpired within an individual. They cannot be conjured up by a sinner, for they can only be accomplished through divine agency.

Four Lines of Biblical Evidence for Monergistic Regeneration

We see this from four different angles of biblical evidence. First, although people are completely responsible to repent and believe, the Bible is clear that they will not do so unless God in his grace gives them the ability to do what they can't do themselves due to their rebellion. Consider the great promises of the New Covenant to Israel, promises that are fulfilled ultimately through Christ in the life of his people, the church. The Lord promised his people, "I will sprinkle clean water on you, and you shall be clean from all your uncleannesses, and from all your idols I will cleanse you. And I will give you a new heart, and a new spirit I will put within you. And I will remove the heart of stone from your flesh and give you a heart of flesh" (Ezek. 36:25–26). Similarly, he encouraged them that

> Behold, the days are coming, declares the LORD, when I will make a new covenant with the house of Israel and the house of Judah, not like the covenant that I made with their fathers on the day when I took them by the hand to bring them out of the land of Egypt, my covenant that they broke, though I was their husband, declares the LORD. For this is the covenant that I will make with the house of Israel after those days, declares the LORD: I will put my law within them, and I will write it on their hearts. And I will be their God, and they shall be my people. And no longer shall each one teach his neighbor and each his brother, saying, "Know the LORD," for they shall all know me, from the least of them to the greatest, declares the LORD. For I will forgive their iniquity, and I will remember their sin no more. (Jer. 31:31–34)

---

3. Ibid., 111–12.

This promise of radical renewal of God's people was fulfilled in Christ, as the epistle to the Hebrews reminds us (Heb. 8:8–12). It shows that God is the author of the change: "I will make," "I will put," "I will write," with the result that "they shall all know me." God is the one who regenerates his people.

Second, God is the author of regeneration according to various New Testament texts that show the two conditions of salvation—repentance and faith—are gifts of God to his people. The elect repent and believe because God has granted them to repent and believe. Jesus taught "that no one can come to me unless it is granted him by the Father" (John 6:65). Paul stresses that repentance itself is a gift from God: "the Lord's servant must not be quarrelsome but kind to everyone, able to teach, patiently enduring evil, correcting his opponents with gentleness. God may perhaps grant them repentance leading to a knowledge of the truth" (2 Tim. 2:24–25). On this text, John Piper comments,

> But if God *gives* him repentance, he cannot resist because the very meaning of the gift of repentance is that God has changed our heart and made it willing to repent. In other words the gift of repentance is the overcoming of resistance to repentance. . . . Resistance to repentance is replaced by the gift of repentance.[4]

Similarly, notice how many times the apostle Paul thanks God for the faith that believers exercise:

- I thank my God through Jesus Christ for all of you, because your faith is proclaimed in all the world. (Rom. 1:8)
- because I have heard of your faith in the Lord Jesus and your love toward all the saints, I do not cease to give thanks [to God] for you. (Eph. 1:15–16)
- We always thank God, the Father of our Lord Jesus Christ, when we pray for you, since we heard of your faith in Christ Jesus and of the love that you have for all the saints. (Col. 1:3–4)
- We give thanks to God always for all of you, constantly mentioning you in our prayers. . . . For we know, brothers, loved by God, that he has chosen you, because our gospel came to you not only in word, but also in power and in the Holy Spirit and with full conviction. (1 Thess. 1:2–5)

Paul thanks *God* for the faith these Christians were expressing. He does this because God granted faith to these believers. People must repent and believe. And the Lord graciously grants what he requires.

---

4. John Piper, *Five Points: Towards a Deeper Experience of God's Grace* (Fearn, UK: Christian Focus, 2013), 31 (italics original).

Third, the language of the New Testament demonstrates that God is the actor in a person's salvation and that the individual is passive until the Lord has regenerated him or her. "Regeneration" ("the washing of regeneration and renewal of the Holy Spirit" [Titus 3:5]) and being "born of God" teach that God is the active agent and that we are passive. The "bringing forth" and "creating" language—such as in James 1:18 ("Of his own will he brought us forth by the word of truth") and Ephesians 2:10 ("we are his workmanship, created in Christ Jesus for good works")—show that God is the active agent in our salvation.[5] God is active and we are the passive recipients of his efficacious grace in regeneration.

Fourth, the syntax and grammar of 1 John proves that regeneration precedes faith. Notice these texts:

- If you know that he is righteous, you may be sure that everyone who practices righteousness has been born of him. (1 John 2:29)
- No one born of God makes a practice of sinning, for God's seed abides in him, and he cannot keep on sinning because he has been born of God. (1 John 3:9)
- Beloved, let us love one another, for love is from God, and whoever loves has been born of God and knows God. (1 John 4:7)
- Everyone who believes that Jesus is the Christ has been born of God, and everyone who loves the Father loves whoever has been born of him. (1 John 5:1)

In each instance, the individual "has been born" of God. This is a perfect tense verb, "denoting an action that precedes the human actions of practicing righteousness, avoiding sin, loving, or believing."[6] Thomas Schreiner's observations are cogent:

> No evangelical would say that before we are born again we must practice righteousness, for such a view would teach works-righteousness. Nor would we say that first we avoid sinning, and then are born of God, for such a view would suggest that human works cause us to be born of God. Nor would we say that first we show great love for God, and then he causes us to be born again. No, it is clear that practicing righteousness, avoiding sin, and loving are all the consequences or results of the new birth. But if this is the case,

---

5. Martyn Lloyd-Jones, *Great Doctrines of the Bible: Three Volumes in One* (Wheaton, IL: Crossway, 2003), 2:75–76.
6. Thomas R. Schreiner, "Does Regeneration Necessarily Precede Conversion?" https://9marks.org/article/does-regeneration-necessarily-precede-conversion/.

then we must interpret 1 John 5:1 in the same way, for the structure of the verse is the same as we find in the texts about practicing righteousness (1 John 2:29), avoiding sin (1 John 3:9), and loving God (1 John 4:7). It follows, then, that 1 John 5:1 teaches that first God grants us new life and then we believe Jesus is the Christ.[7]

Summary

Salvation comes from God. In his grace, he sovereignly changes our hearts and minds so that we love him and his truth. After the Lord powerfully regenerates us, we exercise faith. Regeneration precedes conversion.

REFLECTION QUESTIONS

1. How would you explain the doctrine of regeneration in your own words?

2. Why do you think Arminians insist that faith precedes regeneration?

3. Based on the biblical texts noted in this chapter, do you think there is any warrant to the Arminian belief noted above?

4. If regeneration precedes faith, how should you respond to your heavenly Father who has granted you repentance and faith?

5. If regeneration precedes faith, how do you think you should pray for unbelievers you know?

---

7. Ibid. Peterson and Williams concur, noting, "The perfect-tense verb in 1 John 5:1, 'has been born,' indicates that the new birth is the cause of faith in Christ, even as the new birth is the cause of godliness and love. . . . As a result of God's grace in regeneration, all those who have been born of God believe savingly in the Son of God" (Robert A. Peterson and Michael D. Williams, *Why I Am Not an Arminian* [Downers Grove, IL: InterVarsity Press, 2004], 189).

Will Christians Persevere in the Faith?

Biblical Calvinism is rooted in the loving character of the sovereign, personal, triune God who loves his people with a never-ending love from eternity past to eternity future. The particularity of God's love is a Calvinistic axiom. This truth is highlighted in the doctrine of perseverance. The Father chose his elect people to belong to him for eternity; the Son lived a perfect life on their behalf and died in their place; the Spirit grants them new life and sustains them until their glorification. God's people will persevere because God will uphold them.

The Doctrine Stated

The Westminster divines taught perseverance when they argued,

> They, whom God hath accepted in His Beloved, effectually called, and sanctified by His Spirit, can neither totally nor finally fall away from the state of grace, but shall certainly persevere therein to the end, and be eternally saved.
>
> This perseverance of the saints depends not upon their own free will, but upon the immutability of the decree of election, flowing from the free and unchangeable love of God the Father; upon the efficacy of the merit and intercession of Jesus Christ, the abiding of the Spirit, and the seed of God within them. (WCF 17.1, 2)

The perseverance of God's elect is a biblical truth. For example, Paul encouraged a group of Christians that "he who began a good work in you will bring it to completion at the day of Jesus Christ" (Phil. 1:6). There was no uncertainty here. The same apostle spoke of the end of a Christian's pilgrimage in such certain terms that he could speak of a future event in the past tense: "those whom he predestined he also called, and those whom he called he also justified, and those whom he justified *he also glorified*" (Rom. 8:30; italics added). God has predestined, called, and justified his people. But their glorification is a future event. While it is future for us, though, it is so certain that the Lord can speak of it in the past tense. He does that because our future glorification is secured. Nothing we experience in this life "will be able to separate us from the love of God in Christ Jesus our Lord" (Rom. 8:39). By his sovereign power, our heavenly Father will hold on to his children and keep them in the faith.

To demonstrate that Christians will be kept by the power of God for salvation, we will traverse three steps. First, we will discuss the biblical truth that God preserves his people. Second, we will highlight the manner in which compatibilism comes into play when we think about Christians' persevering. Then we will look at several instances of those who abandoned Jesus in the pages of the New Testament, asking if we have reason to think they ever had been saved. The cumulative force of these lines of biblical reasoning will show us that true believers will persevere in the faith.

God's Preservation of the Saints

God will preserve his people. Whatever happens—death, life, persecution, "anything else in all creation"!—God will not let his people go. We saw this truth in Romans 8 and in Philippians 1. Jesus taught the same thing when he said,

> All that the Father gives me will come to me, and whoever comes to me I will never cast out. For I have come down from heaven, not to do my own will but the will of him who sent me. And this is the will of him who sent me, that I should lose nothing of all that he has given me, but raise it up on the last day. (John 6:37–39)

Notice the connections Jesus makes here. The Father gives some to the Son; those come to the Son; all those who come will never be lost because Jesus won't cast them out. This is God's will. It will be done. Jesus will hold his people fast, and he will keep them from ever falling completely away from him.

Our Lord also taught,

> My sheep hear my voice and I know them, and they follow me. I give them eternal life, and they will never perish, and no one will snatch them out of my hand. My Father, who has given them to me, is greater than all, and no one is able to snatch them out of my Father's hand. I and the Father are one. (John 10:27–30)

Again Jesus grounds the preservation of his people in the authority of the Father. The Father—the greatest of all—has given the sheep to Jesus; the sheep listen and follow the Son; they have eternal life and will have it forever. Why? Because Jesus gave them life, and no one can tear them away from him or the Father. They will not eternally perish.

> And Paul told the Corinthians,
>> I give thanks to my God always for you because of the grace of God that was given you in Christ Jesus . . . as you wait for the revealing of our Lord Jesus Christ, *who will sustain you to the end, guiltless in the day of our Lord Jesus Christ.* God is faithful, by whom you were called into the fellowship of his Son, Jesus Christ our Lord. (1 Cor. 1:4, 7–8; italics added)

The apostle is filled with thanksgiving because of God's grace that has been poured out on these believers. They have come to Jesus. And Jesus (note: it's not the Corinthians ultimately, but Christ) will sustain them. He will present them guiltless at the final judgment.

Without denying Christians' responsibility to persevere in the faith, the Bible stresses God's role in preserving his people in their faith. The world, the flesh, and the devil will combat against their very souls. But when all else seems to give way, the one thing that will sustain them is their heavenly Father's sovereign power. He will preserve his people in the faith.

The Role of Compatibilism in Perseverance

God will preserve his people. At the same time, Christians are responsible for continuing to trust in Jesus, to persevere. Both truths are true, and neither one negates the other. We will notice this compatibilism in two instances.[1]

Few declarations of God's sovereign goodness in saving his people surpass Paul's exclamation in Colossians 1:21–22: "And you, who once were alienated and hostile in mind, doing evil deeds, he has now reconciled in his body of flesh by his death, in order to present you holy and blameless and above reproach before him." God is the one who saves his people. They were trapped in their sin, unable and unwilling to save themselves. God sovereignly—independently—saved them. But that is not all. Paul continues, noting the believers' role in their perseverance in the faith. They will be reconciled to God "if indeed you continue in the faith, stable and steadfast, not shifting from the hope of the gospel that you heard" (Col 1:23). The conditional particle, "if," is significant, highlighting believers' obligation to keep trusting in Jesus and not to allow themselves to drift away from him. God is sovereign and will

---

1. On compatibilism, see Questions 10–12.

accomplish his will. Christians are responsible to keep trusting in Jesus. Both are true, as Douglas Moo confirms,

> [Paul] wants to confront the Colossians with the reality that their eventual salvation depends on their remaining faithful to Christ and to the true gospel. Only by continuing in their faith can they hope to find a favorable verdict from God on the day of judgment. . . . God does, indeed, by his grace and through his Spirit, work to preserve his people so that they will be vindicated in the judgment; but, at the same time, God's people are responsible to persevere in their faith if they expect to see that vindication.[2]

Jude similarly stresses the role of compatibilism in perseverance. He revels in God's power to keep his children in the faith. He writes "to those who are called, beloved in God the Father and kept for Jesus Christ" (v. 1). And he concludes the letter with this wonderful, hopeful benediction:

> Now to him who is able to keep you from stumbling and to present you blameless before the presence of his glory with great joy, to the only God, our Savior, through Jesus Christ our Lord, be glory, majesty, dominion, and authority, before all time and now and forever. Amen. (vv. 24–25)

God will keep his children from stumbling. He will present them blameless before his glorious throne. This is true. Yet, these Christians still have a responsibility. Jude charges them to "build yourselves up in your most holy faith; pray in the Holy Spirit; keep yourselves in the love of God, waiting for the mercy of our Lord Jesus Christ that leads to eternal life" (vv. 20–21). God has loved them, and his love will sustain them to the end. Yet, they are responsible to keep themselves in the arms of God's love. Thomas Schreiner observes,

> Jude represented well the biblical tension between divine sovereignty and human responsibility. On the one hand, believers only avoid apostasy because of the grace of God. On the other hand, the grace of God does not cancel out the need for believers to exert all their energy to remain in God's love.[3]

---

2. Douglas J. Moo, *The Letters to the Colossians and to Philemon*, Pillar New Testament Commentary (Grand Rapids: Eerdmans, 2008), 144.
3. Thomas R. Schreiner, *1, 2 Peter, Jude*, New American Commentary (Nashville: B&H, 2003), 183–84.

Both truths are true, and we will be spiritually weak if we neglect either of these verities.

Not All "Christians" Are Christians

Some of us have known people we thought were Christians who abandoned the faith. Doesn't this call into question what we've seen about God's preservation of his people? I don't want for a moment to suggest that this is an easy issue, but I think there are two possible solutions to this difficulty. The individual might be a believer who will be brought back to repentance and faith in the future. Or, the reality might be that he or she was never a Christian. In fact, the New Testament teaches that not everyone who claims the name "Christian" is really a true disciple of Jesus Christ.

Jesus knew this. He warned of "false prophets" who would come. Outwardly they look like sheep, even though inwardly they are "ravenous wolves" (Matt. 7:15). The only way to know finally if they are truly Christians is to examine the evidence of their lives. Their fruit will demonstrate if they are a good tree or not (Matt 7:16–20). In this context Jesus warns,

> Not everyone who says to me, "Lord, Lord," will enter the kingdom of heaven, but the one who does the will of my Father who is in heaven. On that day many will say to me, "Lord, Lord, did we not prophesy in your name, and cast out demons in your name, and do many mighty works in your name?" And then will I declare to them, "I never knew you; depart from me, you workers of lawlessness." (Matt. 7:21–23)

Another time, after Jesus said some difficult things, "many of his disciples" began grumbling. John tells us that "Jesus knew from the beginning who those were who did not believe" (John 6:60–61, 64). "After this many of his disciples turned back and no longer walked with him" (John 6:66). The conclusion we are forced to draw is simple, yet significant: not everyone who claims to be a Christ-follower, and indeed even looks like a disciple of Jesus to our eyes, is truly a born again believer in Jesus. The person may be self-deceived, or he or she may be intentionally deceptive. Either way, the individual is not truly redeemed.

This is similar to John's words in 1 John 2 where the apostle speaks of the reality of "many antichrists." These false teachers once seemed to be part of the church, but that proved to be untrue because of their abandonment of the fellowship: "They went out from us, but they were not of us; for if they had been of us, they would have continued with us. But they went out, that it might become plain that they all are not of us" (1 John 2:18–19). John does not say that these false teachers lost their faith. Rather, he reasons in an *ex post facto* manner. Their abandonment of the fellowship proves that they were never truly part of the church. In a similar manner, Paul speaks of Demas, ostensibly a Christian. He laments that "Demas, in love with this present world, has deserted me" (2 Tim 4:10). Presumably, Demas had been identified as a believer, but his desertion of Paul due to his love affair with the world proved that he was not a Christian in the first place.

Summary

The last section was not meant to downplay the glory of God's preservation of his people but, rather, to offer an explanation as to why sometimes it seems as if his people fall away. We need to hold on to the overwhelming truth of Scripture that the Lord knows those who belong to him (2 Tim. 2:19). More than that, since he knows those who trust in Christ for salvation, calls them to himself in love, seals them with his Spirit, and speaks of their eternal future with him as a completed reality, they should have every confidence that "he who began a good work in you will bring it to completion at the day of Jesus Christ" (Phil. 1:6). This is the truth the Bible gloriously presents. God's people will persevere because he will keep them. May reading this chapter assist you to "make your calling and election sure" (2 Peter 1:10). Consider Christ's claims on his people as well as the fruits that need to characterize them before you assume you are a believer. Remember, "you will recognize them by their fruits" (Matt. 7:20).

REFLECTION QUESTIONS

1. What encouragement do you take from biblical truths like Romans 8:30 and Philippians 1:6?

2. How would you respond to the charge that the Calvinistic doctrine of God's preservation of the elect negates the significance of our persevering in the faith?

3. How would you express the compatibility of God's preservation of his people and our perseverance in your own words?

4. Have you known a person you thought was a Christian who abandoned the faith? How has this chapter helped you process that difficult situation?

5. Why do you think God requires us to persevere if he has promised to preserve us?

PART 3

Additional Theological Questions

What Is Hyper-Calvinism?

The Bible everywhere assumes that in salvation God is completely sovereign and people are truly responsible. This is "compatibilism."[1] According to this truth, God uses "means" to accomplish his end of saving his people—the gospel preached, heard, and trusted (Rom. 10:8–15). An extreme reaction to the errors within the Arminian system called hyper-Calvinism denies that God uses the means of preaching, hearing, and trusting to convert his people. Hyper-Calvinism is the unbiblical denial of Christians' responsibility to preach the gospel as well as of non-Christians' responsibility to repent and believe in Jesus.

The Logic of Hyper-Calvinism and Arminianism

Hyper-Calvinism is similar to Arminianism in one central way. They both operate with the same logical, and ultimately unbiblical, paradigm. Though the Bible unflinchingly teaches compatibilism, these truths are not easy to hold together. Both Arminians and hyper-Calvinists deny they can be held together; one of them has to be jettisoned in favor of the other one. Arminians so stress human responsibility (i.e., libertarian human freedom) that they functionally deny God's sovereignty in the area of salvation. Hyper-Calvinists go the opposite route; they over-emphasize God's supreme sovereignty in salvation to the point that they deny human responsibility. Both systems are logical and self-consistent. But they are both unbiblical and fail to take into account the whole counsel of God.[2]

---

1. See Questions 10–12.
2. Another way of seeing the similarity between hyper-Calvinism and Arminianism is to say, as John Piper does, that they both stand "on the same pretended logic against Scripture. Both argue that it is absurd and cruel to require of any man what is beyond his power to perform" (*Andrew Fuller: Holy Faith, Worthy Gospel, World Mission* [Wheaton, IL: Crossway, 2016], 40).

The Effects of Hyper-Calvinism

Hyper-Calvinism's grave errors quench evangelism. Joseph Ivimey correctly labelled hyper-Calvinism a "non-invitation, non-application scheme" since it limited a preacher's ability to invite people to Jesus or to apply the gospel to them in any way.[3] Hyper-Calvinists teach that the elect will become "sensible" of their desperate state outside of Christ (as the Spirit brings conviction when the preacher recounts the gospel narrative). Only these "sensible" sinners should be told to repent and receive Christ. If a preacher invites non-sensible sinners to Christ (i.e., those in whom he has no reason to believe the Spirit is graciously at work), he is telling them to do something they can in no way do; in effect, he is making them more guilty than they were before. So he must avoid pressing the claims of the gospel on such non-Christians. The system seems logical. But it is grossly unbiblical.

"Calvinism inevitably leads to hyper-Calvinism" is a charge sometimes made against Calvinism. The charge, though, is invalid. Given the logical similarities of the two systems, a Calvinist could become an Arminian as readily as he or she could defect to hyper-Calvinism. The drift to hyper-Calvinism is not foreordained. Additionally, we acknowledge that some (maybe most?) Calvinists don't do enough evangelism. We need to call this what it is: sin and disobedience. Calvinists need to be more zealous in evangelizing. But I am unconvinced that there's something unstable in Calvinism that leads its adherents not to witness to the lost. We could ask our Arminian brothers and sisters if they think they are doing enough evangelism. Some (maybe most?) Arminians don't evangelize as much as they should. (As someone who's been both an Arminian and a Calvinist, I can say that I have never felt that I was telling enough people about Jesus. And none of my Arminian or Calvinistic friends ever thought they "had arrived" in this area.) Does this mean they've fallen prey to hyper-Arminianism? Of course not. It just means they're sinners and need to be more obedient to the Lord. Either way, the solution is not to turn to Arminianism in order to motivate obedience in evangelism.

Towards a Definition of Hyper-Calvinism, and an Antidote

Hyper-Calvinism has two theological tenets with several corresponding results. The first tenet is eternal justification, the belief that the covenant of grace is so secure, being built on the foundation of God's election, that the elect are viewed by God as being justified from eternity. In this scheme there is no biblical warrant to call sinners to faith since the Lord has already eternally decreed that they would have faith. This is unbiblical. Jesus and the apostles regularly called on sinners to believe (e.g., Mark 1:15; Acts 16:31). In addition, Paul's exposition shows that faith is the means by which a person experiences God's blessing, and without which no one is justified. The apostle

---

3. Joseph Ivimey, *A History of the English Baptists* (London: B. J. Holdworth, 1811–30), 3:272.

proclaims, "Abraham believed God and it was credited to him as righteous-ness" (Rom. 4:3). And he asserts, "Since we have been justified through faith, we have peace with God through our Lord Jesus Christ. Through him we have also obtained access by faith into this grace in which we stand, and we rejoice in the hope of the glory of God" (Rom. 5:1–2). One must exercise personal faith to be God's child. Paul often refers to what believers "once were" before coming to Christ. They were at that point not justified (see Eph. 2:1–3; Col. 1:21–22). Eternal justification is an unbiblical notion.

The second tenet is antinomianism, the belief that since Christ bore the penalty of sin and perfectly fulfilled the law for the elect, Christians are not required to obey his moral law. The whole New Testament (think of Paul's outrage at the question, "Are we to sin because we are not under law but under grace?" in Rom. 6:15), though, shows this to be wrong. Believers are to be perfect as our Father in heaven in perfect (Matt. 5:48).[4]

These two unbiblical doctrines lead to four (non)evangelistic practices of hyper-Calvinists. First, they advocate pressing the claims of the gospel only on "sensible sinners," as we have seen. Only when an unbeliever starts to exhibit con-cern as the preacher recounts the history of the life and death of Jesus (without, of course, ever calling unbelievers to come to faith!) can the preacher know the sinner is elect. At that point the preacher can begin to encourage the unbeliever that the promises of the gospel are for her personally and call her to faith.

The nineteenth-century Baptist luminary, Charles Spurgeon, rebuffed this false idea, proving that gospel invitations were universal for everyone—"sensible" or not—and that the preacher hadn't done his job until he called all his listeners to repentance and faith. God will receive sinners into his family if they will repent and believe. From Acts 3:19 ("Repent ye therefore and be converted, that your sins may be blotted out"), Spurgeon proclaimed:

> Peter preached the Christ of the gospel—preached it per-sonally and directly at the crowd who were gathered around him. . . . Grown up among us is a school of men who say that they rightly preach the gospel to sinners when they merely deliver statements of what the gospel is [that is, the hyper-Calvinists], and the result of dying unsaved, but they grow furious and talk of unsoundness if any venture to say to the sinner, "Believe," or "Repent." To this school Peter did not believe—into their secret he had never come, and with their assembly, were he alive now, he would not be joined.[5]

---

4. See Question 38.
5. Charles Spurgeon, "Apostolic Exhortation," in C. H. Spurgeon, *The Metropolitan Tabernacle Pulpit, Sermons Preached and Revised by C. H. Spurgeon, During the Year 1868*, vol. 14, of *The New Park Street Pulpit and Metropolitan Tabernacle Pulpit* (Pasadena, TX: Pilgrim,

Spurgeon maintained that the apostles "delivered *the* gospel, the same gospel to the dead as to the living, the same gospel to the non-elect as to the elect. The point of distinction is not in the gospel, but in its being applied by the Holy Ghost, or left to be rejected of men."[6] Gospel invitations are for everyone, not for a false category of "sensible" sinners.

Second, and related to this, hyper-Calvinists hold that there is no universal warrant for everyone to come to Christ. They deny the universal "warrant of faith." Before coming to Christ, sinners must sense some "warrant" in themselves for thinking that Christ's invitations are addressed to them personally. This usually takes the form of an impression of some biblical text in their minds that they believe was given to them directly by the Lord, proving that he had a special concern for them. This is wrong. The warrant for the unconverted to trust in Christ rests on nothing in themselves; the warrant lies in the invitation of Christ. Based on that, everyone has a duty to come to Christ.

Again, Spurgeon is helpful:

> "Repent and be baptized every one of you," said Peter. As John Bunyan puts it—one man might have stood up in the crowd and said, "But I helped to hound him to the cross!" "Repent and be baptized *every one of you.*" "But I drove the nails into his hands!" saith one. "*Every one of you,*" says Peter. "But I pierced his side." "*Every one of you,*" said Peter. "And I put my tongue into my cheek and stared at his nakedness and said, 'If he be the Son of God, let him come down from the cross!'" "*Every one of you,*" said Peter. "Repent and be baptized every one of you." I do feel so grieved at many of our Calvinistic brethren; they know nothing about Calvinism I am sorry to say, for never was any man more caricatured by his professed followers than John Calvin. Many of them are afraid to preach from Peter's text. . . . When I do it, they say, "He is unsound." But I do not care for that; I know the Lord has blessed my appeals to all sorts of sinners, and none shall stay me in giving free invitations as long as I find them in this Book.[7]

1970), 194. This and the following sermon excerpts from Spurgeon are found in Iain H. Murray, *Spurgeon v. Hyper-Calvinism: The Battle for Gospel Preaching* (Edinburgh: Banner of Truth, 1995), 71, 75–76, 82, 89–90.

6. Charles Spurgeon, "Degrees of Power Attending the Gospel," in C. H. Spurgeon, *The Metropolitan Tabernacle Pulpit, Sermons Preached and Revised by C. H. Spurgeon, During the Year 1865*, vol. 11, of *The New Park Street Pulpit and Metropolitan Tabernacle Pulpit* (Pasadena, TX: Pilgrim, 1970), 495 (italics original).

7. Charles Spurgeon, "The Silver Trumpet," in C. H. Spurgeon, *The New Park Street Pulpit and Metropolitan Tabernacle Pulpit, Containing Sermons Preached and Revised by the Rev. C.*

Third, and related to the first two consequences, hyper-Calvinists assume that unbelievers are not responsible to come to Christ. Their logic is simple: sinners cannot be required to do what they are not able to do. Since they're sinful and unable to convert by their own power, they can't be required to convert. As we have seen, though, even though humankind fell and became enslaved to sin, that does not limit our responsibility to come to Christ. God is sovereign, *and* people are responsible.[8]

Spurgeon expansively noted,

> The system of truth is not one straight line, but two. No man will ever get a right view of the gospel until he knows how to look at the two lines at once. . . . Now, if I were to declare that man was so free to act, that there is no presidence of God over his actions, I should be driven very near to atheism; and if, on the other hand, I declare that God so overrules all things, as that man is not free to be responsible, I am driven at once to Antinomianism or fatalism. That God predestinates, and that man is responsible, are two things that few can see. They are believed to be inconsistent and contradictory; but they are not. It is the fault of our weak judgment. . . . it is my folly that leads me to imaging that two truths can ever contradict each other.[9]

Fourth, the theological justification for the other three points is the hyper-Calvinistic claim that God does not love all people. If God has chosen an elect people, hyper-Calvinists assert, then he can have no desire for the salvation of any others. To speak as though he loved the non-elect is to deny the particularity of his grace, they maintain. Biblical Calvinists, on the other hand, believe that God loves all persons, even if he loves certain ones differently. We can legitimately say, therefore, that God desires the salvation even of those whom he's not elected to life. We may struggle to reconcile these truths, but we must hold them both since they are equally taught in the Bible.[10]

Spurgeon is perceptive at this point:

> Lost sinners who sit under the sound of the gospel are not lost for want of the most affectionate invitation. God says he

---

H. Spurgeon, During the Year 1861, vol. 7, of *The New Park Street Pulpit and Metropolitan Tabernacle Pulpit* (Pasadena, TX: Pilgrim, 1969), 148–49 (italics original).

8. See Questions 9–12.
9. Charles Spurgeon, "Sovereign Grace and Man's Responsibility," in C. H. Spurgeon, *The New Park Street Pulpit, Containing Sermons Preached and Revised by the Rev. C. H. Spurgeon, Minister of the Chapel, During the Year 1858*, vol. 4, of *The New Park Street Pulpit* (Pasadena, TX: Pilgrim, 1969), 337.
10. See Question 5.

stretches out his hands. . . . Now, was God sincere in his offer?
God forgive the man who dares to say he was not. God is undoubtedly sincere in every act he did. He sent his prophets, he
entreated the people of Israel to lay hold on spiritual things,
but they would not, and though he stretched out his hands
all the day long, yet they were "a disobedient and gainsaying
people" and would not have his love.[11]

Summary

We have driven a nail into the ugly coffin of hyper-Calvinism. There is no
biblical warrant for this extreme error which borders on fatalism with a thin
biblical guise. God is holy and will judge everyone since we're all sinners. In
his love he sent his only Son to die for sinners. If they will repent and believe,
they will have eternal life. This is what the apostles preached. And this is what
we must proclaim as well. May the Lord protect us from ever becoming either
theoretical or functional hyper-Calvinists and withholding this life-giving
gospel from anyone.

REFLECTION QUESTIONS

1. How would you describe hyper-Calvinism in your own words?

2. Do you think that hyper-Calvinism and Arminianism have the same root
   error? What is it?

3. Does holding to compatibilism protect one from falling into the error of
   hyper-Calvinism? If so, what protection does it offer?

4. Do you know any hyper-Calvinists? Is their doctrine and practice similar
   to that described in this chapter? Which of Spurgeon's responses to hyper-
   Calvinism would be most helpful for them to hear?

5. Do you have any hyper-Calvinist tendencies? Identify them, ask the Lord
   to forgive you for them, and seek to share the gospel boldly with everyone
   you can reach.

---

11. Spurgeon, "Sovereign Grace and Man's Responsibility," 341.

If God Is Sovereign, Is He Responsible for Evil?

Christians face three realities:

1. God is all-powerful and controls everything in creation.
2. Evil is real.
3. God is good.

We don't ultimately understand how these three truths can be reconciled, but we put the testimony of Scripture above our meager intellectual deficiencies. God is sovereign and good. Under his good sovereignty, evil exists.

Toward a Solution: The Storyline of Scripture

We must let the Bible give us the parameters for considering God and evil. In fact, the Bible is pretty chaste about all sorts of details regarding evil. Apparently God, for example, isn't interested in telling us exactly how evil entered into creation. God created the world good. At the end of the creation account, "God saw everything that he had made, and behold, it was very good" (Gen. 1:31). Then, seemingly out of nowhere, evil slithered into the pristine creation for "the serpent was more crafty than any other beast of the field that the LORD God had made" (Gen. 3:1). This serpent proceeded to tempt Eve to rebel against her Creator and then Adam also fell into sin (Gen. 3:1–6). We should note here what Anthony Hoekema called "the riddle of sin."

> The fact that we can discern these stages in the temptation and fall of our first parents, however, does not mean that we have in the Genesis narrative an explanation for the entrance of sin into the human world. What we have here is the biblical narrative of the origin of sin, but not an explanation for

that origin. One of the most important things we must remember about sin, both in the life of man and in that of the
angels, is that it is inexplicable. The origin of evil is . . . one of
the greatest riddles of life.[1]

The consequences of sin's entrance into the world were immediate—
Adam and Eve's relationship was fractured (3:7), and their relationship with
their good Creator was also broken (3:8–13, 16–19). Adam's sin had devastating consequences for the whole human race, whom he had represented
when he plunged into sin. Now all are born sinful and guilty (Rom. 5:12–21).
Yet God immediately promised the Messiah who would destroy the works of
Satan and ultimately crush him (Gen. 3:15).

These opening three chapters of the Bible encompass much of the story
of redemptive history. Genesis 1 and 2 deal with creation. God is the supreme
Lord; he's the Creator with rights over everything and everyone in his universe.
Genesis 3 discusses the fall. Satan's wiles and our first parents' rebellion plunge
us all into the status of being guilty rebels against our good Creator. We see the
reality of self-centered rebels painted in vivid colors throughout the pages of the
Old Testament as well as the New. Then, in Genesis 3:15, we get a glimmer of
hope: God will not leave us in our sin to pay the penalty we deserve for our rebellion. No, he will send a redeemer who will deal with the consequences of our
treachery. Genesis 1–3 provides us an overview of creation, fall, and redemption.

It's remarkable that God gives us no data about how we get from the "it
was very good" of Genesis 1:31 to the "crafty" serpent of Genesis 3:1. We
might surmise what we thought happened. Scripture might give us a few
hints, at best. What we hold on to are these revealed truths: God is the sole
Creator and both he and his original creation are good. Under his sovereignty,
he lets sin enter into the creation which disrupts the good order of the original design. Satan is real, but he's a controlled creature and is not a rival deity.
In his mercy, God promises a Redeemer who will rescue his people from the
misery of sin and the clutches of evil.

The "Givens" of Evil

Even though evil is mysterious, Scripture teaches us at least seven truths
that should bound our consideration of it. The first "given" of evil is that
all people experience it. Whether it's in the form of "natural evil" ("God's
curse, the pains brought into the world by the Fall") or "moral evil" ("sin,
the transgression of God's law"), we all experience the effects of evil.[2] It is

---

1. Anthony A. Hoekema, *Created in God's Image* (Grand Rapids: Eerdmans, 1986), 130–31.
2. John M. Frame, *The Doctrine of God* (Phillipsburg, NJ: P&R, 2002), 168. "Natural" evil is
   a result of "moral" evil (ibid., 161; also see D. A. Carson, *How Long, O Lord? Reflections on
   Suffering and Evil* [Grand Rapids: Baker, 1990], 43).

difficult to grasp why nonsensical evil plagues us and those we love.[3] In those moments we can become emotionally weary and unable to answer the "Why, Lord?" question with any sense of perspective. We sometimes wonder about God's involvement in evil. John Feinberg captures the pain inherent in the question:

> The religious problem of evil isn't primarily an intellectual problem but is fundamentally an emotional problem! People wrestling with evil . . . do not need an intellectual discourse on how to justify God's ways to man in light of what's happening. . . . This, on the other hand, is a problem about how someone experiencing affliction can live with this God who doesn't stop it.[4]

Because of the traumatic effect of evil in our lives we must make sure the Bible, not our emotions, is our resource in answering the question.[5]

Second, whatever else we know, we know who God has revealed himself to be. God is absolutely sovereign, as we have seen throughout this book. Nothing that occurs in the world falls outside of his absolute control. "Whatever the LORD pleases, he does, in heaven and on earth, in the seas and all deeps" (Ps. 135:6). Additionally, God is good. The Lord himself is the standard of what goodness is, for he is "the Rock, his work is perfect, for all his ways are justice. A God of faithfulness and without iniquity, just and upright is he" (Deut. 32:4). Since all God's ways are just, and since he has no iniquity, we must let him be the standard of goodness, instead of what we are convinced on the basis of our finite intelligence should be the case.[6]

Third, given the reality that God is the Creator and we're his creatures, we must not attempt to judge what God has the right to do or not do. Think about Job's sufferings. His children died. He suffered incredible physical pain. His own wife even encouraged him to curse God so that the Lord would put him out of his misery. God had given Satan free reign to do whatever he wanted to do to Job short of killing him. After suffering all this evil, Job questioned God. So God "answered Job out of the whirlwind and said: 'Who is this that darkens council by words without knowledge? Dress for action like a man; I

---

3. Robert W. Yarbrough, "Christ and the Crocodiles: Suffering and the Goodness of God in Contemporary Perspective," in *Suffering and the Goodness of God*, eds. Christopher W. Morgan and Robert A. Peterson (Wheaton, IL: Crossway, 2008), 24.

4. John S. Feinberg, "A Journey in Suffering: Personal Reflections on the Religious Problem of Evil," in *Suffering and the Goodness of God*, eds. Christopher W. Morgan and Robert A. Peterson (Wheaton, IL: Crossway, 2008), 219.

5. D. A. Carson, *How Long, O Lord? Reflections on Suffering and Evil* (Grand Rapids: Baker, 1990), 96.

6. Frame, *Doctrine of God*, 161–62.

will question you, and you make it known to me'" (Job 38:1–3). Compared to the Lord, Job is nothing (38:4–40:2). God is not done, though, for he prosecutes Job for daring to question the Lord's right to do all that he had done (40:6–8). Frame's evaluation is correct: "God is not subject to the ignorant evaluations of his creatures."[7] After hearing the Lord's charges against him, Job confesses, "I have uttered what I did not understand, things too wonderful for me, which I did not know" (42:3). Did Job suffer the trauma of evil? Most certainly. But at the end of the day the Lord reserves the right to do his pleasure without being accountable to any of his creatures. Our Creator has the prerogative to do what he wants. He is not accountable to us.

Fourth, spelling out the implications of the Creator-creature divide more, Frame notes that "it is significant that the potter-clay image appears in the one place in Scripture where the problem of evil is explicitly addressed" in Romans 9:19–21:

> You will say to me then, "Why does he still find fault? For who can resist his will?" But who are you, O man, to answer back to God? Will what is molded say to its molder, "Why have you made me like this?" Has the potter no right over the clay, to make out of the same lump one vessel for honored use and another for dishonorable use?

This demonstrates that here the "answer to the problem of evil turns entirely on God's sovereignty" for it shows us that God's "prerogatives are far greater than ours."[8] We must not sit in judgment over the Lord.

Fifth, time and time again the Bible shows us that the Lord often uses evil to accomplish his good purposes. Supremely, God employs it to bring glory to himself, the thing that he is most concerned to do.[9] He also uses evil to manifest his justice and mercy (Rom. 3:26); to redeem his elect through the evil inflicted on his Son in their place (1 Peter 3:18); to confront unbelievers with the reality of their predicament so that they will seek God's forgiveness (Luke 13:1–5; John 9); and to lovingly discipline his children (Heb. 12:5–11).[10]

Sixth, God is completely sovereign over evil. He doesn't have a "hands off" policy towards sin as if he idly watches evil without being sovereign over it. God is completely holy so he never does evil. Yet no evil occurs that God does not sovereignly control. Even though he's not the author of sin in the sense that he never sins, he plans it and uses it. God completely controls evil, as Scripture says:

---

7. Ibid., 181.
8. Ibid.
9. Yarbrough, "Christ and the Crocodiles," 31.
10. See Carson, *How Long?*, 66–68, 70–73, 183–84.

See now that I, even I, am he, and there is no god beside me;
I kill and I make alive; I wound and I heal; and there is none
that can deliver out of my hand. (Deut. 32:39)

I am the LORD, and there is no other, besides me there is no
God; I equip you, though you do not know me, that people
may know, from the rising of the sun and from the west, that
there is none besides me; I am the LORD, and there is no other.
I form light and create darkness, I make well-being and create
calamity, I am the LORD, who does all these things. (Isa. 45:5–7)

Bruce Ware's comments on this passage are apropos: "Although God controls
both light and darkness (Isa. 45:7), God's own nature is exclusively *light and
not darkness* (1 John 1:5)."[11] Since God is holy, "[w]hile evil never flows from
the nature of God, it is in all cases controlled by the agency of God."[12]

The murder of the innocent Son of God was the most evil act in history.
Who did it? Of course, sinners did. But God was also involved. He handed
over his Son to death, as Luke reminds us: "this Jesus, delivered up according
to the definite plan and foreknowledge of God, you crucified and killed by the
hands of lawless men" (Acts 2:23); "Herod and Pontius Pilate, along with the
Gentiles and the people of Israel" did "whatever [God's] hand and plan had
predestined to take place" (Acts 4:27–28). In this instance, as in so much else
that occurs in our lives, we must never judge God as if we know better than
he does. Remember "the depth of the riches and wisdom and knowledge of
God! How unsearchable are his judgments and how inscrutable his ways! For
who has known the mind of the Lord, or who has been his counselor?" (Rom.
11:33–34). In a mysterious way, the Bible tells us that evil is completely under
the control of our good, wise, sovereign God. We need to rest there.

Seventh, evil and the pain and suffering that go along with it are going to
end. Our omnipotent Father will punish evildoers along with Satan and his
evil agents and bring about a new creation (Rev. 15:3–4; 21:1–4). Things will
be restored to their original purity, free from all evil. One antidote to dealing
with the reality of evil, then, is to follow the Scripture's lead and take a long-
view. Our suffering now is real, but it will end when the Lord wipes every tear
from our eyes.

Practical Consequences

Throughout this book (and, indeed, throughout Scripture) we are confronted with mysteries that we cannot explain. But rather than eschew the

---

11. Bruce A. Ware, *God's Greater Glory: The Exalted God of Scripture and the Christian Faith*
(Wheaton, IL: Crossway, 2004), 102 (italics original).
12. Ibid., 106.

Trinity or Christ's human-divine nature because we cannot explain them—rather than deny either divine sovereignty or human responsibility since we can't reconcile them—we trust the Lord that he is different than we are and that what seems mysterious to us is perfectly clear to him. So, we hold to the reality that God is good and sovereign and that in his good sovereignty he rules over evil and uses it for good purposes until the day when he will finally conquer it. Now, in the interim while evil intrudes in God's good creation, we are called to trust him.

Given that evil is traumatic, some people are tempted to believe in a God who wishes he could control evil but can't. However, God is not impotent. He controls everything, absolutely everything, both good and evil. We don't trust in an impotent deity who wishes things could be different than they are. No, we trust in almighty God, our Creator whose ways are not our ways, the one who is our exceedingly loving heavenly Father.

REFLECTION QUESTIONS

1. How do you think the storyline of Scripture helps us to process the reality of evil in our experience?

2. Why do you think that God doesn't tell us how evil intruded into his good creation?

3. Can you think of purposes for evil other than the ones noted in this chapter?

4. Do you think it's better to say God "causes" evil or that he "permits" it? Why?

5. Do you agree with William Cowper's sentiments in "God Moves in a Mysterious Way"? Why?

> God moves in a mysterious way his wonders to perform;
>   He plants his footsteps in the sea, and rides upon the storm. . . .
> Blind unbelief is sure to err, and scan his work in vain;
>   God is his own interpreter, and he will make it plain.

What Is the "Order of the Decrees"?

Calvinists believe that God has one, unified plan—or decree—about all things, including our salvation. This decree, contra Arminianism, is not contingent upon anything we do. It is a sovereign decree. However, Calvinists disagree among themselves about how we should conceive the logical ordering of the parts of this single decree. Supralapsarians stress the rights of God to elect and reprobate apart from anything in the person, while infralapsarians stress God's justice in choosing and damning those he already considers to be sinners.

God's Decree

God's "decree" is his eternal plan, that is, what he determined, willed, purposed, ordained (these are synonyms of one another) would happen. According to the *Westminster Shorter Catechism*, "The decrees of God are his eternal purpose, according to the counsel of his will, whereby, for his own glory, he hath foreordained whatsoever comes to pass" (Q. 7). As Robert Dabney observes, "When God was looking forward from the point of view of His original infinite prescience, there was but one cause, Himself."[1] Given the reality that God is God, he has a decree:

> That God acts upon a plan in all his activities, is already given in Theism. On the establishment of a personal God, this question is closed. For person means purpose: precisely what distinguishes a person from a thing is that its modes of action are purposive, that all it does is directed to an end and proceeds through the choice of means to that end.[2]

---

1. Robert L. Dabney, *Systematic Theology* (1878; Edinburgh: Banner of Truth, 1985), 212.
2. Benjamin B. Warfield, *The Plan of Salvation*, rev. ed. (Grand Rapids: Eerdmans, 1942), 14.

God's decree has at least five qualities. First, it is one, united decree. Since there is one God, the decree "is one act of the divine mind; and not many." Second, since God is eternal, so is his decree. Third, God's decree is universal, encompassing everything, including the free actions of his moral creatures: "God must have foreordained, and so foreknown all events, including [free agents'] volitions." Fourth, the decree is essential, meaning that "God's purpose is in every case absolutely sure to be effectuated." Lastly, God's decree is absolute. It might include conditions to be met by his moral creatures, but if it does he decreed not only the condition but the meeting of the condition by his creatures.[3]

The Positions

In the sixteenth and seventeenth centuries, both Socinians and Arminians questioned God's eternal, sovereign decree regarding people's salvation; therefore, Calvinists began clarifying how they conceived the logical ordering of God's decree.[4] This was a logical challenge since there is only one decree, as A. A. Hodge reminds us:

> We believe that the Decree of God is one single, eternal intention. There cannot be an order of succession in His purpose. The whole is one choice. . . . The question, therefore, as to the Order of Decrees is *not* a question as to the order of acts in God's decreeing, but it *is* a question as to the true relation sustained by the several parts of the system which he decrees to one another.[5]

Nonetheless Calvinists tried to understand how properly to relate God's determination to elect some for salvation and to reprobate others to perdition with his determination to create them and to permit the fall of humankind into sin. How these three "decrees"—creation, fall, and election/reprobation—are related led to two different Calvinistic answers.

Supralapsarians (Latin *supra lapsum*, "above or prior to the fall") believe God's decree to elect some for salvation and to reprobate others precedes his decree to create humanity and to permit the fall. Louis Berkhof maintains that supralapsarianism is logically oriented, proceeding "on the assumption that in planning the rational mind passes from the end to the means in a retrograde movement, so that what is first in design is last in

---

3. Dabney, *Systematic Theology*, 214–19.
4. Socinians denied both the deity of Christ and God's prior knowledge of all future things, which, they believed, would negate human free will.
5. A. A. Hodge, *Outlines of Theology* (1879; Edinburgh: Banner of Truth, 1972), 230 (italics original).

accomplishment."[6] Since the last thing God effects is the separation of his people from the non-elect, that was the first thing he intended; it was his first decree. Supralapsarianism arose to protect God's absolute sovereignty in salvation and damnation. Both election and reprobation were eternal choices of God, and both were determined by nothing outside of himself. (However, supralapsarians taught that God decreed the condemnation of the reprobate with their sin in mind. Those holding this position admit that things are extremely complicated from our perspective.[7])

Infralapsarians (Latin *infra lapsum*, "below or subsequent to the fall")—always the majority voice among Calvinists—teach that God first decreed to create humanity; then he decreed to permit the fall. Only then, out of this viewed-as-fallen humanity, did he decree to choose some for salvation and to condemn others.[8] Infralapsarianism follows more closely the historical process: first God created, then permitted the fall, then dealt with his fallen creatures.[9] The infralapsarian position arose to guard God's character. He decreed to elect *sinners*. He decreed to reprobate *sinners*. He can be charged with no wrongdoing in either action.

Supralapsarianism arranges God's decrees in this fashion:

1. God's decree to manifest his glory in the execution of (a) mercy in the salvation of the elect and (b) justice in the damnation of the reprobate
2. his decree to create humanity
3. his decree to permit the fall

Infralapsarianism differs, teaching God's:

1. decree to create humanity
2. decree to permit the fall
3. decree to elect some of the fallen race, leaving others in their native corruption to justly be condemned for their sin

They both agree that after these first three come the following divine decrees:

4. decree to send Christ for the salvation of the elect

---

6. Louis Berkhof, *Systematic Theology*, 4th ed. (Grand Rapids: Eerdmans, 1941), 119.
7. Ibid., 121.
8. Warfield identifies the difference between the two views in this way: "Whether God discriminates between men in order that he may save some [infralapsarianism]; or whether he saves some in order that he may discriminate between men [supralapsarianism]" (*Plan of Salvation*, 27).
9. Berkhof, *Systematic Theology*, 120.

5. decree to send the Holy Spirit to bring Christ's salvation to the elect
6. decree to sanctify the elect[10]

J. V. Fesko summarizes the differences between these two arrangements:

> The question ultimately hinges upon how a theologian un-
> derstands the object of predestination. According to a basic
> supralapsarian position man is predestined *creabilis et labilis*
> (creatable and fallible). In other words, man is a creatable
> possibility and is capable of falling into sin. According to a
> basic infralapsarian position man is predestined *creatus et
> lapsus* (created and fallen). In the former, God does not take
> into account man's fall into sin in the decree of election; in the
> latter, the fall is factored into the eternal decree of election.[11]

The Positions Evaluated

We must be chaste in trying to read God's mind, remembering that "the
secret things belong to the LORD our God" (Deut. 29:29) and "who has known
the mind of the Lord, or who has been his counselor?" (Rom. 11:34). Dabney
was probably right to lament, "In my opinion this is a question which never
ought to have been raised."[12] Since, though, the matter has been addressed, we
need to ask, What does Scripture say?

In fact, the two positions are quite close to each other in their disagreement with Arminianism. These commonalities include "(1) the universal corruption and sinfulness of mankind; (2) the election of certain people out of
the wretched state of sin; (3) effectual grace that works through the gift of
faith given by God alone; (4) and the primacy of the gospel and the Scriptures
as the only means of salvation and God's revelation to mankind."[13]

Supralapsarianism, though, is incorrect for two reasons. First, God did
not decree the election and reprobation of creatable persons, for there is no
such category as "creatable" persons in God's eternal rationality. It errs in asserting that "the objects of predestination" were "men conceived *in posse* [i.e.,
as possibilities] only; and in making creation a means of their salvation or
damnation." In reality, "an object must be conceived as existing, in order to

---

10. Francis Turretin, *Institutes of Elenctic Theology*, 3 vols., trans. George Musgrave Giger,
    ed. James T. Dennison, Jr. (Phillipsburg, NJ: P&R, 1992), 1:341–50; Warfield, *Plan of
    Salvation*, 23–31.
11. J. V. Fesko, "Lapsarian Diversity at the Synod of Dort," in *Drawn into Controversie: Reformed
    Theological Diversity and Debates Within Seventeenth-Century British Puritanism*, eds.
    Michael A. G. Haykin and Mark Jones (Göttingen: Vandenhoeck & Ruprecht, 2011),
    100–1.
12. Dabney, *Systematic Theology*, 233.
13. Fesko, "Lapsarian Diversity," 122.

have its destiny given to it."[14] Supralapsarianism is illogical. Second, it impugns God's character, for it avers that God created some of humankind for the purpose of condemning them, without viewing them as having already sinned. We have to remember that our Lord is just, desiring all to be saved, not delighting in punishing sinners.[15] For this reason, the Calvinistic confessional tradition is consistently infralapsarian, even though Calvinists have never seen fit to condemn supralapsarianism as heresy.[16]

Infralapsarianism is the correct view for at least two reasons. First, when God elected his people for salvation he viewed them as already sinful. "Before the foundation of the world," God chose us "that we should be holy and blameless before him" (Eph. 1:4). Why did we need to be chosen to be holy if God did not already conceive us as being sinful and blameworthy? Paul's words make sense only in an infralapsarian view. Ephesians 1 is also filled with language of being united with Christ (vv. 3, 4, 5, 6, 7, 9, 10, 11, 12), all to the end that God's wonderful grace would be magnified (v. 6). Why would those-yet-to-sin need to be united to the Savior? How could their salvation result in the praise of God's grace unless it was an expression of his incredible mercy to *sinners*?[17]

Second, Scripture tells us from beginning to end that God condemns only those he views as guilty. He is a righteous judge, who will always do what is just (Gen. 18:25). There is no fault in God in his dealings with man. We must remember that

> He created all His creatures at first in holiness and happiness; that He gave them an adequate opportunity to stand; that He has done nothing to make the case of the non-elect worse than their own choice makes it, but on the contrary,

---

14. Dabney, *Systematic Theology*, 233.
15. Turretin identifies these errors in supralapsarianism: it suggests that God's first act towards a part of humanity is hatred; it questions his holiness since it has God creating some in the state of integrity to damn them; it seems impossible for God to exercise either mercy or justice to those who are not guilty; finally, it seems to make sin come into the world as a means of God's decreeing to damn some of humanity (*Institutes of Elenctic Theology*, 1:342–44).
16. J. V. Fesko, *The Theology of the Westminster Standards: Historical Context and Theological Insights* (Wheaton, IL: Crossway, 2014), 116–17.
17. Warfield's defense of infralapsarianism on this count is trenchant: "The actual dealing with men which is in question, is, with respect to both classes alike, those who are elected and those who are passed by, conditioned on sin: we cannot speak of salvation any more than of reprobation without positing sin. . . . There must be sin in contemplation to ground a decree of salvation, as truly a decree of punishment. We cannot speak of a decree discriminating between men with reference to salvation and punishment, therefore, without positing the contemplation of men as sinners as its logical prius" (*Plan of Salvation*, 26).

sincerely and mercifully warns them by conscience and His word against that wicked choice.[18]

God condemns *sinners*. For this reason supralapsarianism is incorrect, as Robert Letham notes: "Those passed by are ordained to wrath *for their sin*. In short, all who endure everlasting death do so justly, in keeping with their sin. Their own free choice freely echoes God's decree." This is because there is "a marked disparity between election and preterition (passing by). The latter is directly connected with the sin of the nonelect and in perfect accord with God's justice. Election, on the other hand, is entirely a matter of free grace and love."[19] Indeed, God's ordination of some to dishonor and wrath, "is inflicted 'for their sin' and is in full conformity with his glorious justice."[20]

We must note the distinct asymmetry that exists between God's election in grace of his people and his reprobation in justice of the damned. As Letham observes, there is

> disparity between election and reprobation. Election is by grace and is rooted in Christ; reprobation, or preterition (passing by) is in connection with sin and God's justice. There is asymmetry, not a parallel. Ultimately, both depend on the unchangeable, wise, holy, eternal will of God, but in themselves they differ considerably.[21]

We will do well to remember this asymmetry and allow Scripture (not our faulty logic) to guide our thinking both about God's dealings with his elect and with others. We must also recall that though God knows who the elect and the reprobate are, we don't. He's "the only census taker of heaven."[22] Our responsibility is to pray for unbelievers, to tell them the gospel, and to call them to repentance and faith, reminding them that God sent his Son to die for sinners like them.

Summary

At first glance we might not think there is much edification in discussing the order of the decrees. But as we reflect on the biblical warrant for the infralapsarian position, we should pause and marvel once again that God chose us to be his adopted children in union with Christ when he viewed us as sinful

---

18. Dabney, *Systematic Theology*, 240.
19. Robert Letham, *The Westminster Assembly: Reading Its Theology in Historical Context* (Phillipsburg, NJ: P&R, 2009), 187.
20. Ibid., 183.
21. Ibid.
22. Timothy George, *Amazing Grace: God's Pursuit, Our Response*, 2nd ed. (Wheaton, IL: Crossway, 2011), 89.

and deserving only his condemnation. How astounding that he is compassionate and merciful and that he did not treat us as our sins deserve!

REFLECTION QUESTIONS

1. Are you an infralapsarian or a supralapsarian? Why?

2. Do you believe Christians should try to understand the logical arrangement of God's eternal decree? Why?

3. Why do you think Calvinists have treated the differences between infralapsarianism and supralapsarianism as a minor disagreement between family members? Do you think this is the right approach? Why?

4. Can you think of other Scripture that supports either the infralapsarian or the supralapsarian position?

5. Do you think there are the practical benefits of being either an infralapsarian or a supralapsarian? If so, what are they?

Does God Have Two "Wills"?

The Bible teaches us that from our perspective God's will (which is always one, simple determination) should be understood in a twofold sense. First is his revealed-to-us (in Scripture) will; second is his hidden-from-us, known-only-to-himself secret will. This twofold understanding leads to the conclusion that there are two wills in God regarding human salvation. At the same time that he desires the salvation of all persons, our Lord determines to save only his chosen ones.

God's Will

God is a unified person. He is not tugged in different directions as we so often are due to our sin, our ignorance, and our fickleness. He has all power to do whatever he desires to do. Therefore, God's will is simply, according to John Frame, "anything he wants to happen."[1] God's will has no causes outside his wise decision that something should occur.

God's will absolutely shall come to pass since it is his good pleasure and is accompanied by unlimited power and perfect wisdom. So, the Lord declares, "My counsel shall stand, and I will accomplish all my purpose" (Isa. 46:10). Paul exudes with joy, reflecting on the fact that God "predestined us for adoption through Jesus Christ, according to the purpose of his will" (Eph. 1:5). He rejoices that in Christ "we have obtained an inheritance, having been predestined according to the purpose of him who works all things according to the counsel of his will" (Eph. 1:11). God's will is what he wants to happen, what pleases him, and what he determines to have happen according to his wise counsel. God's will shall be done.

---

1. John M. Frame, *The Doctrine of God* (Phillipsburg, NJ: P&R, 2002), 528.

God's Two Wills

God's will, then, is one, for his will takes place according to his "decree," his "determination," his "counsel," his "purpose." "Our God is in the heavens; he does all that he pleases" (Ps. 115:3). "Whatever the LORD pleases, he does, in heaven and on earth, in the seas and all deeps" (Ps. 135:6). Everything that happens in the whole universe occurs because of God's pleasure and because it is his will. However, Robert Dabney alerts us to the fact that, in another sense, the Bible portrays to us what can be understood as two seemingly conflicting wills in our God:

> God's will is absolutely executed over all free agents; and yet Scripture is full of declarations that sinful men and devils disobey His will! There must be, therefore, a distinction between His secret and revealed, His decretive and preceptive will. All God's will must be, in reality, a single, eternal, immutable act. The distinction, therefore, is one necessitated by our limitation of understanding, and relates only to the manifestation of the parts of this will to the creature.[2]

For this reason, many theologians have spoken of a distinction between the Lord's secret will and his revealed will. On the one hand, God has an eternally planned will ("decreed" or "secret" because it has been ordained from eternity and is known perfectly only to him) which will surely come to pass. It is God's decree, "his eternal purpose, by which he foreordains everything that comes to pass."[3] On the other hand, God has a will in which he tells us what he desires for us to do. That is why it is also called his "revealed" or "preceptive" will, since it has been made known to us and comes to us in the form of commands or expectations of how we should live before God; but he does not sovereignly decree that we shall do this will. Frame concludes that, "God's decretive will cannot be successfully opposed; it will certainly take place. It is possible, however, and often the case, for creatures to disobey God's preceptive will."[4]

This is no esoteric theological nitpicking without any practical implications. Rather, we must keep God's secret will and revealed will distinct in our thinking, Dabney insists, for the dissimilarity protects God's integrity as well as human responsibility:

---

2. Robert L. Dabney, *Systematic Theology*, 2nd ed. (1878; Edinburgh: Banner of Truth, 1985), 161.
3. John M. Frame, *Systematic Theology: An Introduction to Christian Belief* (Phillipsburg, NJ: P&R, 2013), 347.
4. Ibid.

> Every man is impelled to make [the distinction]; for other-
> wise, either alternative is odious and absurd. Say that God
> has no secret decretive will, and He wishes just what He
> commands and nothing more, and we represent Him as a
> Being whose desires are perpetually crossed and baffled: yea,
> trampled on; the most harassed, embarrassed, and impotent
> Being in the universe. Deny the other part of our distinction,
> and you represent God as acquiescing in all the iniquities
> done on earth and in hell.[5]

We yearn for biblical, not just logical, proof. And, in fact, Scripture is
filled with teachings that require something like this distinction. The Bible
teaches that God has a secret, or decreed, will which will surely come to pass.
Notice these examples:

> As for you, you meant evil against me, but God meant it for
> good, to bring it about that many people should be kept alive,
> as they are today. (Gen. 50:20)

> So then he has mercy on whomever he wills, and he hardens
> whomever he wills. You will say to me then, "Why does he
> still find fault? For who can resist his will?" (Rom. 9:18–19)

> In him we have obtained an inheritance, having been predes-
> tined according to the purpose of him who works all things
> according to the counsel of his will. (Eph. 1:11)

In these texts God "means" that a certain result would come about because of
people's actions even though they had no idea that was the purpose of what
they were doing. He "wills" to have mercy on some and to harden others, even
though we don't know who the objects of either of these choices are. His "will"
is guided by his "purpose" and his "counsel"; it will inevitably happen. These
are instances of God's secret will.

Additionally, numerous texts use similar terms to refer to God's revealed,
or preceptive, will. Here are a few examples:

> Not everyone who says to me, "Lord, Lord," will enter the
> kingdom of heaven, but the one who does the will of my
> Father who is in heaven. (Matt. 7:21)

---

5. Dabney, *Systematic Theology*, 161.

> If anyone's will is to do God's will, he will know whether the teaching is from God or whether I am speaking on my own authority. (John 7:17)

> For this is the will of God, your sanctification. (1 Thess. 4:3)

People must do the Father's "will" to enter into eternal life. They should strive to do God's will, but whether they will do so or not, Jesus does not tell us. God's revealed "will" is that believers should be holy, even though we can think of numerous examples to the contrary.

According to this distinction between the decreed and the revealed wills of God, we are right in asserting that at times God wills something that he disapproves. Jesus's death, for instance, was, according to John Piper, "a morally evil act inspired immediately by Satan (Luke 22:3)." At the very same moment, though, it occurred "according to the definite plan and foreknowledge of God (Acts 2:23)." Piper concludes that "there is a sense in which God willed the delivering up of his Son, even though the act was sin."[6] God's hardening of Pharaoh's heart is similar. On the one hand, God's "will is that Pharaoh let the Israelites go." But the Lord also says to Moses, "but I will harden his heart, so that he will not let my people go." We must surmise, then, that there is "the 'will of command' ('Let my people go!') and the 'will of decree' ('God hardened Pharaoh's heart')."[7] The distinction between the decreed and revealed wills of God is eminently biblical.

God's Two Wills in Salvation

Our discussion so far has been leading us up to this point, for we can legitimately believe that God has two wills when it comes to human salvation. Consider two statements Jesus made:

> O Jerusalem, Jerusalem, the city that kills the prophets and stones those who are sent to it! How often *would I have gathered* your children together as a hen gathers her brood under her wings, and you would not! (Luke 13:34; italics added)

> I thank you, Father, Lord of heaven and earth, that you have hidden these things from the wise and understanding and revealed them to little children; yes, Father, for such was *your gracious will*. All things have been handed over to me

---

6. John Piper, "Are There Two Wills in God?," in *Still Sovereign: Contemporary Perspectives on Election, Foreknowledge, and Grace*, eds. Thomas R. Schreiner and Bruce A. Ware (1995; Grand Rapids: Baker, 2000), 111.
7. Ibid., 113–14.

> by my Father, and no one knows the Father except the Son
> and anyone to whom the Son *chooses to reveal* him. (Matt.
> 11:25–27; italics added)

How could our Lord say both of these seemingly contradictory declarations? We know he's not schizophrenic, nor is he lying. The conclusion we come to, then, is that Jesus in some sense really willed both of these things. He really desired all in Jerusalem to be saved. At the same time, he willed that only certain people in Israel would be saved. Based on Jesus's words, we conclude that it is appropriate to say there are two wills in God when it comes to salvation.

From this, we discern that there are two types of biblical texts. There are those that teach God's universal saving will and desire for all to be saved, such as this: "Have I any pleasure in the death of the wicked, declares the Lord God, and not rather that he should turn from his way and live?" (Ezek. 18:23; compare Ezek. 13:11, and John 3:16). There are also texts that teach God's unconditional election of particular individuals to salvation. We remember Romans 9:15–16, for instance: "For he says to Moses, 'I will have mercy on whom I have mercy, and I will have compassion on whom I have compassion.' So then it depends not on human will or exertion, but on God, who has mercy."[8] Piper notes that when we hold together texts such as Deuteronomy 28:63 ("as the Lord took delight in doing you good and multiplying you, so the Lord will take delight in bringing ruin upon you and destroying you") and Ezekiel 18:23, we are struck by "the inescapable fact that in some sense God does not delight in the death of the wicked (Ezek. 18), and in some sense he does (Deut. 28:63; 2 Sam. 2:25)."[9]

In other parts of this book, we have noted abundant proof of the sovereign particularity of salvation. Dead sinners are raised to life because God effectually calls them to himself. At the same time, we must not neglect the biblical teaching that our God yearns for all his image bearers to come to Christ for salvation, even if (mysteriously to us) he does not choose to act savingly on his yearning. Notice these two texts which show the Lord's real desire for sinners to be saved:

> This is good, and it is pleasing in the sight of God our Savior,
> who desires all people to be saved and to come to the knowl-
> edge of the truth. (1 Tim. 2:3–4)

> The Lord is not slow to fulfill his promise as some count slow-
> ness, but is patient toward you, not wishing that any should
> perish, but that all should reach repentance. (2 Pet. 3:9)

---

8. See the entire context of Romans 9:6–23.
9. Piper, "Two Wills in God," 118–19.

Along with Jesus's yearning for the salvation of Jerusalem and God's desire for Israel to be saved, they prove to us that our sovereign God truly desires the salvation of everyone.

Both Arminians and Calvinists admit that there are (from our perspective) these two sorts of wills in God (as long as they remember at the same time that God's will is one and simple). But evangelical Arminians do not believe God's desire for the salvation of all persons will lead to universalism. Rather, they reason something like this: "What does God will more than saving all? The answer given by Arminians is that human self-determination and the possible resulting love relationship with God are more valuable than saving people by sovereign, efficacious grace."[10] In this scheme, God's will to let humans (aided by prevenient grace) make their libertarian choice for Jesus takes priority over his will to save people.[11] Calvinism is different. For Calvinists, according to Piper, "the greater value is the manifestation of the full range of God's glory in wrath and mercy (Rom. 9:22–23) and the humbling of man so that he enjoys giving all credit to God for his salvation (1 Cor. 1:29)."[12] Arminians emphasize the priority of libertarian human freedom. Calvinists emphasize the priority of divine sovereign freedom. Piper is correct:

> Since not all people are saved we must choose whether we believe (with the Arminians) that God's will to save all people is restrained by his commitment to human self-determination or whether we believe (with the Calvinists) that God's will to save all people is restrained by his commitment to the glorification of his sovereign grace. (Eph. 1:6, 12, 14; Rom. 9.22–23)[13]

Summary

Submitting to the full counsel of God's Word, recognizing that God's ways are not our ways (Rom. 11:33–34), and struggling to let God be God in our thinking and affections, we must turn away from the apologetic of Arminianism in its desire to alleviate God of any responsibility in the damnation of any humans. It just will not work. Why did God create people he foreknew would not believe the gospel if his supreme desire was to love them savingly? Instead, we must rest in God's revelation of himself in Scripture. Our God has two wills. Because this is so, we can in good conscience and with full conviction take the gospel to the ends of the earth, calling all to faith in Jesus, knowing of our Lord's desire that they would be forgiven. And we

---

10. Ibid., 124.
11. See Frame, *Systematic Theology*, 347.
12. Piper, "Two Wills in God," 124.
13. Ibid., 130.

can trust in the sovereign Spirit to give his elect life. This doctrine is faith-building, evangelism-producing, and creature-humbling.

REFLECTION QUESTIONS

1. Do you agree with Frame that God's will is "anything he wants to happen"? Why?

2. Does the fact that Jesus spoke both Luke 13:34 and Matthew 11:25–27 encourage you? Why?

3. How would you explain the "two wills of God" to someone?

4. Piper has written, "God's emotional life is infinitely complex beyond our ability to fully comprehend."[14] Do you agree with him? Does this have any bearing on your understanding of God's two wills? Why?

5. What practical impact does the reality of God's two wills have in your thinking and acting?

---

14. Ibid., 126.

PART 4

Practical Questions

Why Pray if God Has Ordained All Things?

All Christians—Calvinists and non-Calvinists alike—should pray to our heavenly Father. Indeed, prayer is one of the greatest blessings of a Christian's life. What a joy to know that our mighty God not only hears our prayers but also cares about our concerns (1 Peter 5:6–7)! Scripture is filled with remarkable encouragements for us to come to the Lord in prayer. In fact, the tenets of Calvinism encourage regular and persistent habits of prayer.

Answering Arminian Charges

Sometimes, though, Arminians ask Calvinists, Why pray if you believe God has already ordained all things? This is not a valid critique of biblical Calvinism for at least four reasons. First, no one I know—Calvinist, Arminian, or anyone else—believes that he or she prays enough. We should all pray more. Simply knowing Calvinists who don't pray as they should does not undermine their theology any more than a non-praying Arminian's doctrinal system is shipwrecked by his or her lack of intercession. Second, nothing intrinsic to Calvinism makes its adherents less likely to pray than Arminians. In fact, Arminiansim has the same potential weakness as Calvinism. Arminians, after all, believe that God's knowledge of the future is perfect. He doesn't need any new data from a Christian to move him to do something he wasn't already going to do. Third, some Arminians have a misconception about Calvinism's view of God. They sometimes betray the fact that they think the God Calvinists pray to is a cold, rational force as opposed to the loving, personal God he is.[1] As we have seen throughout this book, however, Calvinists

---

1. See, for example, Glen Shellrude, "Calvinism and Problematic Readings of New Testament Texts, Or, Why I Am Not a Calvinist," in *Grace for All: The Arminian Dynamics of Salvation*, eds. Clark H. Pinnock and John D. Wagner (Eugene, OR: Wipf and Stock, 2015), 38.

believe in a truly personal God, a God who yearns to be in relationship with us. In prayer, we are growing closer to him. Fourth, many Arminian critiques are really not criticisms of Calvinism but of hyper-Calvinism, or fatalism. A fatalist has no reason to bring any petitions to God, for *que sera, sera* ("whatever will be, will be").[2] The heart of biblical Calvinism, though, is that God uses means to accomplish his ends. One of those means—and what a glorious one it is since it brings us into close communion with the God and Father of our Lord Jesus Christ—is the means of prayer. Why pray? Because God uses prayer to accomplish his wonderful purposes in the world and in our lives. And because in the process we grow closer to him.

In the rest of this chapter we will consider five reasons Calvinistic Christians should pray: (1) because God hears us; (2) to grow close to the Lord; (3) for our good; (4) because God fills the Bible with promises; and (5) so that God will accomplish his will.

God Hears Our Prayers

God hears our prayers. Why else would our Lord exhort us, "Ask, and it will be given to you; seek, and you will find; knock, and it will be opened to you. For everyone who asks receives, and the one who seeks finds, and to the one who knocks it will be opened" (Matt. 7:7–8)? Why else would the apostle charge us, "do not be anxious about anything, but in everything by prayer and supplication with thanksgiving let your requests be made known to God" (Phil. 4:6)?

One of the things that distinguishes the true God from idols is that God hears and answers prayer. "To whom will you liken me and make me equal, and compare me, that we may be alike?" the Lord asks. What about an idol? "If one cries to it, it does not answer or save him from his trouble" (Isa. 46:5, 7). Unlike the false gods who can neither hear nor answer, the Lord tells us that "I am God, and there is no other; I am God, and there is none like me, declaring the end from the beginning and from ancient times things not yet done, saying 'My counsel shall stand, and I will accomplish all my purpose'" (Isa. 46:9–10). The true God is the one who declares, "before they call I will answer; while they are yet speaking I will hear" (Isa. 65:24). God hears our prayers.

Pray to Have a Closer Relationship with God

Our heavenly Father yearns for his children to have an intimate, personal relationship with him. We notice this in Jeremiah 9:23–24: "Let not the wise man boast in his wisdom, let not the mighty man boast in his might, let not the rich man boast in his riches, but let him who boasts boast in this, that he understands and knows me, that I am the LORD who practices steadfast love, justice, and righteousness in the earth. For in these things I delight, declares the LORD." Jesus's words—"This is eternal life that they may know you and

---

2. See Question 31.

Jesus Christ whom you have sent" (John 17:3)—also show that God wants us to be in relationship with him.

Prayer allows Christians to become more intimately related with their heavenly Father. We understand this from the analogy to human communication. I have a much closer relationship with my wife and sons than I do with my cat. Among other reasons for this, I can talk to them and they can understand and respond to me. There's a give and take as we learn about each other, ask questions, make comments, and open up and share not only our ideas but our hopes and our feelings. Those words convey our inmost heart. Speaking is one of the most intimate of all human exercises. It is a baring of the soul to another person.

The same applies to prayer in our relationship with the Lord. John Calvin saw this as clearly as anyone in the history of the church. He calls prayer, "the chief exercise of faith," the avenue "by which we daily receive God's benefits."[3] Calvin encourages us to pray, for in prayer "is a communion of men with God by which, having entered the heavenly sanctuary, they appeal to him in person."[4] This communion we have with God in prayer is essentially relational.

Calvin also points out that prayer is the means by which a believer experiences the Lord as being "wholly present" to him. In this sense, communion with God is the ultimate goal of prayer. "Words fail to explain how necessary prayer is, and in how many ways the exercise of prayer is profitable," Calvin avers, for among other things, "it is by prayer that we call him to reveal himself as wholly present to us.[5] In prayer we experience intimate fellowship with God.

Pray for Your Own Good

According to Calvin, we don't fundamentally pray because God needs to be awakened by us, "as if he were drowsily blinking or even sleeping until he is aroused by our voice." No, God knows everything. He doesn't need us to pray; rather he "ordained it not so much for his own sake as for ours." Prayer benefits us in several ways. "First, that our hearts may be fired with a zealous and burning desire ever to seek, love, and serve him." We also pray in order to "embrace with greater delight those things which we acknowledge to have been obtained by prayers." Finally, we pray in order to "confirm [God's] providence, while we understand not only that he promises never to fail us, and of his own will opens the way to call upon him at the very point of necessity, but also that he ever extends his hand to help his own, not wet-nursing them with words but defending them with present help."[6]

---

3. John Calvin, *Institutes of the Christian Religion*, ed. John T. McNeill, trans. Ford Lewis Battles (Philadelphia: Westminster, 1960), 3.20.
4. Ibid., 3.20.2
5. Ibid.
6. Ibid., 3.20.3.

Why pray? Because it is for your good! You will experience a closeness to the Lord as you pray and as you notice his answers to your prayers. So, Calvin encourages his readers, "our most merciful Father, although he never either sleeps or idles, still very often gives the impression of one sleeping or idling in order that he may thus train us, otherwise idle and lazy, to seek, ask, and entreat him to our great good."[7]

Pray according to God's Promises

Since God is fully sovereign, he both makes promises and has the power and wisdom to keep those pledges he's made. Prayers offered according to his promises in Scripture, then, are acknowledgements that he is the majestic King, the one who alone will always keep his promises. Christians should pray God's promises.

Jeremiah 29 and Daniel 9 offer a wonderful example of the necessity of praying God's promises. Many Israelites were exiled in Babylon. God's gracious plan for his people was his promise to restore them to Jerusalem after 70 years of exile (29:10–11). This was not a naked promise though. Part of God's plan to restore his people was that they should pray, seeking his aid in their distress (Jer. 29:12–13). He promised that when they called out to him, he would bring them back to the land (29:14).

And this is exactly what Daniel, one of the exiles, did. He knew God's promise; he saw that the 70 years of exile was completed (Dan. 9:2). So Daniel prayed, calling out to God to remember his promise, reminding him that he is "the great and awesome God, who keeps covenant and steadfast love" (9:3–4). He reminded the Lord that he would receive praise when he answered Daniel's prayer, for it would be seen that God is a promise-keeping God. Therefore, Daniel asked the Lord to act ultimately "for your own sake" (9:17, 19), to redeem the city "called by your name" (9:18). D. A. Carson notes the dynamics of prayer at work here: "When Daniel becomes aware from Scripture just when the close of the exile would take place, far from resting and waiting for the promises to come true, he prays for such fulfillment. The peculiar dynamic between God's sovereignty and human responsibility in the Bible never retreats to fatalism. The promises of God are incentives to intercession."[8]

Calvin stresses God's sovereign promises as powerful incentives to prayer. It is, he asserts, "by the benefit of prayer that we reach those riches which are laid up for us with the Heavenly Father." In prayer, Christians appeal to God "concerning his promises" so that they may experience "that what they believed was not vain, although he had promised it in word alone." Calvin's

---

7. Ibid.
8. D. A. Carson, *For the Love of God: A Daily Companion for Discovering the Treasure of God's Word*, vol. 2 (Wheaton, IL: Crossway, 1999), Oct. 24.

conclusion is stunning: "We see that to us nothing is promised to be expected from the Lord, which we are not also bidden to ask of him in prayers."[9]

Consider one example. From the great commission we know that all authority is in Christ's hands and he charges his people to take the gospel to all people groups (Matt. 28:18–20). And we know that in heaven, redeemed people from "every nation, from all tribes and peoples and languages" will worship their Savior, Jesus (Rev. 7:9). We should, therefore, pray in faith that the Lord would fulfill his promise and bring lost people out of darkness among all the people groups of the world and that he would use cross-cultural missionaries we have sent out to accomplish his will, according to Romans 10:14–15. God's sovereign promises should fuel our prayers.

Prayer as God's Means to Do His Will

The heart of biblical Calvinism is that God uses means to accomplish his ends. Prayer is one of the glorious means the Lord invites us to employ so that he will "work all things according to the counsel of his will" (Eph. 1:11). Reflect on Paul's epistle to the Colossians. The apostle thanks God for his work in saving the believers in Colossae. Note that the things they truly do—their faith and their love—Paul thanks God for doing. This is another example of compatibilism. Ultimately, Paul knows that apart from God's work in these Christians' lives they would not have faith or love. So he thanks the Lord for them (Col. 1:3–4). Paul writes that he is constantly praying for these believers, that God would allow them to know him better so that they would please him as they persevere in endurance (1:9–11). And the apostle expresses his confidence that this will happen, for God is sovereign in upholding and taking care of his people (1:12–14). He concludes by urging the church to pray for him, that he would be bold in sharing the gospel (4:2–4). God will accomplish his purposes in these people's lives. So Paul prays.

Summary

Calvinists (and all Christians!) should pray regularly and persistently. In fact, no one has more reason to pray than a Calvinist. When we pray, we know that we're communicating with our all-knowing, all-powerful, and good heavenly Father. He desires what is best for us and promises that he will accomplish his wise purposes in our lives (Rom. 8:28–39). Conversely, Calvinists who are not regularly praying need to examine themselves to make sure they are not, in fact, practical fatalists. We end with D. M. Lloyd-Jones's warning and admonition in this regard:

> Unhappily it is often the case that those who understand the doctrines of grace most clearly are the very persons who are

---

9. Calvin, *Institutes*, 3.20.2.

most guilty of misunderstanding them to this extent, that they cease to pray. . . . But a right understanding of apostolic teaching leads a person to pray more than ever, not less. The Apostle Paul was a great man of prayer; and teachers of his type have been men of prayer throughout the centuries.[10]

REFLECTION QUESTIONS

1. Do you think any of the Arminian charges against Calvinists' praying are warranted?

2. Do you think Arminians have the same five reasons as Calvinists to pray? Which one(s)?

3. Have you experienced God as "wholly present" to you in prayer? Does this encourage you to pray more?

4. In addition to the Great Commission in Matthew 28, what other biblical promises do you think Christians should pray?

5. Why bother praying if God is not absolutely sovereign?

---

10. D. M. Lloyd-Jones, *Romans: An Exposition of Chapter 8:17–39, The Final Perseverance of the Saints* (Grand Rapids: Zondervan, 1975), 145.

Do Calvinists Practice Evangelism and Missions?

Even though Arminians and others sometimes assume that the "logic" of Calvinism results in the lack of evangelism and missions, Calvinists have historically been active in sharing their faith both locally and cross-culturally. Biblical Calvinism recognizes that God uses means to accomplish his ends—including the means of his people going and sharing the gospel indiscriminately with unbelievers so that those whom the Lord is calling to himself will believe. Calvinists refuse to follow the "logic" of the grave error of hyper-Calvinism which asserts that God will save his elect without the means of gospel preaching.[1] In this chapter we will notice that Calvinists have been active in missions from their beginning in the sixteenth century and that they are responsible for the beginning of the modern missions movement in the English-speaking church, the movement that happily is continuing in our day.

A caveat is in order as we begin. There are Calvinists (just like there are Arminians) who aren't faithful in evangelism and missions. Both as an Arminian and a Calvinist, I have never felt that I was doing "enough" in these areas—and that's after a summer in Europe doing street evangelism and living in the 10/40 window. All of us—Arminian or Calvinist—need to be more active in evangelism and missions. A non-evangelistic Calvinist does not disprove Calvinism any more than a non-evangelistic Arminian disproves Arminianism.

Missions during the Reformation and Puritan Era

Calvinists in the sixteenth century didn't engage in missionary activity the way evangelicals do in our day for two reasons. First, they had little political power and were combatting revived and powerful Catholicism. Stephen Neill notes that "in the Protestant world, during the period of the Reformation,

---

1. See Question 31.

there was little time for thought of missions. Until 1648, the Protestants were fighting for their lives; only the Peace of Westphalia in that year made it certain that Protestantism would survive."[2] Second, most Calvinists were landlocked, lacking the natural means to send missionaries across oceans to the nations, as Glenn Sunshine observes:

> For most of the sixteenth century, Catholic powers such as Spain, Portugal, and the Italian city-states had trading connections and colonies in Asia, Africa, and the New World, while the Protestant powers did not. So while Catholics were able to engage in extensive missionary activity around the globe in the sixteenth century, Protestants had little opportunity to do so until later. In the few instances where they did have access to mission fields, the Protestants were involved in cross-cultural evangelism.[3]

John Calvin had a heart for missions. His writings and sermons are filled with exhortations like this one that Christians should "daily desire that God gather churches unto himself from all parts of the earth; that he spread and increase them in number."[4] In fact, Calvin's Geneva was zealous in sending church planters into hostile Catholic territory in France. Even though some were martyred, between 1555 and 1563 Geneva sent out at least 88 young men, and probably closer to 150.[5] Through these zealous evangelists the church grew dramatically. According to Pierre Courthial, "In 1555 there were five organized Reformed churches in France; in 1559, the year the first national synod assembled in Paris, there were nearly 100; and by 1562 they numbered 2,150."[6] That is remarkable church growth, fueled by aggressive Calvinist church-planters. In addition to this, when Geneva was given the opportunity to send cross-cultural missionaries on an expedition to the coast of Brazil, Calvin unhesitatingly sent them.[7]

---

2. Stephen Neill, *A History of Christian Missions*, 2nd ed. (New York: Penguin, 1991), 187.
3. Glenn Sunshine, "Protestant Missions in the Sixteenth Century," in *The Great Commission: Evangelicals and the History of World Missions*, ed. Martin I. Klauber and Scott M. Manetsch (Nashville: B&H, 2008), 14.
4. John Calvin, *Institutes of the Christian Religion*, eds. John T. McNeill, trans. Ford Lewis Battles (Philadelphia: Westminster, 1960), 3.20.42. On Calvin's missionary zeal, see Michael A. G. Haykin and C. Jeffrey Robinson Sr., *To the Ends of the Earth: Calvin's Missional Vision and Legacy* (Wheaton, IL: Crossway, 2014), 27–64.
5. Robert M. Kingdon, *Geneva and the Coming Wars of Religion in France, 1555–1563* (Geneva: Droz, 1955), 14.
6. Pierre Courthial, "The Golden Age of Calvinism in France," in *John Calvin: His Influence in the Western World*, ed. W. Stanford Reid (Grand Rapids: Zondervan, 1982), 77.
7. Haykin and Robinson, *To the Ends of the Earth*, 71–72.

Calvin was not alone in missionary zeal among early Calvinists. Gisbertus Voetius (1589–1676), one of the representatives at the Synod of Dort, became a passionate advocate of international missions. He wrote the first Protestant theology of missions, urging fellow Calvinists to go, preach to non-believers, establish churches, and thus glorify God.[8] His understanding of cross-cultural missions, like that of most in his day, was tied to sending Christian workers alongside European traders. Nonetheless, the gospel went out.

A flowering of evangelistic and missionary zeal occurred in the seventeenth and eighteenth centuries among Calvinists in the English Puritan tradition.[9] The *Westminster Larger Catechism* teaches that Christ gave "the commission to preach the gospel to all nations" (Q. 53). It also urges Christians to pray for "the gospel [to be] propagated throughout the world" (Q. 191). English Puritan luminaries like Jospeh Alleine and John Flavel urged an indiscriminate, aggressive preaching of the gospel.[10] This evangelistic and missionary passion made its way to New England Puritans like Jonathan Edwards, who wrote such works as *An Humble Attempt* (urging prayer for revival) and *The Diary of David Brainerd* (on the endeavors of a missionary to reach the native American population with the gospel), which was Edwards' best-selling book during his lifetime.[11] Not only did Edwards write about missions and evangelism; he was an evangelistic preacher whose sermons ignited the First Great Awakening which also was fueled by George Whitefield and numerous other Calvinistic evangelists.[12]

The "Means" of Calvinism and the Modern Missions Movement

Regrettably, many Calvinists in England in the eighteenth century abandoned biblical Calvinism for hyper-Calvinism.[13] Andrew Fuller (1754–1815), a Baptist, was one of them. He was raised in a hyper-Calvinistic church where the logic of this anti-evangelistic system didn't allow the pastor ever to address unbelievers directly. Fuller labored under this "nonapplication, noninvitation"

---

8. Jan A. B. Jongeneel, "Voetius, Gisbertus [or Gijsbert Voet]," in *Biographical Dictionary of Christian Missions*, ed. Gerald H. Anderson (Grand Rapids: Eerdmans, 1999), 708.
9. See Iain H. Murray, *The Puritan Hope: Revival and the Interpretation of Prophecy* (Carlisle, PA: Banner of Truth, 1971), and Haykin and Robinson, *To the Ends of the Earth*, 75–90.
10. Joseph Alleine, *A Sure Guide to Heaven* (Edinburgh: Banner of Truth, 1960); John Flavel, "England's Duty under the Present Gospel Liberty," in *The Works of John Flavel* (Edinburgh: Banner of Truth, 1968), 4:3–268.
11. Jonathan Edwards, *An Humble Attempt to Promote Explicit Agreement and Visible Union of God's People in Extraordinary Prayer, For the Revival and Religion and the Advancement of Christ's Kingdom on Earth (1746); Jonathan Edwards, The Life and Diary of David Brainerd (1749).*
12. See Thomas S. Kidd, *The Great Awakening: The Roots of Evangelical Christianity in Colonial America* (New Haven, CT: Yale University Press, 2007).
13. See Peter Toon, *The Emergence of Hyper-Calvinism in English Nonconformity, 1689–1765* (1967; Eugene, OR: Wipf and Stock, 2011).

system (as he called it) until he was finally converted apart from any pleading on his pastor's part. Becoming a pastor himself, Fuller began studying the Bible. He was struck by the numerous times in both testaments of Scripture that lost people are implored to come to the Lord for salvation. The consistent testimony of the Bible is that eternal blessings are held out for everyone who comes to God for forgiveness. The result of his biblical investigation was one of the most important books in modern Evangelicalism, *The Gospel Worthy of All Acceptation, or The Duty of Sinners to Believe in Jesus Christ,* first published in 1785.

In the introduction, Fuller said that three things led him to abandon hyper-Calvinism: the overwhelming number of commands in Scripture for people to turn to God for forgiveness; missionary biographies like that of David Brainerd; and the distinction Jonathan Edwards made in *Freedom of the Will* between moral inability and natural ability. These considerations led Fuller to his six main points:

1. Unconverted sinners are commanded, exhorted, and invited to believe in Christ for salvation.
2. Every man is bound cordially to receive and approve whatever God reveals.
3. Though the gospel, strictly speaking, is not a law but a message of pure grace, yet it virtually requires obedience and such an obedience as includes saving grace.
4. The want of faith in Christ is ascribed in Scripture to men's depravity and is itself represented as a heinous sin.
5. God has threatened and inflicted the most awful punishments on sinners for their not believing on the Lord Jesus Christ.
6. Other spiritual exercises which sustain an inseparable connexion with faith in Christ are represented as the duty of men in general.[14]

The book was earth-shattering. Fuller's younger friend, William Carey, loved it and caught its vision. Carey extended Fuller's vision to include the nations and, in 1791, published *An Inquiry into the Obligation of Christians to Use Means for the Conversion of the Heathen.* This was a clarion call for the Baptists of his day to leave their homeland and take the gospel out to other peoples. The next year, The Particular Baptist Society for the Propagation of the Gospel Amongst the Heathen was formed, and in 1793, Carey, his family, and some others left England for India. The modern missions movement in

---

14. Andrew Fuller, "The Gospel Worthy of All Acceptation, or The Duty of Sinners to Believe in Jesus Christ," in *The Complete Works of Andrew Fuller,* ed. Joseph Belcher (1845; Harrisonburg, VA: Sprinkle, 1988), 2:328–416. Also see Paul Brewster, *Andrew Fuller: Model Pastor-Theologian* (Nashville: B&H, 2010).

the English-speaking world was born.[15] In 1812, Adoniram Judson (1788–1815) set sail from Massachusetts birthing the American impulse for world missions.[16]

What was at the heart of the shift in these men's minds from hyper- to biblical Calvinism? It was the simple, and biblical, notion that God usually uses "means" to accomplish his will. Fuller had passionately pleaded with other pastors: "The truth is, we wait for we know not what; we seem to think 'the time is not come, the time for the Spirit to be poured down from on high.' . . . We pray for the conversion of the world and yet we neglect the ordinary means by which it can be brought about. . . . How shall they hear without a preacher? And how shall they preach except they be sent?" There you have it. God uses "means." God has ordained "means" for the salvation of his elect, and the church needed to be diligent in the use of these "means." The "means," of course, was the sending of missionaries and the preaching of the gospel.[17]

God uses the means of preaching to edify Christians and keep them trusting in Jesus. He uses the means of prayer to change his people and to do his will. He uses the means of sunshine and rain to grow crops. He uses the means of food and water to sustain and grow people physically. And he uses the means of preaching the gospel to save his elect. It is no more inconsistent for Calvinists to share the gospel than it is for a loving mother to feed her infant. Without the gospel—just like without food—there will be no life.[18]

And it is because of their vision of God's glory that Calvinists since the Protestant Reformation have been willing to suffer to take the gospel to the lost. In the words of John Piper,

> Missions is not the ultimate goal of the church. Worship is. Missions exists because worship doesn't. Worship is ultimate, not missions, because God is ultimate, not man. When this age is over, and the countless millions of the redeemed fall on their faces before the throne of God,

---

15. See Timothy George, *Faithful Witness: The Life and Mission of William Carey* (Birmingham, AL: New Hope, 1991).

16. See Courtney Anderson, *To the Golden Shore: The Life of Adoniram Judson* (Valley Forge, PA: Judson, 1987); and John Piper, *Filling Up the Afflictions of Christ: The Cost of Bringing the Gospel to the Nations in the Lives of William Tyndale, Adoniram Judson, and John Paton* (Wheaton, IL: Crossway, 2009), 85–108.

17. Andrew Fuller, "Instances, Evil, and Tendency of Delay, in the Concerns of Religion," in *The Complete Works of Andrew Fuller*, ed. Joseph Belcher (1845; Harrisonburg, VA: Sprinkle, 1988), 1:147–48.

18. For evidence that Calvinists have been motivated by a desire that God would be glorified through missions, see Kenneth J. Stewart, *Ten Myths about Calvinism: Recovering the Breadth of the Reformed Tradition* (Downers Grove, IL: InterVarsity Press, 2011), 123–48.

missions will be no more. It is a temporary necessity. But worship abides forever.[19]

Brothers and sisters, may the Lord embolden us with a biblical vision of himself—his beauty and majesty—so that we will take the gospel to the nations, for God's glory.

Summary

Calvinists have been at the forefront of the modern missions movement. Calvinism led to an aggressive church-planting effort in France, ignited the English Puritan movement, created the evangelistic zeal of the First Great Awakening in the American colonies, spurred on the modern missions movement, and continues in our day to fuel many who are willing to leave everything to go around the world (or across the street) for the sake of the gospel. If the only evangelistic Calvinists we could drum up were George Whitefield (1714–70) or Charles Spurgeon (1834–92), the Arminian retort that "they are the exception that proves the rule" might have some substance. But the host of Calvinists—past and present—who care deeply for evangelism and are engaged in missions in different ways proves the lie to that statement.[20]

REFLECTION QUESTIONS

1. What most surprised you while reading this chapter? Why?

2. How would you explain in your own words the Calvinistic belief that God uses "means" to accomplish his goals?

3. Can you think of other historical examples of Calvinistic evangelists and missionaries?

4. Can you think of other reasons people often assume Calvinists don't "do" missions besides confusing Calvinism with hyper-Calvinism?

5. How has reading this chapter spurred you on to greater faithfulness in evangelism and missions?

---

19. John Piper, *Let the Nations be Glad! The Supremacy of God in Missions* (Grand Rapids: Baker, 1993), 11.

20. A useful overview of the history of missions can be found in Zane Pratt, M. David Sills, and Jeff K. Walters, *Introduction to Global Missions* (Nashville: B&H, 2014), 95–134.

Can Calvinists Freely and Genuinely Offer the Gospel to All People?

The New Testament is filled with both apostolic examples and exhortations for Christians to share the gospel indiscriminately with everyone they can reach with the saving message of Christ. From Jesus's commission, "Go therefore and make disciples of all nations" (Matt. 28:19) and his charge that "whoever believes in [the Son] should not perish but have eternal life" (John 3:16), to Peter's encouragement always to be "prepared to make a defense to anyone who asks you for a reason for the hope that is in you" (1 Peter 3:15) and the example of early church, "Now those who were scattered [from the persecution of the Jerusalem church] went about preaching the word" (Acts 8:4)—the New Testament guides Christians to call sinners to faith and repentance in Jesus. We make a *bona fide* ("in good faith") offer of salvation to all people, because if they will repent and believe, they will be saved. The particularity of Calvinism should not hinder aggressive, promiscuous gospel preaching.

Apostolic Evangelism

Peter and Paul were evangelistic preachers, calling on all their hearers to repent and trust in Jesus. Notice how they charged their listeners that they must respond to the gospel summons, that they were responsible to believe in Jesus and come to him for salvation. After his Pentecost sermon, Peter's listeners "were cut to the heart, and said to Peter and the rest of the apostles, 'Brothers, what shall we do?'" (Acts 2:37). Peter's response was expansive, not constrained. He cried out, "Repent and be baptized every one of you in the name of Jesus Christ for the forgiveness of your sins, and you will receive the gift of the Holy Spirit. For the promise is for you and for your children and for all who are far off, everyone whom the Lord our God calls to himself" (2:38–39). Peter was not done. He continued, pleading with the crowd: "with many other words he bore witness and continued to exhort them, saying,

'Save yourselves from this crooked generation'" (2:40). So here we have three chief actors: God calls, Peter exhorts and pleads, and the listeners must respond in faith. Peter's expansiveness was not limited by the reality that only those God calls will come to faith.

Paul was also equally indiscriminate in his gospel appeals. One time he addressed a crowd, urging them all: "The times of ignorance God overlooked, but now he commands all people everywhere to repent, because he has fixed a day on which he will judge the world in righteousness by a man whom he has appointed; and of this he has given assurance to all by raising him from the dead" (Acts 17:30–31). And in fact "some men joined him and believed" (17:34). Later, when Paul testified before King Agrippa, he confronted the ruler: "do you believe the prophets?" Luke tells us, "And Agrippa said to Paul, 'In a short time would you persuade me to be a Christian?' And Paul said, 'Whether short or long, I would to God that not only you but also all who hear me this day might become such as I am—except for these chains'" (Acts 26:27–29). The apostle Paul was pointed and direct in his appeals for all people to come to Christ for forgiveness.

God's Character and Evangelism

Can God want something (all people's salvation) that does not come to fruition? According to John Murray, "It would appear that the real point in dispute in connection with the free offer of the gospel is whether it can properly be said that God *desires* the salvation of all men."[1] But the Lord really does yearn for the salvation of all people:

> The gospel is not simply an offer or invitation, but also implies that God delights that those to whom the offer comes would enjoy what is offered in all its fulness. And the word "desire" has been used in order to express the thought epitomized in Ezekiel 33:11, which is to the effect that God has pleasure that the wicked turn from his evil way and live. It might as well have been said, "It pleases God that the wicked repent and be saved."[2]

In other words, Murray notes, God has "a real attitude, a real disposition of lovingkindness inherent in the free offer to all; in other words, a pleasure or delight in God, contemplating the blessed result to be achieved by compliance with the overture proffered and the invitation given."[3]

---

1. John Murray, "The Free Offer of the Gospel," in *Collected Writings of John Murray* (Edinburgh: Banner of Truth, 1983), 4:113 (italics original).
2. Ibid., 4:114.
3. Ibid.

Murray marshals much biblical support for this view. Matthew 5:44–48 shows that "presupposed in God's gifts bestowed upon the ungodly there is in God a disposition of love, kindness, [and] mercifulness."[4] Deuteronomy 5:29 is an instance of God's "earnest desire or wish or will that the people of Israel were of a heart to fear him and keep all his commandments always. . . . [It is] an instance of desire on the part of God for the fulfilment of that which he had not decreed, in other words, a will on the part of God to that which he had not decretively willed."[5] Matthew 23:37 ("O Jerusalem, Jerusalem, the city that kills the prophets and stones those who are sent to it! How often would I have gathered your children together as a hen gathers her brood under her wings, and you would not!") demonstrates that Jesus "often wished the occurrence of something which did not come to pass and therefore willed (or wished) the occurrence of that which God had not secretly or decretively willed."[6] This is a stark instance, and Murray points out that

> Our Lord in the exercise of his most specific and unique function as the God-man gives expression to a yearning will on his part that responsiveness on the part of the people of Jerusalem would have provided the necessary condition for the bestowal of his saving and protecting love, a responsiveness, nevertheless, which it was not the decretive will of God to create in their hearts.[7]

Ezekiel 18:23, 32, and 33:11 mean what they say. God's word in 33:11 ("I have no pleasure in the death of the wicked") "admits of no limitation or qualification; it applies to the wicked who actually die in their iniquity."[8] Similarly 18:23 means that "it is true absolutely and universally that God does not delight in the death of the wicked"[9]

Murray concludes that God's character and will is the foundation of our gospel summons:

> The full and free offer of the gospel is a grace bestowed upon all. Such grace is necessarily a manifestation of love or lovingkindness in the heart of God. . . . The grace offered is nothing less than salvation in its richness and fulness. The love or lovingkindness that lies back of that offer is not anything less; it is the will to that salvation. In other words, it is

---

4. Ibid., 4:116.
5. Ibid., 4:117–18.
6. Ibid., 4:119.
7. Ibid., 4:120.
8. Ibid., 4:122.
9. Ibid., 4:124.

Christ in all the glory of his person and in all the perfection of his finished work whom God offers in the gospel.[10]

Calvinism Fuels Evangelism

The reality is that apostolic evangelism was fueled—not hindered—by belief in God's particular election and Christ's particular atonement. We see this, for instance, in Paul's ministry in Corinth. Paul had been rebuffed by some there (Acts 18:6) but had seen some fruit from his evangelism (18:8). Then the Lord came to him in a vision, saying "Do not be afraid, but go on speaking and do not be silent, for I am with you, and no one will attack you to harm you, for I have many in this city who are my people. And [Paul] stayed a year and six months, teaching the word of God among them" (18:9–11). It's remarkable that the Lord said he had a definite group ("many") whom he already identified as belonging to himself. Because Paul knew there were many who would come to Christ, he stayed and preached! We could compare this instance to a previous one where the Holy Spirit directed Paul and Timothy not to take the gospel to Asia and Bithynia but rather to go to Macedonia; and they went there, "concluding that God had called us to preach the gospel to them" (Acts 16:6–10).

We also see Calvinistic impulses spurring on evangelism in the epistle to the Ephesians. The particularity of God's grace dominates chapters 1 and 2. God chose and predestined particular people for adoption out of his special love for them (ch. 1), and then he graciously raised those elect ones to life and granted them faith (ch. 2). Obviously Paul knew and believed this. So his request at the end of the letter is illuminating: pray "also for me, that words may be given to me in opening my mouth boldly to proclaim the mystery of the gospel, for which I am an ambassador in chains, that I may declare it boldly, as I ought to speak" (Eph. 6:19–20). God chose and gave life. Knowing this, Paul evangelized.

The *Bona Fide* ("in Good Faith") Offer

Arminians sometimes assert that Calvinists can't make a good faith offer of the gospel to everyone since Calvinists don't believe God will assist everyone to receive Christ. Therefore, Arminians charge, the Calvinist "offer" is not sincere. Roger Nicole dismisses this critique, noting that Arminians believe "God foreknows all things and would be unable to offer the gospel sincerely to those he knows will refuse."[11] Judged by their criticism of Calvinists' "free offer," Arminians are in the same bind.

---

10. Ibid., 4:132.
11. Roger Nicole, "Covenant, Universal Call and Definite Atonement," *Journal of the Evangelical Theological Society* 38 (1995): 409.

More importantly, Nicole elaborates what is required of an offer to make it sincere. He notes perceptively it is just this:

> that if the terms of the offer be observed, that which is offered be actually granted. In connection with the gospel offer the terms are that a person should repent and believe. Whenever that occurs, salvation is actually conferred. There is not a single case on record in the whole history of mankind where a person came to God in repentance and faith and was refused salvation.[12]

Since the terms of the offer are real (if sinners will repent and believe they will be saved), and since it is not the fault of the one offering the gospel if his listeners are unwilling to believe (for "the disability under which sinners labor is not forcibly produced by direct action of God but is self-induced so that they, rather than God, are rightly charged with their own plight, dramatically revealed in their obduracy in the presence of the gospel call"), the offer is a sincere one.[13]

Summary

The Bible gives us every reason to sow the seed of the gospel freely and widely. This is just what the divines at the Synod of Dort said many years ago: "Moreover, it is the promise of the gospel that whoever believes in Christ crucified shall not perish but have eternal life. This promise, together with the command to repent and believe, ought to be announced and declared without differentiation or discrimination to all nations and people, to whom God in his good pleasure sends the gospel."[14] J. I. Packer reminds us what this gospel message (he calls it the "old gospel") is that we should preach far and wide to everyone we can reach:

> Christ Jesus, the sovereign Lord, who died for sinners, now invites sinners freely to himself. God commands all to repent and believe; Christ promises life and peace to all who do so. . . . men despise and reject [these invitations] and are never in any case worthy of them, and yet Christ still issues them. He need not, but he does. . . . He whose death has ensured the salvation of all his people is to be proclaimed everywhere as

---

12. Ibid., 409–10.
13. Ibid., 409.
14. Canons of Dort, 2.5.

a perfect Saviour, and all men invited and urged to believe on him, whoever they are, whatever they have been.[15]

May God lead us to greater faithfulness in preaching this life-giving gospel to everyone we can reach.

REFLECTION QUESTIONS

1. How would you explain the "free offer of the gospel" in your own words?

2. Can you think of other biblical support for offering the gospel freely to all persons?

3. Roger Nicole asserted, "Our Lord specifically promised: 'Whoever comes to me I will never drive away' (John 6:37). If the question be raised 'Who is going to come?', the answer is 'All that the Father gives me will come to me' (John 6:44). Far from undermining the sincere offer of the gospel, the doctrine of definite atonement undergirds the call. It provides a real rather than a hypothetical salvation as that which is offered. It does not expect the fulfillment of an unrealizable condition on the part of the sinner as a prerequisite for salvation. But it confidently looks to God who initiates the offer and can also raise sinners from death to life and thus enable them in sovereign grace to repent and to believe so that they will appropriate the benefit secured for them by the death of Christ."[16] Do you agree that definite atonement should not be a hindrance to the free offer of the gospel? Why?

4. Are there reasons you feel constrained not to press the claims of the gospel on everyone? How do John 3:16–18 and Acts 17:30–31 help you in this regard?

5. Has reading this chapter provoked you to desire to be more faithful in evangelism? How will you push yourself to greater faithfulness in this area?

---

15. J. I. Packer, "'Saved by His Precious Blood': An Introduction to John Owen's *The Death of Death in the Death of Christ*," in *A Quest for Godliness: The Puritan Vision of the Christian Life* (Wheaton, IL: Crossway, 1990), 141–42.

16. Nicole, "Covenant, Universal Call and Definite Atonement," 410.

Do Calvinists Pursue Personal Holiness?

Calvinism's opponents sometimes argue that Calvinists don't have any reason to pursue personal holiness. After all (it's charged), why should they strive for godliness since they believe God has predestined them for salvation apart from anything they do? However, like all Bible-believing Christians, Calvinists maintain that they are responsible to strive "for the holiness without which no one will see the Lord" (Heb. 12:14). In fact, Calvinism contains several impulses that should encourage Christians to pursue sanctification.

Calvinism, the Bible, and Holiness

We begin with the Bible. Three important biblical texts stress God's sovereign grace and its powerful effect of changing Christians so that they will be more holy. In prior questions we noted that grace is always specific (directed towards individuals) and also effective (it does what God intends it to do). One purpose of God's grace is to make us more like Jesus.

Ephesians 1 demonstrates that God's sovereignty and our pursuit of holiness should function together. Paul stresses that God chose his elect "that we should be holy and blameless before him" (v. 4). Clinton Arnold is correct that the Greek phrasing here "expresses the purpose or goal of the election."[1] God elected his people for the purpose of holiness. Calvinists who don't seek to be holy betray that; they do not honor the God of their salvation.

We see the same thing in Ephesians 2. God powerfully raises dead people to spiritual life, unites them with Christ, and joins them with Christ in the heavenly places so that they will display his grace. All this is an outworking of God's grace: "But God . . . made us alive together with Christ—by grace

---

1. Clinton E. Arnold, *Ephesians*, Zondervan Exegetical Commentary on the New Testament (Grand Rapids: Zondervan, 2010), 81.

you have been saved" (2:4–5). Grace continues to be effective in Christians' lives after they are converted because not only did God save them by grace, but also because "we are his workmanship, created in Christ Jesus for good works, which God prepared beforehand, that we should walk in them" (2:10). God graciously prepares the works and we do them. Calvinists who delight in God's sovereignty in salvation need to realize that the Lord chose them so that they would be holy. If they are unwilling to walk in good works (2:10), they should question if they have indeed been recipients of God's gift of salvation (2:8).

In Titus 2, Paul also speaks of the role of God's grace in our holiness. Divine grace has come, bringing salvation (v. 11). Apart from God's grace, none of us would be saved. But grace does more than free us from God's eternal judgment. God's grace is also active, "training us to renounce ungodliness and worldly passions, and to live self-controlled, upright, and godly lives" (v. 12). Christ came to redeem a people, "to purify for himself a people for his own possession who are zealous for good works" (v. 14). The beauty of our pursuit of holiness, then, is that the source doesn't rise up from within us. The source is God's powerful grace. He acts, and we respond. More than that, he gives the power we lack in order to energize us to seek holiness. These three texts prove that God's sovereign grace saves a people who will be marked by personal holiness.

The New Testament is clear that who we are by God's grace must come before what we seek to do by God's grace. In other words, the biblical pattern is that indicatives come before imperatives. Think about Ephesians. Chapters 1 through 3 describe in rich detail what God has done for his people in Christ. It's only then, in chapter 4, that Paul tells the Christians how they should live— "I therefore, a prisoner for the Lord, urge you to walk in a manner worthy of the calling to which you have been called" (Eph. 4:1). Paul teaches the same thing in Romans. After his doctrine-packed summary of what God has done on behalf of believers in the first eleven chapters, he exhorts them, "I appeal to you therefore, brothers, by the mercies of God, to present your bodies as a living sacrifice, holy and acceptable to God, which is your spiritual worship" (Rom. 12:1). And note Paul's words to the Colossians. Again, after telling them of Christ's work on their behalf (chapters 1–2), he implores them, "If then you have been raised with Christ, seek the things that are above, where Christ is, seated at the right hand of God" (Col. 3:1). Paul's "therefore" and "if then" show the order in the apostle's mind. First comes God's work for us; then out of gratitude to the Lord in faith, hope, and love, and empowered by the Spirit, we pursue holiness.

And we must seek to be godly. The New Testament is saturated with imperatives related to holiness that Christians must follow. Surely J. C. Ryle is correct, then, when he summarizes much of the New Testament's teaching about personal holiness:

The Lord Jesus has undertaken everything that His people's souls require; not only to deliver them from the *guilt* of their sins by His atoning death, but from the *dominion* of their sins, by placing in their hearts the Holy Spirit; not only to justify them, but also to sanctify them. He is, thus, not only their "righteousness," but their "sanctification." (I Cor. i.30.) Let us hear what the Bible says: . . . Christ loved the Church, and gave Himself for it; that He might sanctify and cleanse it."—"Christ gave Himself for us, that He might redeem us from all iniquity, and purify unto Himself a peculiar people, zealous of good works."—"Christ bore our sins in His own body on the tree, that we, being dead to sins, should live unto righteousness."—"Christ hath reconciled (you) in the body of His flesh through death, to present you holy and unblameable and unreproveable in His sight." (John xvii.19; Ephes. v.25; Titus ii.14; I Peter ii.24; 51-Coloss. i.22.) Let the meaning of these five texts be carefully considered. If words mean anything, they teach that Christ undertakes the sanctification, no less than the justification of His believing people.[2]

Compatibilism and Personal Holiness

Compatibilism provides a helpful lens through which to view our pursuit of holiness. Two texts will bear this out. In 2 Peter, the apostle reminds believers that God's "divine power has granted us all things that pertain to life and godliness" (1:3). God's sovereignty is all-encompassing in our lives; without sovereign grace we would lack life and the ability to be godly. Then Peter goes on to implore the Christians to "make every effort" to add all sorts of character qualities to their lives (1:5–7), and he concludes with the exhortation: "Therefore, brothers, be all the more diligent to make your calling and election sure, for if you practice these qualities you will never fall" (1:10). Believers must work hard ("make every effort") and have a plan to grow in holiness so that they can be assured of their salvation. They must act. Yet, they strive because God's almighty grace provides them with everything they need for godliness. Peter doesn't flinch from holding God's sovereignty and human responsibility together without trying to tease out their exact relationship.

Neither does Paul in Philippians 2:11–12. He tells the church to "work out your salvation with fear and trembling, for it is God who works in you, both to will and to work for his good pleasure." The "salvation" intended here refers to believers' final standing with God at judgment, so Paul is

---

2. J. C. Ryle, *Holiness: Its Nature, Hindrances, Difficulties, and Roots* (Westwood, NJ: Fleming H. Revell, n.d.), 17 (italics original).

certainly dealing with weighty matters. Which is it—God's work, or ours—that's essential? Both. Moisés Silva comments, "the point here is not merely that both the human and the divine are stressed, but that in one and same passage we have what is perhaps the strongest biblical expression of each element." Regarding "our conscious activity in sanctification," on the one hand, he argues, "our salvation, which we confess to be God's from beginning to end, is here described as something that we must bring about." On the other hand, "the divine influence is said to extend not only to our activity, but to our very wills—a unique statement, though the idea is implied in other passages (e.g., John 1:13; Rom. 9:16)."[3] We must strive for holiness. And we can only do so because God is at work in our lives to give us the desire to be like him in purity. May God grant us the grace to know this reality more and more in our lives.

Calvinism and Sanctification

In line with the biblical material we've already surveyed, the Westminster Confession of Faith provides a brief Calvinistic discussion of personal holiness in chapter 13, "Of Sanctification." The Confession both discusses what sanctification is and also upholds the importance of sanctification in a Christian's experience. We notice seven truths it teaches.

First, the Confession reminds us that God's grace must precede our attempts to be righteous; switch the order and all kinds of things will go wrong. So it is only we "who are once effectually called, and regenerated, having a new heart, and new spirit created in them" (13.1) who are to pursue holiness. Second, those who are called and regenerated by the Spirit will actually be changed people. They will "really and personally" be "further sanctified," meaning that they will experience tangible changes in their lives (13.1). Third, these changes will happen due to the power of Christ at work in our lives—"through the virtue of Christ's death and resurrection, by His Word and Spirit dwelling in them" (13.1). The promise for Christians' growth in holiness, then, is that changed lives are not dependent on us. Sanctification will occur in us due to Christ's power, not ours.

Fourth, the presence of the Spirit in believers' lives will have two results. The Spirit will lead us to mortify, or put to death, our sin—"the dominion of the whole body of sin is destroyed, and the several lusts thereof are more and more weakened and mortified." And he will also empower us in the process of vivification, i.e., making ourselves more and more alive to Christ and righteousness—"they [are] more and more quickened and strengthened in all saving graces, to the practice of true holiness, without which no man shall see the Lord" (13.1). Fifth, this rejuvenating work of the Spirit in Christians'

---

3. Moisés Silva, *Philippians*, Baker Exegetical Commentary on the New Testament (Grand Rapids: Baker, 1992), 139–40.

lives will affect every part of who we are: "This sanctification is throughout, in the whole man" (13.2). As sin has affected every part of who we are as persons, so the Spirit's work of recreating us will affect every part of us. Yet, sixth, this work of recreating us will not be done completely in this earthly life. Sanctification is "imperfect in this life, there abiding still some remnants of corruption in every part; whence ariseth a continual and irreconcilable war, the flesh lusting against the Spirit, and the Spirit against the flesh" (13.2). Nonetheless, seventh, there should be tangible progress in believers' holiness throughout our lives: "In which war, although the remaining corruption, for a time, may much prevail; yet, through the continual supply of strength from the sanctifying Spirit of Christ, the regenerate part doth overcome; and so, the saints grow in grace, perfecting holiness in the fear of God" (13.3). The Confession, then, gives no platform for ungodly living on the pretense that it doesn't matter due to God's sovereign election.

Westminster accords with John Calvin's emphasis on the necessity of personal holiness in the Christian's life. The Catholic church had charged that the logic of Protestantism—with the priority it gave to the sovereign action of God in salvation and the stress it placed on a sinner's justification before God by faith alone apart from any good works—would necessarily lead to licentious living. Calvin, though, disagreed vehemently with this Catholic assertion and answered it at length in the *Institutes*. In justification,

> by faith we grasp Christ's righteousness, by which alone we are reconciled to God. Yet you could not grasp this without at the same time grasping sanctification also. For he 'is given unto us for righteousness, wisdom, sanctification, and redemption' [I Cor. 1:30]. Therefore Christ justifies no one whom he does not at the same time sanctify. These benefits are joined together by an everlasting and indissoluble bond, so that those whom he illumines by his wisdom, he redeems; those whom he redeems, he justifies; those whom he justifies, he sanctifies.[4]

Because of God's rich and gracious kindness to us in Christ, believers have both the power at work in us through the Holy Spirit to live changed lives and the sustaining impulse of gratitude to our Lord that should motivate us in our pursuit of holiness. May we strive for tangible holiness that is both our joy and also the goal of our life in Christ.

---

4. John Calvin, *Institutes of the Christian Religion*, Library of Christian Classics, 2 volumes, ed. John T. McNeill, trans. Ford Lewis Battles (Philadelphia: Westminster, 1960), 3.16.1.

REFLECTION QUESTIONS

1. Do biblical texts we looked at—like Ephesians 1 and 2 and Titus 2—encourage you in your pursuit of personal holiness? Why?

2. How do you balance emphasizing the imperatives to be holy while also resting in the indicatives of what God has graciously done for you in Christ?

3. Is the concept of compatibilism helpful for you to consider as you strive for sanctification?

4. Is there any warrant to the Arminians' charge that Calvinists have no reason to try to grow in grace?

5. What specific ways has reading this chapter encouraged you to intensify your striving after "the holiness without which no one will see the Lord" (Heb. 12:14)?

Does Calvinism Lead to Doubts about Assurance of Salvation?

Some people assume Calvinists cannot have assurance, or confidence, that they will finally go to heaven. After all, it's charged, how can they know for sure that before the creation of the world, of his sovereign will alone, God had chosen them for salvation? But following the New Testament's teaching on assurance, Calvinism teaches that through all the tumultuous ups and downs of life, Christians can have deep-seated confidence that they are children of almighty God. Because the Lord is sovereign and has set his never-ending love on his people as shown in the death of Christ for them, they can know they are Christians.

Assurance in the Bible

The New Testament regularly tells us that Christians can have assurance of their saving faith in Jesus. Paul, for instance, exclaimed, "I am not ashamed, for I know whom I have believed, and I am convinced that he is able to guard until that Day what has been entrusted to me" (2 Tim. 1:12). The apostle was convinced that the Lord would sustain him until the final day of his salvation. He knows this because of God's sovereignty in salvation, for the Lord has "saved us and called us to a holy calling, not because of our works but because of his own purpose and grace, which he gave us in Christ Jesus before the ages began" (1:9). To Paul, the Lord's sovereignty in election and calling was not a hindrance to the experience of assurance. Exactly the opposite, it was the foundation of a Christian's hope.

First John, especially, is filled with "we know" statements that are to give John's readers means of coming to assurance that they are truly believers. J. I. Packer perceptively notes that

John specifies right belief about Christ, love to Christians and righteous conduct as objective signs of being a child of God and knowing him savingly (1 Jn. 2:3–5, 29; 3:9f., 14, 18f.; 4:7; 5:1, 4, 18). Those who find these signs in themselves may assure (lit., persuade) their hearts in the presence of God when a sense of guilt makes them doubt his favour (1 Jn. 3:19). But absence of these signs shows that any assurance felt is delusive (1 Jn. 1:6; 2:4, 9–11, 23; 3:6–10; 4:8, 20; 2 Jn. 9; 3 Jn. 11).[1]

Romans 8:28–39 also persuades us that Christians can have assurance of salvation. We know God is working in us and that we "are called according to his purpose" (8:28) because of the foreknew-predestined-called-justified-glorified chain (8:29–30) we have seen previously.[2] The glorious truths that Calvinism revels in don't hinder assurance; they actually promote it. They do so, because, as Paul records, they are all centered on Christ. God's purpose in predestination is that we might "be conformed to the image of his Son" (8:29). Since he has given us Christ, God will give us everything we need to be like Christ; no one and nothing can be effectively against us (8:31–32). Nothing can condemn us before God because Christ died; he rose; and he's seated at the Father's right hand and is even now praying for us (8:33–34). The most important thing in the universe is that Christ loves us and died for us. And nothing can ever remove God's people from his love (8:35, 39). Even the most horrendous things we can imagine, even death itself, can't pull us away "from the love of God in Christ Jesus our Lord" (8:35–39).

Do Calvinistic emphases hinder our search for assurance of salvation? Romans 8:28–29 proves the exact opposite. The ground for one of Scripture's great promises of assurance is God's eternal choice of us as well as certainty of our present relationship with him by faith in Christ (8:29–30). Both of these assurances are centered on Christ (not on our fluctuating feelings), showing that in Paul's mind rather than robbing us of assurance, God's sovereignty fosters it.[3]

Assurance in Calvinism

John Calvin and the tradition that takes his name spent a great deal of time discussing aspects of Christian assurance of salvation since, in many ways, we might cast the Protestant Reformation largely as a debate between Catholics—who taught that (apart from a very rarified few, the "saints") a

---

1. J. I. Packer, "Assurance," in *New Bible Dictionary*, 2nd ed., ed. J. D. Douglas (Leicester: InterVarsity Press, 1982), 98.
2. See Questions 19–21.
3. For an insightful discussion of this passage and its practical ramifications, see J. I. Packer, "The Adequacy of God," in *Knowing God* (Downers Grove, IL: Inter-Varsity Press, 1973), 230–54.

Christian could not have certainty of salvation in this life—and Protestants, who believed Christians could be persuaded in this life that they were going to heaven. That constellation of doctrines usually associated with the Reformation—beliefs such as justification by faith alone, predestination, the Eucharist, and the authority of the church and the Bible—really were orbiting around the simple question asked by countless individuals in the sixteenth century, "Am I a Christian?" This practical, pastoral query is what the Reformation sought to answer definitively. The Catholic Church disagreed with Protestant assertions. At the Council of Trent (1545–63), the Catholics taught that justification by faith alone (*sola fide*) was an erroneous doctrine; since persons can lose their salvation, "If any one saith, that a man, who is born again and justified is bound by faith to believe that he is assuredly in the number of the predestinate: let him be anathema."[4]

A few years after Trent denied assurance to almost all Christians, the Protestant Heidelberg Catechism (1563) asked the question, "What is your only comfort in life and death?" (Q. 1). The answer given assures believers of their future with the Lord:

> That I am not my own, but belong with body and soul, both in life and in death, to my faithful Saviour Jesus Christ. He has fully paid for all my sins with His precious blood, and has set me free from all the power of the devil. He also preserves me in such a way that without the will of my heavenly Father not a hair can fall from my head; indeed, all things must work together for my salvation. Therefore, by His Holy Spirit He also assures me of eternal life and makes me heartily willing and ready from now on to live for Him.

The parallels with Romans 8 are important. Certainty of salvation centers on Jesus Christ; he is the means (so to speak) to arriving at assurance since it's only through his sacrifice for us that we can know that we are forgiven of our sins, which is what we are seeking in our quest for assurance. No matter what happens to us ("both in life and in death"), we can have confidence that we belong to Christ due to his death for us. Indeed, the entire Trinity is integral to our assurance. The Father providentially guards us. The Son has died for us and intercedes for us. The Spirit assures us of salvation and leads us to follow Christ more wholly.

The Puritan tradition spent a great deal of time speaking about assurance of salvation, especially helping those with troubled consciences to discern if

---

4. *The Canons and Decrees of the Council of Trent*, "On Justification," Canon 15, in Philip Schaff and David S. Schaff, eds., *The Creeds of Christendom: With a History and Critical Notes*, rev. ed. (1931; Grand Rapids: Baker, 1990), 2:113.

they were truly believers. The Westminster Confession of Faith, in this tradition, contains a separate section, chapter eighteen, titled "Of the Assurance of Grace and Salvation." We have used this confession throughout our study as a helpful summary of the Calvinistic doctrine of salvation. We have seen it stress the sovereign, eternal decree of God as the bedrock of his people's salvation. The first observation we need to make about it, then, is simply that the Calvinistic authors of the Confession did not think that assurance of salvation was antithetical to Calvinism.

The Confession makes several important points about certainty of salvation. First, it's possible for Christians to have assurance in this life. Believers—defined here as "such as truly believe in the Lord Jesus, and love him in sincerity, endeavoring to walk in all good conscience before him"—"may in this life be certainly assured that they are in a state of grace" (18.1). Second, believers have three avenues for attaining assurance, as the Confession notes in a very important paragraph:

> This certainty is not a bare conjectural and probable persuasion, grounded upon a fallible hope; but an infallible assurance of faith, founded upon the divine truth of the promises of salvation, the inward evidence of those graces unto which these promises are made, the testimony of the Spirit of adoption witnessing with our spirits that we are the children of God; which Spirit is the earnest of our inheritance, whereby we are sealed to the day of redemption. (WCF 18.2)

With pastoral wisdom and with awareness that the Christian's experience of assurance may not be constant, or may be lacking almost completely (18.3, 4), the Confession's authors say there are three means of arriving at "infallible assurance" (18.2). First is the reality of the death of Christ for sinners on the cross along with God's word that whoever believes in him will be saved. This is "the divine truth of the promises of salvation." There is, second, indication that the gospel has taken root in Christians' lives to such an extent that they are changed and can see the progress of sanctification. This is "the inward evidence of those graces unto which these promises are made." Third, there is the secret working of the Spirit in believers' lives whereby they know that they are Christians ("the testimony of the Spirit of adoption witnessing with our spirits that we are the children of God").

Note that one of the three (Christ's work of salvation) is objective while the other two are experienced subjectively. This is significant, for our subjective feelings or experiences can shift dramatically, and they can be drastically influenced by our circumstances (e.g., all the problems we saw that might plague Christians noted in Rom. 8:35–39). We may go through extended periods of time where it is difficult to see evidences of grace in our lives. God may even at times, for his mysterious purposes, act by "withdrawing the light of his countenance and suffering even such as fear him to walk in darkness and to have no light" (18.4). Why he takes away the sense of his fatherly love (and we must be clear here: it's just the "sense," not the reality, of his affection that's withdrawn) we don't know. But either way, the Christian at this time cannot rely on the testimony of the Spirit as a means of acquiring assurance. All he or she can rely on is the one stable, never-changing rock that anchors his or her soul: the reality that God is a gracious sovereign who has sent his only Son into the world to live and die and rise again in the place of his people, and that all they need do is look outside of themselves to Christ and they will be saved.

In other words, it is the gospel, the promise of salvation of almighty God, that is the objective, never-changing facet of assurance of salvation. No matter how I feel, or how I evaluate myself, the reality of Christ's effective salvation never changes. We can think of these three means of salvation as the wheels on a big wheel tricycle. The tricycle needs all three wheels (evidence of sanctification, testimony of the Spirit, saving work of Christ) to function well. But the big wheel, the one that pulls the other two along, is the most significant one. The tricycle can limp along without one or both of the small wheels in the back, but it won't work at all without the large wheel. In the same way, our experience of assurance of salvation will be weak and limpid if we're only looking at the small wheels. But when we look to the finished work of Christ on the cross for us, along with the assurance of the saving character of God that accompanies it, we have real assurance of salvation.[5]

Practical Implications of Calvinism for Assurance

Rather than being a hindrance to assurance, Calvinism's belief in the absolute, particular sovereignty of our heavenly Father, the complete atonement procured for us by the Son, and the fact of a new heart given to us by the Holy Spirit can sustain us through the trials of life. As we have seen, the New Testament admonishes us to have assurance of salvation. Yet, there are many foes ready to quash the reality of our eternal destiny. Satan is a tremendously powerful and wily foe who seeks to damn us (e.g., Eph. 6:10–18; 1 Peter 5:8–9). All around us the world plots how to ruin our faith (e.g., John 17:14; 1 Cor. 2:12; Gal. 4:3). Beyond that, the sin we continue to struggle with would cause us to abandon Christ if it were allowed to run its course (e.g., Gal. 5:19–21). Only a power outside of us—our heavenly Father—can keep us in his love. Knowing him intimately, and trusting in his goodness and wisdom and power, is the means to being persuaded we are, and will remain, believers.

---

5. I first heard this tricycle illustration from Thomas R. Schreiner. On the relationship of perseverance to assurance of salvation, see his *Run to Win the Prize: Perseverance in the New Testament* (Wheaton, IL: Crossway, 2010).

REFLECTION QUESTIONS

1. D. A. Carson defines "Christian assurance" as "a Christian believer's confidence that he or she is already in a right standing with God, and that this will issue in ultimate salvation."[6] Do you agree with his definition? Why?

2. Did any of the discussion of the New Testament's teaching on assurance surprise you? Why?

3. Why do you think some people insist that Calvinism necessarily leads to loss of assurance of salvation?

4. How do you think Romans 8:28–39 can aid someone you know (maybe yourself) who has struggled with doubting his or her relationship with the Lord?

5. Richard Sibbes wrote that, "A holy despair in ourselves is the ground of true hope. In God the fatherless find mercy. . . . Christ's sheep are weak sheep."[7] Do you agree with him? Why?

---

6. D. A. Carson, "Reflections on Assurance," in *Still Sovereign: Contemporary Perspectives on Election, Foreknowledge, and Grace*, eds. Thomas R. Schreiner and Bruce A. Ware (Grand Rapids: Baker, 2000), 248.

7. Richard Sibbes, *The Bruised Reed and Smoking Flax*, in *Works of Richard Sibbes*, ed. Alexander B. Grosart (1862; Edinburgh: Banner of Truth, 1973), 1:48.

Do the Questions in This Book Matter?

The questions and answers in this book truly matter. They matter not because it is absolutely essential for a Christian to know what Calvinism is or to label him- or herself a "Calvinist." They don't matter so that we can win debates with our Arminian friends over sovereignty and free will. They matter for much more important and practical reasons.

The questions matter because they fundamentally deal with who God is and whether or not we can trust him given our finitude and our sinfulness. They matter because we are pilgrims traversing the turmoil of this world on our way to our eternal home. Knowing God and who he is—and knowing who we are in relation to him—will sustain us in our journey, with both joy and confidence. Believing that our God is sovereign to save his people will lead us to worship him. It will motivate us to lay down our lives to take the gospel to unreached peoples. Does it matter if you're a 3-, 4-, 4½-, or 5-point Calvinist? Yes, because only one of them is correct. And, yes, because these biblical truths have all the practical implications in the world. Calvinism matters for three important reasons.

The Truths of Calvinism Help Us to Know God

First of all, the biblical truths of Calvinism help us to know the Lord. And there is no more important thing in the world than for a human being to know God. The Bible says so.

> Thus says the LORD: "Let not the wise man boast in his wisdom, let not the mighty man boast in his might, let not the rich man boast in his riches, but let him who boasts boast in this, that he understands and knows me, that I am the Lord who practices steadfast love, justice, and righteousness in the earth. For in these things I delight, declares the Lord." (Jer. 9:23–24)

> And this is eternal life, that they know you, the only true
> God, and Jesus Christ whom you have sent. (John 17:3)

Pastors and theologians have long stressed this. A. W. Tozer's words are true, and challenging because of their truth:

> What comes into our minds when we think about God is the
> most important thing about us. . . . Worship is pure or base
> as the worshiper entertains high or low thoughts of God. For
> this reason the gravest question before the Church is always
> God Himself, and the most portentous fact about any man is
> not what he at a given time may say or do, but what he in his
> deep heart conceives God to be like. We tend by a secret law
> of the soul to move toward our mental image of God. This is
> true not only of the individual Christian, but of the company
> of Christians that composes the Church. Always the most re-
> vealing thing about the Church is her idea of God.[1]

J. I. Packer is equally incisive:

> Knowing about God is crucially important for the living
> of our lives. . . . The world becomes a strange, mad, painful
> place, and life in it a disappointing and unpleasant business,
> for those who do not know about God. Disregard the study
> of God, and you sentence yourself to stumble and blunder
> through life blindfolded, as it were, with no sense of direc-
> tion and no understanding of what surrounds you. This way
> you can waste your life and lose your soul.[2]

The questions and answers in this book teach us at least these biblical truths about God:

- God saves his people by his will and power alone.
- God loves all persons, and he loves his elect uniquely and savingly.
- God's grace monergistically saves sinners, sovereignly overcoming all their resistance.[3]
- God eternally predestined all persons' eternal destinies, electing his children for salvation.

---

1. A.W. Tozer, *The Knowledge of the Holy* (New York: HarperCollins, 1961), 1.
2. J. I. Packer, *Knowing God* (Downers Grove, IL: InterVarsity Press, 1973), 19.
3. Monergism is the biblical reality that God is the sole actor in saving spiritually dead people whom he's elected to be his own. See Question 21.

- God elected persons based on his love and wisdom alone, not on anything he foresaw in his children.
- God the Son accomplished the salvation of the elect by his death on the cross.
- God the Holy Spirit sovereignly regenerates his elect when they are dead in their sin through the preaching of the gospel.
- God graciously and sovereignly preserves his people throughout the course of their lives.

Since our greatest need is to know God, and since the Bible reveals these truths about God and his ways, we need to learn these realities. Not only should we know them, but we should cherish them, for God delights in them himself.[4] God tells his people, "I the LORD do not change" (Mal. 3:6). That means that the way the Lord acted toward sinners in the days of the patriarchs, in the period of Israel's theocracy, during the earthly ministry of Jesus, and through the apostles and the early church as recorded in the New Testament is the same way he acts towards sinners and needy people today. Packer is correct:

> God's ways do not change. He continues to act toward sinful men and women in the way that he does in the Bible story. Still he shows his freedom and lordship by discriminating between sinners, causing some to hear the gospel while others do not hear it, and moving some of those who hear it to repentance while leaving others in their unbelief, thus teaching his saints that he owes mercy to none and that it is entirely of his grace, not at all through their own effort, that they themselves have found life.[5]

I do not believe, nor have I said anywhere in this book, that Arminianism is heresy. Evangelical Arminians are children of the same God as Calvinists, they trust in the same gospel of Christ, they are indwelt by the same Spirit. Yet it matters whether at the end of the day God sovereignly saves us of his own free will or if he does a lot to make our salvation possible and leaves the rest up to our libertarian free will. Calvinism gives us hope, and it causes us to praise our Lord. John Calvin wrote,

> We shall never be clearly persuaded, as we ought to be, that our salvation flows from the wellspring of God's free mercy until we come to know his eternal election, which illumines

---

4. See John Piper, *The Pleasures of God: Meditations on God's Delight in Being God* (Portland, OR: Multnomah, 1991).
5. Packer, *Knowing God*, 79.

God's grace by this contrast: that he does not indiscriminately adopt all into the hope of salvation but gives to some
what he denies to others.[6]

Calvinists praise God for saving them, when all they deserved was eternal
damnation. Arminians are inconsistent (and biblical!) in praising God for
their salvation and writing wonderful Calvinistic hymns like "And Can it Be
That I Should Gain," which has lyrics like these:

> Long my imprisoned spirit lay
> Fast bound in sin and nature's night
> Thine eye diffused a quick'ning ray
> I woke, the dungeon flamed with light;
> My chains fell off, my heart was free;
> I rose, went forth and followed Thee.[7]

In order for us to trust in God and to praise him in a manner more and more
consistent with the Bible's presentation of who he is, we should hold on to the
truths about God that Calvinism asserts.

The Truths of Calvinism Help Us to Know Ourselves

Second, the biblical truths of Calvinism not only teach us about God, but
they also give us insight into who we are. Among other truths, in this book
we have noticed that

- Although we are created in God's image, we rebelled against his
  rightful rule and alienated ourselves from him.
- In our unregenerate condition, we have real freedom and that
  freedom expresses itself in our constant rebellion towards the Lord.
- As creatures we are responsible to submit to everything the Lord reveals of himself to us in Scripture and not to determine what he can
  be like or what he can do.
- Compatibilism gives us the correct lens through which to read the Bible,
  holding together God's absolute sovereignty and our true responsibility.

John Calvin began the *Institutes of the Christian Religion* with this memo-
rable line: "Nearly all wisdom we possess, that is to say, true and sound wisdom,

---

6. John Calvin, *Institutes of the Christian Religion*, Library of Christian Classics, 2 volumes,
   ed. John T. McNeill, trans. Ford Lewis Battles (Philadelphia: Westminster, 1960), 3.21.1.
7. Charles Wesley, "And Can It Be That I Should Gain" (1738). J. I. Packer has noted on
   several occasions the happy inconsistency of Arminians both singing and praying like
   Calvinists. See, e.g., J. I. Packer, *Evangelism and the Sovereignty of God* (Downers Grove, IL:
   InterVarsity Press, 1961), 11–17.

consists of two parts: the knowledge of God and of ourselves."[8] He was right. And he was right that there is a correlative relationship between the two sorts of knowledge. In knowing ourselves better (especially the obligations we're under as God's creatures, our transgression of his law, and our consequent inability to save ourselves), we know God better. And in knowing God better (his lordship, love, and provision for us in Christ), we know ourselves more fully, and more correctly. The truths of Calvinism remind us that we are marred, fractious people. Since he saved such wretched and responsible people as us, God's grace, love, patience, kindness, and mercy stand out ever more clearly and starkly in contrast. It's these biblical truths Calvinism delights in.

The Truths of Calvinism Help Us to Live Life to God's Glory and for Our Joy

Third, we have also seen throughout this book that Calvinism is much more than just a system of esoteric ideas that have no impact on "real life." As believers, we want to be able to say with Paul that "I have been crucified with Christ. It is no longer I who live, but Christ who lives in me. And the life I now live in the flesh I live by faith in the Son of God, who loved me and gave himself for me" (Gal. 2:20). But we are unable to say this with confidence, with the pronouns that Paul uses—"me"—if our standing with God is up to us. We can't rest in this truth if we don't know that Jesus died for us particularly. But because of biblical Calvinism,

- We can trust God to keep his promises.
- We can pray hopefully that God will save sinners.[9]
- We can read the Bible and know that the Lord holds us accountable for how we respond to him in obedience and faith.
- We must preach the gospel indiscriminately to all people.
- We can take the gospel to the hardest-to-reach, most resistant people groups on the planet because our sovereign God has chosen a people to be his own, and Christ has died for those people, and the Holy Spirit will accompany our preaching of the gospel to them with his life-giving power.
- We are responsible to persevere in faith and obedience to the Lord throughout all the days of our lives, knowing that he will preserve and sustain his people.
- We must strive for holiness in our lives, not out of fear that God will reject us otherwise, but out of gratitude that he has been merciful to us.

---

8. Calvin, *Institutes*, 1.1.1.
9. Packer reminds us that "When you pray for unconverted people, you do so on the assumption that it is in God's power to bring them to faith." Arminians often do this (even if they vocally oppose Calvinism) because "the Christian is at his sanest and wisest when he prays" (*Evangelism and the Sovereignty of God*, 15).

- We can trust in our heart of hearts—no matter the real difficulties and deep discouragements we face—that our good, merciful, long-suffering heavenly Father will never let anything in all creation separate us from the love he has for us in Christ Jesus our Lord.

So, whether or not you agree with Calvinism, don't fall prey to the lie that this "heady theology" has no bearing on "real life." It couldn't be more practical. Instead, in conclusion listen to the words of Martin Luther, who expresses the ideas of Calvinism as well as any Calvinist ever has:

> If I am ignorant of what, how far, and how much I can and may do in relation to God, it will be equally uncertain and unknown to me, what, how far, and how much God can and may do in me, although it is God who works everything in everyone (1 Cor. 12:6). But when the works and power of God are unknown, I do not know God himself, and when God is unknown, I cannot worship, praise, thank, and serve God, since I do not know how much I ought to attribute to myself and how much to God. It therefore behooves us to be very certain about the distinction between God's power and our own, God's work and our own, if we want to live a godly life.[10]

REFLECTION QUESTIONS

1. Do you think the truths Calvinism seeks to protect matter? Why?

2. What truths about God that Calvinism asserts are most significant to you? Why?

3. How does Calvinism specifically help you to know yourself better?

4. If Calvinistic truths don't impel you to be more active and hopeful in sharing the gospel, why don't they?

5. How do you think Arminians would respond to this chapter? Where do you think their ideas would differ from those of Calvinists?

---

10. Martin Luther, *On the Bondage of the Will*, in *Luther and Erasmus: Free Will and Salvation*, ed. E. Gordon Rupp and Philip S. Watson (Philadelphia: Westminster, 1969), 117.

Select Bibliography

This bibliography is not comprehensive. The footnotes throughout the book will alert readers to those resources I have used to come to my conclusions. The resources below are the ones I would highlight for someone who wants to begin to understand Calvinism better. The list includes twelve resources—eleven books and one introduction to a book—arguing for Calvinism in a biblical manner as well as a recent comprehensive defense of the Arminian position.

Boettner, Lorraine. *The Reformed Doctrine of Predestination*. Grand Rapids: Eerdmans, 1957.

Carson, D. A. *How Long, O Lord? Reflections on Evil and Suffering*. Grand Rapids: Baker, 1990.

Gibson, David, and Jonathan Gibson, eds. *From Heaven He Came and Sought Her: Definite Atonement in Historical, Biblical, Theological, and Pastoral Perspective*. Wheaton, IL: Crossway, 2013.

Horton, Michael. *Putting Amazing Back Into Grace: Embracing the Heart of the Gospel*. Rev. ed. Grand Rapids: Baker, 2011.

Murray, Iain. *The Forgotten Spurgeon*. 2nd ed. Edinburgh: Banner of Truth, 1973.

Murray, John. *Redemption Accomplished and Applied*. Grand Rapids: Eerdmans, 1955.

Nicole, Roger. *Our Sovereign Saviour: The Essence of the Reformed Faith*. Fearn, UK: Christian Focus, 2002.

Olson, Roger E. *Arminian Theology: Myths and Realities*. Downers Grove, IL: InterVarsity, 2006.

Packer, J. I. *Evangelism and the Sovereignty of God*. Downers Grove, IL: InterVarsity, 1961.

_____. "'Saved by His Precious Blood': An Introduction to John Owen's *The Death of Death in the Death of Christ*." In *A Quest for Godliness: The Puritan Vision of the Christian Life*. Wheaton, IL: Crossway, 1990, 125–48.

Piper, John. *The Pleasures of God: Meditations on God's Delight in Being God*. Portland, OR: Multnomah, 1991.

Schreiner, Thomas R., and Bruce A. Ware, eds. *Still Sovereign: Contemporary Perspectives on Election, Foreknowledge, and Grace*. Grand Rapids: Baker, 2000.

_____. *The Grace of God, The Bondage of the Will*. Vol. 2: *Historical and Theological Perspectives on Calvinism*. Grand Rapids: Baker, 1995.

Scripture Index

Genesis
1:1 .... 35, 89
1:1–2 40
1:14–19 208
1:28 18
1:31 237
1–2 50
1–3 238
3:1–19 237
3:15 238
3:16–17 91
4:1 160
12:1–3 212
18:19 160
18:25 .... 148, 247
22:13 195
45:5–8 96
50:20 .... 96, 253

Exodus
2:25 160
7:3 97
7:13 97
7:22–23 97
8:15 97
32:30 137
34:6 .... 53, 168
34:6–7 36

Leviticus
4:13 137
16 195

Deuteronomy
5:29 275
7:6–8 161
7:7–8 .... 37, 51, 54, 153, 212
10 212
10:14–15 51
10:14–16 212

10:15–16 161
18:5 153
28:63 255
29:4 97
29:18–20 98
29:29 .... 41, 42, 168, 246
30:6 .... 98, 212
30:19–20 98
32:4 239
32:39 .... 90, 241

Joshua
24:14 91

1 Samuel
2:25 96
10:24 153
16:7 79

2 Samuel
2:25 255
6:21 153

1 Kings
17:18 137

Ezra
6:22 97

Job
37:5 42
38:4–11 36
38–42 240

Psalms
1:1 91
1:6 160
4:7 79
13:2 79
19:1–4 214
25:10 110
25:17 79

27:8 79
37:4 79
49:3 79
51:4 137
51:9 137
53:1 79
57:7 79
88:18 96
95:3–6 41
105:26 153
106:8 36
106:23 153
107:1 5
115:3 .... 11, 30, 90,
                      104, 165, 252
135:6 .... 36, 90, 239, 252
139:1–16 41
139:16 .... 90, 153
144:3 160
147:5 42

Proverbs
2:2 79
16:4 165
16:9 165
16:33 .... 95, 144
19:21 95
20:24 165
21:1 .... 85, 92, 165
21:2 92

Ecclesiastes
1:13 93

Isaiah
6:3 40
6:5 40
10:5–12 92
40:12 41
40:15 41

40:23...............................41
42:1..............................153
42:8................................43
43:6–7.............................37
44:24...............................36
45:5–7............................241
45:7..........................90, 165
46:5–10..........................262
46:9–11..........................153
46:10.............................251
49:3................................37
53.................................195
53:6................................29
53:11–12.........................196
54:13.............................209
55:1................................91
55:3................................91
65:24.............................262
66:1–2.............................40

Jeremiah
1:5..........................153, 160
4:4................................212
9:23–24 .... 54, 262, 291
10:23.............................165
13:11..............................37
18.................................165
29:10–14.........................264
31:31–34 ....209, 219
31:33–34...........................54
33:3................................42

Lamentations
3:37–38 90

Ezekiel
13:11.............................255
18:23.......................255, 275
18:25–29..........................169
18:32.............................275
33:11................. 50, 274, 275
36:22–23...........................37
36:24–26..........................209
36:25–26..........................219
36:32..............................37

Daniel
4:34–35............................90
4:35..............................165
9:2–19............................264

Hosea
11:8–9 48
13:5..............................160

Amos
3:2................................160
3:6................................165

Jonah
2:9.......................10, 25, 162

Malachi
3:6................................293

Matthew
1:21..........................12, 137
5:44................................91
5:44–48..........................275
5:45................................49
5:48..............................233
7:7–8.............................262
7:15–20..........................227
7:17–18............................76
7:18................................72
7:20..........................76, 228
7:21..............................253
7:21–23..........................227
7:23.........................160, 161
8:17..............................196
10:29.....................36, 50, 90
11:25–27 ....255, 257
11:25–30 ....99, 163
11:28.............................215
11:29.............................216
13.................................130
15:19..............................79
19:24.............................212
19:26.............................212
20:28.............................196
22:1–14..........................215
22:14.............................153
22:37..............................97
23:37.......................216, 275
25:46.............................137
26:28.............................198
28:18–20 ....214, 265
28:19.............................273

Mark
1:5................................182
1:15........................218, 232
2:6................................79
7:21..............................139

10:45.......................188, 196
14:24.............................197
15:28.............................196

Luke
1:1–4..............................93
1:51................................79
2:51................................79
9:45................................96
13:1–5...........................240
13:34.......................254, 257
14:23.............................215
18:13.............................199
22:3................................254
22:20..............................54
24:47.............................218

John
1.................................64
1:9...................62, 63, 183
1:10–11 ....63, 213
1:12................................99
1:12–14..........................192
1:13............... 99, 218, 282
1:17................................55
1:29.............. 173, 174, 183
3.................................64
3:3....................11, 77, 217
3:3–8.............................159
3:5...........................77, 139
3:5–8.............................217
3:8.................................12
3:16........... 49, 50, 52, 100,
        117, 121, 127, 174,
        186, 255, 273
3:16–18..........................278
3:16–20..........................213
3:17................................49
3:18................................76
3:20................................63
3:21................................63
3:35................................50
3:36...........................49, 85
4:39..............................183
4:42.......................174, 183
5:21................................99
5:40................................99
5:43................................99
6:28..............................139
6:29................................99
6:34................................77
6:35...........................83, 99

6:37.....................63, 83, 99,
          154, 209, 278
6:37–39 224
6:37–40 191
6:38–39 ....99, 192
6:40....................................99
6:44.........62, 63, 77, 100, 1
          39, 191, 192, 278
6:44–45 ....72, 159, 209
6:45..................................100
6:47..................................100
6:51...............100, 174, 197
6:60–66 227
6:65..........77, 159, 209, 220
6:66....................................72
7:17..................................254
8:34..................................138
8:43....................................72
8:43–44 78
8:47....................................78
9..240
10:11................................197
10:15................................197
10:26–29 154
10:27–30 224
10:36................................183
11:52................................184
12:47................................183
12:49–50 191
13:2....................................79
14:17..................................72
14:30–31 191
15:5..................................118
15:10..................................51
15:16.......................111, 192
16:8....................................62
17:1–26 ....191, 193
17:2..................................158
17:3........................263, 292
17:6........................152, 158
17:9.............. 152, 154, 158,
          183, 189, 192, 281
17:14................................289
17:20................................189
17:24......................37, 158

Acts
1:6–8................................214
2:23................. 86, 241, 254
2:37–40 273
2:38........................91, 218
2:40....................................91

3:19..................................233
4:12..................................141
4:27–28 ....86, 241
5:3......................................79
5:31..................................218
6:5–12 212
7..212
7:51..................................118
8:4....................................273
8:32..................................196
13:38–41 162
13:43..................................55
13:48......................98, 155,
          159, 162, 163
14:19–21 162
15:18................................164
16:6–10 276
16:14......... 62, 98, 207, 218
16:31................................232
17:17................................162
17:24................................214
17:28..................................39
17:30................................215
17:30–31 ....162, 278
17:30–34 274
17:31......................36, 139
18:6–11 ....162, 276
18:27..................................98
20:20–21 162
20:21................................219
20:24..................................55
20:25..................................49
26:16–23 214
26:24–29 162
26:27–29 274

Romans
1:7....................................207
1:8....................................220
1:18..........56, 139, 198, 200
1:18–23 213
1:18–32 ..... 56, 77, 138, 200
1:19–21 214
1:24–27 138
1:30....................................77
1:32..................................139
2:1–3:10 56
2:4......................................49
2:5...........56, 139, 200, 213
2:5–11 36
2:8......................................56
2:8–9................................139

2:12–16 49
2:14–15 214
2:15..................................213
2:16....................................36
3:5................... 56, 139, 200
3:9–20 200
3:10–12 77
3:11....................................77
3:11–12 56
3:12........................77, 213
3:19....................................77
3:21............... 57, 141, 200
3:21–26 56
3:22....................................57
3:23.......................198, 213
3:24....................................57
3:25..........57, 189, 199, 200
3:25–31 ....57, 200
3:26........................57, 240
4:3.........................189, 233
4:15..................................137
4:16–18 189
5:1–2................................233
5:6....................................196
5:8.........................168, 196
5:10.......................139, 188
5:12–21 ....139, 238
5:18..................................174
5:18–19 77
6:3–4................................186
6:15..................................233
6:23............... 137, 139, 198
7..115
8..167
8:1–11 192
8:3....................................198
8:7......................................72
8:7–8.............. 77, 139, 157
8:16–17 133
8:28................. 21, 154, 162
8:28–30 ....152, 161,
          185, 207
8:28–39 ....209, 265,
          286, 290
8:29............... 145, 152, 192
8:30............... 192, 224, 228
8:31–39 166
8:32........................185, 197
8:33–39 185
8:39..........................21, 224
9..121

9:1–6 166
9:6–23 255
9:6–24 192
9:6–29 166
9:11 154
9:11–24 99
9:13 52
9:14 110
9:15–16 255
9:16 282
9:18 165
9:18–19 253
9:19–21 .... 163, 240
9:20–21 .... 41, 107
9:20–24 165
9:22–23 256
10 167
10:8–15 .... 214, 231
10:8–17 .... 99, 161
10:10–17 141
10:14–15 265
11:5 154
11:5–6 55
11:33 .... 30, 90, 110
11:33–34 .... 241, 256
11:33–36 42
11:34 .... 168, 246
11:36 .... 30, 35, 36, 90
12:1 280
15:7 37
15:17–24 162

1 Corinthians
1:4–8 225
1:9 207
1:21 138
1:23–24 215
1:27–29 153
1:29 256
1:30 .... 281, 283
2:7 42
2:12 289
2:14 .... 138, 139,
                            154, 215
3:6–10 97
4:7 .... 58, 161, 162
6:8 137
8:3 160
8:11 198
10:31 37
12:3 72
12:4–6 191

12:6 296
15:1–8 214
15:50 72

2 Corinthians
4:4–6 208
5:14–15 .... 174, 185
5:17 218
5:18–19 183
5:18–21 188
5:19 174
5:21 .... 197, 198
6:11 79
8:9 198
13:14 191

Galatians
1:4 197
1:15 207
2:20 .... 21, 197, 200, 295
3:10 199
3:13 197
4:3 289
4:4–5 205
4:4–6 191
4:9 160
5:19–21 289

Ephesians
1:3 .... 152, 155
1:3–5 154
1:3–6 43
1:3–11 .... 158, 162
1:3–12 247
1:3–14 ..... 56, 155, 163, 192
1:4 .... 51, 52, 143,
                            152, 279
1:4–5 .... 37, 162, 192
1:4–6 37
1:5 .... 152, 154, 155, 251
1:6 .. 154, 155, 161, 162, 256
1:7 192
1:9 .... 154, 155
1:11 .... 85, 90, 152, 154,
                   164, 251, 253, 265
1:12 .... 43, 155, 256
1:14 .... 43, 155, 256
1:15 192
1:15–16 220
2:1 139
2:1–3 .... 57, 77, 138, 233
2:1–7 10

2:1–10 142
2:3 .... 157, 162
2:4 .... 21, 57, 78, 141
2:4–7 50
2:4–8 58
2:4–10 279
2:5 218
2:7 155
2:8 .... 154, 159, 192
2:10 221
2:12 .... 141, 153
4:1 280
4:4–6 191
4:17 .... 91, 138
5:2 197
5:22 91
5:25 .... 51, 91, 197, 281
6:1 91
6:4 91
6:10–18 289
6:19–20 276

Philippians
1:6 .... 223, 228
1:29 159
2:6–7 49
2:11–12 281
2:12 93
2:13 93
4:6 262

Colossians
1:3–4 .... 220, 265
1:12–14 265
1:13–14 188
1:16 35
1:19–20 173
1:20 177
1:21–22 233
1:21–23 225
1:22 281
2:11–14 186
2:13 218
3:1 280
4:2–4 265

1 Thessalonians
1:2–5 .... 163, 220
1:4–5 155
4:3 254
5:9 155

2 Thessalonians
2:13.........................159, 192
2:13–15 99
2:14..................................207
3:5......................................97

1 Timothy
1:15....................................12
2:1...................................184
2:2...................................184
2:3–4......................184, 255
2:4...................................173
2:5–6...............................197
2:6...................................185
2:7...................................185
4:10........................173, 175
6:10.................................138

2 Timothy
1:9.................. 55, 154, 155,
159, 285
1:9–10 192
1:12.................................285
2:19........................160, 228
2:24–25 220
3:4...................................138
3:16...........................40, 93
4:10.................................228

Titus
2:11.................................141
2:11–14 280
2:12.................................137
2:13–14 197
2:14.................................281
3:2...................................184
3:4...................................141
3:4–6..............................192
3:4–7................................57
3:5...................................221

Hebrews
2:9.............. 174, 175, 197
2:9–16 189
2:17........................189, 199
8:6....................................54

8:8–12 220
11:6...................................43
12:5–11 240
12:14......................279, 284

James
1:18.................................221
2:5...................................159

1 Peter
1:1–2...............................192
1:1–5................................43
1:2...................................152
1:3...................................217
1:5.....................................29
2:8...................................165
2:21.................................197
2:22.................................196
2:24........................196, 281
3:4.....................................79
3:15.................................273
3:18.............. 175, 197, 240
5:6–7...............................261
5:7.....................................43
5:8–9...............................289

2 Peter
1:1...................................208
1:2...................................159
1:3–10 281
1:10.............. 153, 208, 228
1:21...................................94
2:1...........................174, 176
2:19.................................138
3:9...................................255

1 John
1:5...................................241
1:6...................................286
2:2.............. 117, 121, 173,
174, 177, 183, 184,
189, 198, 199
2:3–5...............................286
2:4...................................286
2:9–11 286
2:18–19 227

2:23.................................286
2:29.............. 221, 222, 286
3:1...................................160
3:4...................................137
3:6–10 286
3:9.............. 218, 221, 222
3:9–18 286
3:16.................................197
3:19.................................286
4:1...................................183
4:3...................................183
4:7 .... 221, 222, 286
4:8 .... 47, 168, 286
4:8–10 51
4:9...................................183
4:10.............. 189, 198, 199
4:14.................................174
4:16...................................47
4:20.................................286
5:1 .... 221, 222, 286
5:4...................................286
5:18.................................286

2 John
9......................................286

3 John
11.....................................286

Jude
1...............................208, 226
4......................................166
20–21 226
24–25 226

Revelation
4:11....................................36
7:9............................196, 265
13:8.................................166
15:3–4 241
17:8.................................166
20:11–13 36
21:1–4 241
22:1...................................89
22:12.................................85
22:21.................................53